Village, hamlet and field

Village, hamlet and field

Changing medieval settlements in central England

*Carenza Lewis, Patrick Mitchell-Fox
and Christopher Dyer*

MANCHESTER UNIVERSITY PRESS

MANCHESTER AND NEW YORK

distributed exclusively in the USA by St. Martin's Press

Published by Manchester University Press
Oxford Road, Manchester M13 9NR, UK
and Room 400, 175 Fifth Avenue, New York, NY10010, USA

Distributed exclusively in the USA by
St. Martin's Press, Inc., 175 Fifth Avenue, New York, NY10010, USA

British Library Cataloguing-in-Publication Data

A catalogue record for this book is available from the British Library

Library of Congress Cataloging-in-Publication Data
Lewis, Carenza.
  Village, hamlet and field: changing medieval settlements in central England
/ Carenza Lewis, Patrick Mitchell-Fox and Christopher Dyer
     p.   cm.
Includes Index
  ISBN 0-7190-4577-0 *hardback*
  1. Villages–England–History.   2. England–Rural conditions.
3. England–Social conditions–1066–1485.   I. Mitchell-Fox, Patrick.
II. Dyer, Christopher.   III. Title
HN398.E5l49   1997
307.72′ 0942—dc20   96–2689
                                                      CIP

HN
398
.E5
L49
1997

ISBN 0–7190–4577–0 *hardback*

First published 1997

00 99 98 97   10 9 8 7 6 5 4 3 2 1

Typeset by Carnegie Publishing, Preston
Printed in Great Britain by Biddles Ltd, Guildford and King's Lynn

Contents

Figures and tables

Figures

Tables

Note

The county boundaries used in the text and figures are those of 1974, and thus Rutland is treated as part of Leicestershire.

Preface

This book was the result of generous funding of a research project by the Leverhulme Trust, and we wish to record our thanks to that organisation for its assistance, and for the personal encouragement of the Director, Professor Barry Supple. The original formulation of the research was improved by discussion by the committee of the Medieval Settlement Research Group, and the Group subsequently held a succession of seminars at which interim results were given, and from which we received much valuable advice and criticism. The work was located at the University of Birmingham, and we are grateful to the staff of the School of History and the Finance Office for their assistance. The Royal Commission on the Historical Monuments of England agreed to second Carenza Lewis to take part in the project. Dr Joan Thirsk and Professor Glanville Jones supported our application. Research could not have been done without the help of the county archaeologists who made available information from their Sites and Monuments Records and gave much other advice and encouragement. We also received valuable help from the staff of the county record offices.

Services, information and advice have been provided by various individuals: Christine Addison, David Baker, Desmond Bonney, Stephen Coleman, Deborah Cunliffe, Paul Everson, Mike Farleigh, Suzanne Ferguson, Glenn Foard, Harold Fox, David Hall, Fred Hartley, Peter Liddle, Liz Mann, David McOmish, Nancy Moore, Graham Norrie, Andrew Pike, Nesta Rooke, Drew Shotliff, Graham Smith, Paul Snell, Peter Spencer, Alison Taylor, Chris Taylor, Bob Zeepvat.

We are grateful to the following for permission to reproduce illustrations: Bedfordshire Archaeological Unit, Dawson Publishers, Lutterworth Press, the Royal Commission on the Historical Monuments of England and the University of Cambridge Committee for Aerial Photography

C. L., P. M. F., C. D.
October, 1995

Abbreviations

Beds	Bedfordshire
Bucks	Buckinghamshire
BCS	W. de G. Birch (ed.), *Cartularium Saxonicum* (London, Whiting, 1885–93)
DB	A. Farley (ed.), *Domesday Book seu Liber Censualis Wilhelmi Primi Regis Angliae* (London, Record Commission, 1783).
DMV	deserted medieval village.
ed., eds	editor, -s.
edn	edition
f., ff.	folio, -s.
Leics	Leicestershire
MVRG	Medieval Village Research Group
NMR	National Monuments Record
Northants	Northamptonshire
OD	Ordnance Survey Datum
OE	Old English
PRO	Public Records Office
RCHM, RCHME	Royal Commission on Historic Monuments, England
S	P. H. Sawyer, *Anglo-Saxon Charters* (London, Royal Historical Society, 1968)
SMR	Sites and Monuments Records [county]
VCH	Victoria County History

The study of villages and landscapes in medieval England

In the 1940s M. W. Beresford and W. G. Hoskins found that the sites of many former medieval villages were still visible as mounds and hollows in modern pasture fields.[1] They worked independently at first, though only a short distance apart, Beresford in Warwickshire and Hoskins in Leicestershire. They were both historians who believed that the study of maps and the physical remains of the past added a further dimension to the documentary record. Their discoveries of deserted medieval villages, and their general approach to the past, set in train a sequence of events that was to open up a new field of enquiry, and to transform the conventional interpretation of the history of the village.

Beresford assembled information about *The Lost Villages of England* into an influential book (published in 1954) and formed with J. G. Hurst the Deserted Medieval Village Research Group. This had the aim of listing, classifying and mapping deserted village sites, and researching into them, notably by collecting plans and aerial photographs which showed streets, boundaries and houses surviving as earthworks, and by excavations on the deserted Yorkshire village of Wharram Percy. Research began with some relatively straightforward and closely focused objectives, which were to show that in the fifteenth and sixteenth centuries large numbers of medieval villages had been deserted (the figure climbed from 1,353 in 1954 to 2,263 in 1968),[2] to explain how and when the desertion had occurred, and to use the sites, uncluttered with modern buildings, to investigate the houses of their peasant inhabitants (Fig. 1.1). Soon enquiries developed in a number of other directions.

It was realised that the selection of deserted villages for study was rather artificial, and in particular large numbers of settlements had not been totally abandoned by their inhabitants, but had merely shrunk, leaving remains of former streets and houses on the edge of existing villages. Furthermore, comparison of inhabited villages with the groundplans of those that had been deserted, suggested that their modern forms preserved important elements of their medieval layout, and should therefore be considered as part of the evidence for earlier villages. As excavations

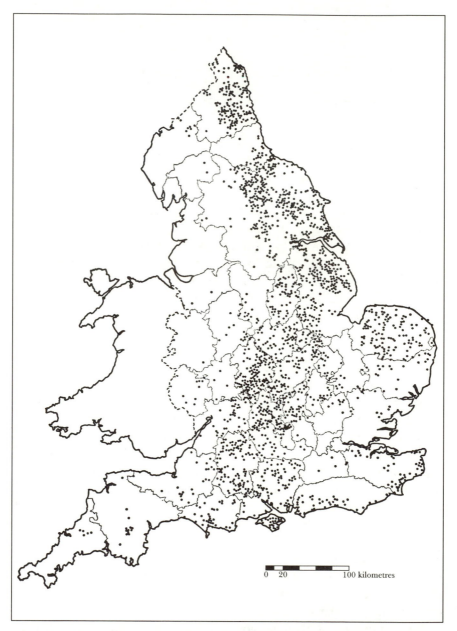

Figure 1.1 Map of deserted medieval villages in England, as known in 1968.

continued at Wharram Percy and many other sites, archaeological research shifted its aims from the recovery of evidence for the houses and material remains of late medieval peasant life (mainly for the period 1200–1500) to understanding earlier phases of the settlement. In recognition of the extension of interest from deserted villages to all villages (whatever their fate may have been after 1400), and from the phenomenon of desertion to the origin and development of the village, the title of the organisation that encouraged and co-ordinated research changed to the Medieval Village Research Group.

However this did not go far enough, because the Group's focus on the village was beginning to seem restricting, and needed to be further widened as the importance of hamlets, farmsteads, granges and other types of settlement was recognised, and in 1986 the Medieval Settlement Research Group was formed from a merger of the former village group and the group devoted to the study of moated sites – in many parts of the country an important type of isolated non-village settlement.[3] By this stage also, a society had been formed to investigate the historic landscape, inspired by the earlier work of W. G. Hoskins. Villages had always been studied in relation to their agricultural land: the original discovery of village sites had been made in the course of Beresford's planning of medieval field systems represented by ridge and furrow. But by the 1980s it was accepted that settlements could only be understood if their landed resources, the boundaries of their territories, the estates within which they lay and their systems of communication were also taken into account.

A once closely focused area of study was becoming very wide, taking in as it did every form of habitation, over a long period, in relation to resources and management; the research was in danger of becoming excessively diffuse. However a new central problem emerged from one of the main discoveries of the 1970s and 1980s. For a long time it had been believed that the village had been brought to England from Germany by Anglo-Saxon settlers in the fifth and sixth centuries.[4] Archaeological thinking before the 1960s was dominated by the notion that any novelty must have spread by diffusion, and that invasions by ethnic groups caused most cultural changes. This chronology of villages also accorded with a deeply rooted historical assumption that the village must have predated the manor; if the manor was thought to have been in existence as early as the seventh century, the village, it was reasoned, must have been formed even earlier.

But the excavation of more and more deserted and shrunken villages which showed very little evidence for occupation earlier than the eleventh or twelfth century, and the discovery of a growing number of hamlets

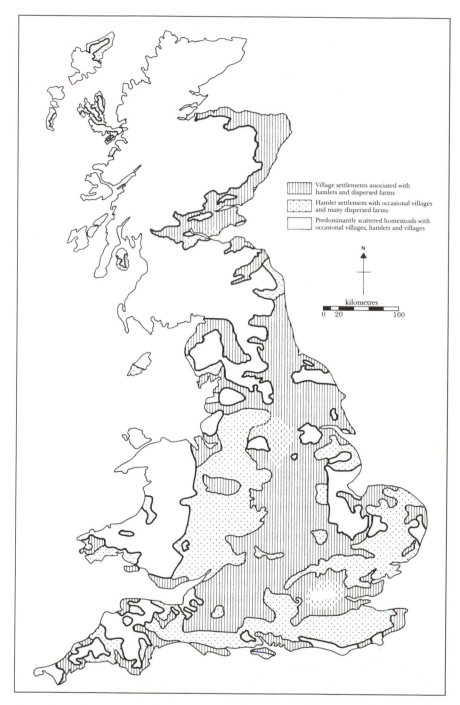

Village settlements associated with
hamlets and dispersed farms

Hamlet settlement with occasional villages
and many dispersed farms

Predominantly scattered homesteads with
occasional villages, hamlets and villages

N

kilometres
0   20   100

Figure 1.2 Map of rural settlements in modern Britain, based on work by Thorpe.

and farmsteads of the pre-Conquest period which had been abandoned by the ninth century, seemed to push forward the origin of the large nucleated village to the period between about 850 and 1200.[5] Research showed that this process of village formation had been restricted to a belt of central England running from the north-east (Northumberland and Durham) to the south-west (Dorset and Wiltshire), and various forms of dispersed settlements were characteristic of the south-east and west of the country (Fig. 1.2).[6] Villages no longer seemed such a 'natural' and stable feature of English life – they appeared to be the localised product of specific times and circumstances, and to be vulnerable to change. Most country dwellers in medieval England, and a growing number after *c*. 1400, did not live in villages. Parallel work in various European countries has shown that village nucleations, and their varied distribution over different regions, are found throughout the continent.[7]

This book aims to extend our understanding of settlement forms. We are concerned with describing the types of settlement, plotting their distribution in a sample English region, and with testing some explanations of the differences between villages and dispersed settlements. By way of introduction this chapter will seek to justify the study by explaining why the subject matters; it will then survey our state of knowledge by looking at the contributions of different disciplines; and it will end by setting out the range of questions and problems that needs to be answered both through the research that this book records, and in future work.

Why study medieval settlements?

Abandoned medieval villages have long attracted public interest. A site where the skeletal plan of the village is still clearly identifiable, and where it is possible to walk down an abandoned street and step through a house doorway visible as a gap in grassed-over foundations, gives the visitor a certain *frisson* of direct contact with the remote past (Fig. 1.3).

People are attracted to live in existing villages because they represent more than a convenient living space – they are a tangible symbol of an ideal rural life: simple, safe, stable and cohesive, and all the more desirable because of their patina of history. Modern planners have attempted to recreate villages, both in the model suburban developments before the first world war, or in the new dormitory settlements of more recent times. This sentimental, mythical version of the village tells us more about modern psychology than about the harsh reality of the middle ages, and would be a weak excuse for embarking on a study of medieval settlements. But the medieval village, at least in its imagined form, is part of

Figure 1.3 Plan of the deserted village of Firsby, Lincolnshire. This is a well-preserved and well-recorded site which exhibits many of the features of a deserted village, and shows some of the interpretations that can be based on the analysis of earthworks. The manor house complex lies to the west. The letter *e* marks the remains of the church, and fish ponds are visible at *d*. The main village street ran from *a* to *b*, and a series of house sites and toft boundaries adjoins it (*g*).

our experience, and consequently its study is not entirely irrelevant to modern life.

From the beginning of scientific history the plans of medieval settlements have been used as evidence for their origins. The early pioneer work was done in the late nineteenth century, by Germans such as Meitzen. In England Seebohm analysed village maps, particularly of Hitchin (Hertfordshire) and its neighbours, to argue the case for the Roman and British origins of medieval society.[8] In Maitland's response, *Domesday Book and Beyond*, two sections of Ordnance Survey maps were used to contrast 'village country' (south of Oxford) with 'a land of hamlets' on the Devon/ Somerset border.[9] With his customary elegant clarity, he contrasted the 'nucleated village [which].. stands in the midst of its fields', with the 'small clusters' of houses with 'no traces of very large fields'. Textbooks have since then sometimes contained a map, or an aerial photograph, of at least one deserted village. All too often, however, they are primarily decorative, and not given the prominence that they deserve as a source on a par with charters or tax lists. If we are concerned with the daily existence of ordinary people, then we cannot neglect considering their living space.

The hierarchy of settlements is a useful way of understanding the ordering of the material and social world of the middle ages. This is a hierarchy based partly on size, from large to small towns, and then to villages of varying population (most would fall between 300 and 30 people, or 60 and 6 households), and finally to hamlets, clusters of farms and individual farmsteads, ending perhaps with shielings, small structures occupied in the summer by people tending animals on upland pastures. The hierarchy could also be arranged in social terms, from the castles, manor houses and granges of the aristocracy to the peasant settlements. But increasingly we also think of settlements ranged according to their degree of planning. Towns were most likely to be arranged in orderly grids and equal sized building plots, with market places, churches and other civic structures sited at their centres. Many villages have neat rows

---

The site is surrounded by ridge and furrow, on which houses and tofts have been superimposed at *h*. Structures have been built over the ridge and furrow at *i* and *j*. A sequence of occupation can be observed, from Roman activity north of the village, a likely early medieval nucleus around the manor house and church, a planned village to the east, and later houses and tofts added between the main planned settlement and the manor house. The structures at *i* and *j* are probably connected with sheep farming after the village had been deserted. The settlement had reached a considerable size by 1086, and declined in the fourteenth, fifteenth and sixteenth centuries.

of measured, uniform tofts (enclosures each containing a house, agricultural buildings, yards and gardens), along streets or greens, and it was once fashionable to distinguish between 'planned' and 'unplanned' or 'organic' settlements, the latter having winding roads and oddly shaped tofts, arranged at irregular intervals. Now we assume that almost all settlements have some degree of organisation behind them – even a toft with boundaries which lack right angles must have been deliberately laid out by someone; and even dispersed settlement can show signs of some regularity, for example when houses lie at intervals along a road, or on the edge of a green.

The physical layout of the settlement can give us insights into social relationships – between the peasant houses and the superior residence of the lord of the manor, and among the peasant dwellings. The clear definition of the toft as a separate space, indeed defended by a ditch and bank, speaks of privacy and distrust of outsiders, but the close proximity of neighbours in a nucleated village, and the provision of communal facilities such as streets, greens, church houses, guild halls and the church or chapel tell us of co-operation in the community.[10] Beyond the village the same division between public and private is apparent in the fields and pastures, with a higher proportion of enclosed fields held by individual tenants in many dispersed settlements.

The settlement is also related to methods of production: the nucleated village and its extensive field system provides evidence for the primacy of grain growing over pastoral activities, while the greens at the centre of some villages and the crofts behind houses tell us something about the management of stock. Some settlements had access to large areas of open pasture in uplands and marshes, often reached by a wide drove way. We have come to associate dispersed settlements with rural industry, though potting or ironworking are also known to have occurred in the back yards of villages.

The settlement is an artefact which gives us some help in understanding medieval ideas and culture. The more regularly planned villages indicate an ordered society, anxious to measure and allocate land rationally, yet the wandering lanes and irregularly arranged tofts in both nucleated and dispersed settlements, speak of a distinct approach to the organisation of space, and a different balance between private and public access to resources.

The study of settlements makes us fully aware of the complexities of medieval society and its institutions. A village, perhaps a single street with a row of houses on each side, standing in a well defined block of land, gives an appearance of simplicity, until we find that its field system was shared with a neighbouring village, and the inhabitants had rights to fuel and pasture in a wood ten miles away. Investigation of the lordship of the village might reveal that it was divided between two or three manors, so that neighbours along the same street owed rents and services to different lords. Instead of a single church serving a parish coinciding with the village territory, we might find two churches standing in one churchyard, or discover that the village church was dependent on another, and the dead had to be carried five miles for burial. The simple coincidence of village, manor and parish was in fact rather unusual, and the complicated divisions and overlaps may tell us something about the chronology of development of the different institutions to which the villagers belonged. But unravelling the different layers of development can be hard to achieve.

Settlement studies also focus our attention on change, or on its absence. No better example of continuity can be found than the streets and property boundaries of a twentieth-century inhabited village, which probably originated in the twelfth century, or earlier. This should not conceal the social transformations that have overtaken the inhabitants and the changes in function of the houses contained within the boundaries. Nor can continuity always be assumed, because so many villages are found to have been replanned or moved over the centuries. But even these additions, shrinkages and shifts cannot be compared with the volatility that was characteristic of settlements before the tenth century. Once we have discovered and described these changes, we must explain them. Invasions were formerly thought to be the overriding factor; now social, economic and political processes seem to provide better answers.

While it is helpful to take a fragment of past culture, such as settlement, and subject it to thorough examination, eventually we must put it back into the jigsaw to see how it fits into the whole picture. The formative period of villages clearly belongs to that great expansive phase of society and civilisation, connected with the 'feudal transformation' or the 'twelfth century renaissance'; deserted villages are rightly linked to the 'crisis of the fourteenth century' and the 'transition from feudalism to capitalism'. But it is still worth keeping the fragments apart to give long-term chronological perspectives. The settlements of the early middle ages owed a great deal to the land clearances and territorial organisation of the prehistoric and Roman periods, and echoes of medieval changes can be found in phases of expansion and contraction, nucleation and dispersal, in earlier millennia.

The state of knowledge

Our studies are multi-disciplinary, but before we can combine the evidence and approaches of different subjects we must understand how the practitioners of history, archaeology, geography, place-names and landscape studies interpret their data and contribute to the study of settlement.

History

Historians have made a modest contribution to settlement studies, but it is worth beginning with history (meaning, in this context the study of the past based on written documents) because it is the oldest of the disciplines, and historical thinking has provided frameworks and chronologies which have influenced the approach of archaeologists and geographers.

Historical writing on the early middle ages (*c.* 400–1200) in England has been preoccupied with the great theme of the political unification of the country or, to use more modern language, the formation of a centralised state. The small kingdoms, that had emerged from the breakdown of the Roman province and the intrusion of groups of Anglo-Saxon migrants, came under the control of overkings from the late sixth century, but the decisive move to unity began in the ninth. Scandinavian invaders then disrupted the northern and eastern kingdoms, and galvanised the kings of Wessex into defending the south and then conquering the rest of the country. Their new kingdom was provided with a well-ordered structure of government with strong links between the crown and the provinces, which though threatened by invasion and civil conflict in the eleventh and twelfth centuries, was developed and strengthened under Norman and Angevin rulers.

Research into early local government has revealed an underlying pattern of administrative units, each covering many square miles, and known by various names such as shires, sokes or lathes.[11] Each depended on some local centre, often a royal vill, to which taxes and tributes were paid, and they have been described as the building blocks from which the early kingdoms were formed. Although these 'land units' relate mainly to administrative history, it has always been assumed that they told us something about early settlement because they contained populations of peasants, and were involved in agriculture in the sense that they provided food for the household of the king or lord. Some are known to have had a federal structure, with subdivisions which became separate territories when the larger units broke down from the ninth century onwards.[12] The written records do not say much about villages or peasants, but the charters of the tenth century show the fragmentation of landholding as estates of relatively small size (assessed at one to five hides and, according to a later source, Domesday Book, usually containing no more than two dozen peasant households) were granted, often to minor aristocrats, the thegns.[13] By the time of Domesday Book in 1086, though the occasional large federal estate survived in the hands of the king or a great church, these small manors were numerous and many villages were divided between two or more lords. By the eleventh century the village had charged upon it responsibilities to the state, in terms of self-policing and the provision of information.[14]

The local organisation of the church followed the pattern of secular government and landholding. The earliest local churches, the minsters, were founded on the land units of the seventh and eighth centuries, and consequently the groups of clergy attached to these well endowed churches were serving large parishes. From the ninth century the lords of the newly independent, smaller territories founded churches which became the close network of parish churches of later medieval and modern times.[15]

Lordship, along with relations between lords and peasants, is presumed to have been much affected by the fragmentation of the large land units. For a long time the assumption that Anglo-Saxon society was characterised by a mainly free peasantry made historians date the development of the manor, in which a demesne was cultivated with the labour services of dependent tenants, to the later part of the pre-Conquest period, and it was believed that manorialisation was continuing into the twelfth and thirteenth centuries.[16] In this view the village was much older than the manor – it reflected the independent, co-operative nature of free peasant communities, and the tendency for the lordship of a village to be divided among a number of manors suggested that the manor had been imposed on the village. In contrast with this interpretation there had always been a 'Romanist' school which assumed that the Roman villa, with its slaves and dependent *coloni*, preceded the manor, and exponents of this view assigned more prominence to lords as organisers of settlement. This approach was revived by H. P. R. Finberg who saw continuity between villas and manors, and showed that the Anglo-Saxon peasant, the *ceorl*, could be burdened with heavy services; Finberg was aided by Glanville Jones who traced the manor back even to pre-Roman antecedents, and emphasised the role of bond hamlets as providing services to estate centres. He also received support from T. H. Aston, who found evidence for the division between demesne and tenant holdings as early as the seventh century.[17] These views continue to be influential – a degree of continuity over the fourth to sixth centuries is generally accepted; powerful lords are given more prominence in interpretation of the early medieval countryside than free peasant communities; and no one believes in a democratic Anglo-Saxon tradition.

However, some recent work has reasserted the view that the manor developed in the later part of the pre-Conquest period. The great estates of the seventh and eighth centuries were mainly involved in collecting tribute, and more intensive exploitation of tenant services with demesne cultivation, though it may have existed to some degree, seems to have become more widespread as it was introduced as the appropriate means of managing the smaller units of landholding of the ninth, tenth and eleventh centuries.[18] On some estates heavy labour obligations may have been imposed as late as the twelfth century.[19] The new type of heavily burdened peasantry consisted partly of slaves who were settled on parcels of demesne land, a process well recorded in the eleventh century, and partly of landholding peasants whose obligations had been increased. The new chronology made the origins of the manor and nucleated village approximately contemporary developments, and would suggest a mechanism by which villages could have been founded by lords, as the lords would presumably have settled their slaves in a compact group of holdings near the manor house. There is, however, an obstacle to regarding villages simply as the creation of lords, because while manors are found everywhere in England, the nucleated village is more localised in its distribution.

English historians have been reluctant to apply the idea of the 'feudal transformation', much used on the continent.[20] There the Carolingian empire wielded much political authority in the eighth and ninth centuries, and its collapse gave opportunities for local lords to seize judicial power and exercise new forms of control over the peasantry. As in England, this period saw the disappearance of slavery, probably as lords found that dependent peasants provided more profitable sources of revenue. But precise parallels are hard to identify, because the centralised state was emerging in England at the same time as it collapsed on the continent, and the English aristocracy consequently had limited powers of independent jurisdiction. All that can be said is that in their different ways the aristocracies on both sides of the Channel were increasing their ability to generate revenue from land. Despite these social and political contrasts, nucleated villages are found both in England and on the continent, and it is thought that they came into existence at similar times.

Continental historians regard the whole period between the tenth and thirteenth centuries as one of economic growth. English historians are more cautious, but there is sufficient evidence of urban expansion from the late ninth century, of the growing intensity in the use of land implied by the smaller units of exploitation, the increased payment of taxes and rents in money, implying a degree of commodity production, and some extension of cultivation, for us to identify the centuries between 850 and 1100 as an expansive period, though inevitably with occasional lulls and setbacks. In the process of internal colonisation during the twelfth and thirteenth centuries both English and continental views co-incide, as assarting of woods and clearance of heaths and moors is well attested everywhere. Yet still there is perhaps more enthusiastic celebration of *les grands défrichements* across the Channel.[21]

Later medieval peasants have been intensively studied, principally using the manorial court rolls which provide English historians with uniquely detailed evidence for every aspect of peasant lives. The issues that have attracted most attention, such as the structure of families, may not have an immediate relevance to settlement history, though here regional differences in inheritance and attitude to property have been noted which may help us to understand variations in settlement form.[22] One focus of interest has been the land market, the recording of which has suggested to one authority that the detailed territorial identity of holdings – that is the definition of the precise boundaries of each parcel of land in the open fields – may have been an innovation of the twelfth century.[23] Before that time, the peasants held shares of land in the open fields which needed no precise identification. Much debate has centred on the village community, and its importance in peasant life in relation to the individual family and holding. Clearly the community was a powerful force in the thirteenth and fourteenth centuries, but its presence was not confined to the regions of nucleated villages and common fields. Indeed, research into interpeasant relations suggests that the men and women who lived in hamlets could enjoy close neighbourly contacts.[24]

Historians have always sought to understand long-term changes in economy and society, sometimes explaining developments by means of social power or the money supply, which have no direct link with rural settlements. An exception was M. M. Postan: both his explanation of the expansion and decline of medieval society, and the subsequent criticisms of his thesis, have used settlement as evidence. Postan attributed the late medieval crisis to the over-expansion of the twelfth and thirteenth centuries, when cultivation was extended over poor marginal soils, which were abandoned after they failed to maintain their productivity.[25] Critics who have examined the 'marginal' lands more closely have shown the skilful way in which the resources of pastures, wetlands and woodlands were exploited.[26] The assumption that a densely peopled landscape must lead to impoverishment and ruin has been shown not to apply to some areas of high population: for example intensive agricultural methods gave employment to the numerous inhabitants of north-east Norfolk.[27]

The debate over Postan's ideas has made historians more sensitive to regional variety than before. Even when experiencing a universal social trend, such as the late medieval demographic decline, the people of the various regions reacted in different ways. In the corn growing midlands, decay of settlements was almost universal, while in the more complex woodland landscapes or on upland pastures, new hamlets and farmsteads were being built, at least partly replacing those that were abandoned.[28] Research on the market suggests that from the thirteenth century com-mercialisation affected every part of the countryside, but especially the vicinities of larger towns, and that the use of land and choice of crops was much influenced by market demand.[29]

The practitioners of local history have made an original contribution to our understanding of regional differences. They began with the defin-ition of the 'farming regions' of the early modern period.[30] The country could be divided into mixed farming, wood pasture, and open pasture regions, further subdivided according to their agrarian economy and social structure. These farming regions resulted partly from changes in the late middle ages, but essential similarities can be observed with the regional patterns revealed by the mapping of plough teams and woodland in Domesday Book.[31] A useful way of classifying landscapes has come from the Leicester local historians, who recognise different *pays* – marshlands, fenlands, wolds, woodlands, champion country and so on.[32] These are helpful in understanding the characteristics of each part of the country, and settlement form plays a part in the definition, with nucleated villages especially characteristic of champion and wold landscapes. They also show the connections between different *pays*, such as the links in the early middle ages between riverside settlements specialising in arable farming and wolds where pasture and woodland products could be obtained. More recently the Leicester historians have become concerned with reconstructing mental horizons and cultural boundaries, and have pointed to the role of watersheds between river basins in defining regions.[33]

Archaeology

Modern archaeological work on medieval settlement began with the excavation of peasant houses on deserted village sites. Regional types have been identified, notably long houses with their combined accommo-dation for people and animals under the same roof, which were built not just in the uplands of the west and north, but also over parts of the midlands. Techniques of building varied from place to place also, and the materials used depended on local availability. The adoption of stone foundations was one of the main developments in the construction of peasant houses during the later middle ages.

Buildings relate to our understanding of the history of settlements in two main ways. Firstly, each household occupied a complex of structures, consisting of a dwelling and agricultural buildings arranged around a yard. This was once thought to have been a late development, but is now recognised throughout the period and shows that a large part of each toft was occupied by structures. Secondly, after a long debate about the durability of peasant buildings, there is now some agreement that while peasant houses were much altered and repaired, the same house often stood on the same site for centuries, and therefore contributed a conservative element to the development of the settlement.[34]

Even while excavators selected house sites for excavation, they came upon evidence for changes in the settlement as a whole. At Wharram Percy, for example, under thirteenth-century peasant houses lay the foundations of a twelfth-century manor house, while at Ashwell in Hertfordshire post holes and beam slots of peasant houses predated the construction of a moated site. Evidently the allocation of space between lords and peasants within a village could change drastically.[35] On one site (Wythemail, Northants) a toft boundary had a house built over it, suggesting a shift in village layout in the late thirteenth century.[36] More commonly toft boundaries were removed when formerly separate holdings were amalgamated, sometimes in a co-ordinated change involving the whole village, as at West Whelpington, Northumberland, in the early fourteenth century.[37] When streets and boundary banks were deliberately excavated in order to throw light on the development of the village plan, archaeologists often found evidence of their continued use from the twelfth to the fifteenth century.[38] But everywhere the excavators could report the absence of pre-Conquest settlements of any size under their deserted villages. The earliest occupation was usually dated to the eleventh or twelfth centuries, and at Thrislington a date as late as *c.*1200 could be proposed for the planned layout of the village.[39]

Relatively few dispersed settlements have been excavated. For a time it was claimed that hamlets on Dartmoor had been continuously occupied by a succession of turf houses beginning as early as the eighth century, but subsequent re-examination of the evidence suggested that some of these sites began in the twelfth or even in the thirteenth century, no earlier than the villages.[40] The myth of the timeless English village was broken. Villages had been created at a relatively late date, and when they had been abandoned within three or four centuries of their foundation, they looked like a transient phenomenon and could even be described as an aberration.[41]

Meanwhile excavation was proceeding on pre-Conquest sites. In 1957 an article on the Anglo-Saxon house had to make much use of continental analogies, but by 1976 a general survey of Anglo-Saxon buildings and settlements could draw on dozens of excavated examples, and the numbers have multiplied since then.[42] The settlements were quite small. Even when they might contain seventy structures, like West Stow in Suffolk, many of the buildings, such as the sunken floored huts or *grubenhauser*, were identified as outbuildings, and not all of the dwellings were occupied at the same time.[43] The pre-Conquest sites were often remote from later villages, even in rather marginal environments, like West Stow's sandy heath, and they had been abandoned after a relatively short period of occupation. An exception to these generalisations, certainly in terms of size, seems to be a settlement on river gravels at West Heslerton in North Yorkshire, which has produced seventy buildings, though interpretation of the site is still proceeding.[44]

Excavations of cemeteries of the pagan Saxon period seem to confirm the results of settlement research. The cemeteries were small, were often located at some distance from later villages, and were abandoned after a century or two – and not just because of conversion to christianity, because some continued in use as christian cemeteries and others ceased to be used before the likely date of conversion.[45] The abandonment and relocation of settlements in this period has been memorably described as the 'seventh century shuffle' or the 'middle Saxon shift', though settlements apparently began and ended their lives throughout the period from the sixth to the tenth century. All this seems to accord with the results from the excavation of later medieval villages, which began their lives after the earlier generation of settlements had been abandoned.

Excavated sites represent a tiny sample of the available archaeological evidence. Much more has been recovered by survey, that is finding and investigating sites from surface remains. The advantage of survey work is that a wider range of sites can be covered in a relatively short time. Fieldwork began on the deserted medieval village sites, for which county lists were compiled in the first two decades of the existence of the Deserted Medieval Village Research Group.[46] These gazetteers had specialised aims, focusing on deserted villages and excluding shrunken sites and any type of non-village settlement. But they had the advantage of consistency, as the same criteria for inclusion were used throughout the country.

Now each county maintains lists of medieval settlement sites in its Sites and Monuments Record, which are more comprehensive. To give an example of the figures that emerge from the new listing, while the gazetteer for Oxfordshire of 1965 contained 103 DMVs, the county archaeologist could report twenty years later that there were 148 deserted sites and 113 cases of shrinkage, out of a total of 617 'nucleated settlements' in the county.[47] No-one has ever attempted to count the deserted hamlets and individual farmsteads on a large scale, but as eighty abandoned house sites are known from one thoroughly studied woodland parish in Worcestershire, the figure for whole counties must run into thousands.[48] Moated sites represent an easily discovered settlement type most densely distributed in the counties where hamlets and farmsteads prevailed (mainly in the south-east and north-west) and more than 5,000 of these are known.[49] Deserted hamlets and farmsteads not surrounded with moats must outnumber these at least tenfold.

The next stage in fieldwork after the discovery and listing of sites is to record the plans, either from an aerial photograph or from a ground level survey, or preferably from a combination of both sources of information. The number of such plans has steadily increased in quality and quantity, drawn by the county archaeologists and groups organised by university external studies departments, but above all by the Royal Commission on Historical Monuments.[50] These surveys record the settlement remains at the last stage of their development, fossilised at the time of desertion (though often altered by the subsequent use of the site), but inevitably reflecting earlier stages of the settlement's history. They can be analysed together with the plans of still existing villages to show the extent of early planning, or replanning, or of planned or unplanned additions. Some villages can be seen to have spilled on to adjacent strips in the open fields, or to have shrunk back to allow cultivation of abandoned tofts. Greens may have been integral parts of an original plan; or greens and market places could be late additions; some greens were eventually filled with houses. Villages may have grown apart – or have been deliberately split, or more often a number of smaller nuclei have come together, to form a famous plan type, the 'polyfocal' settlement.[51] Fieldwork on deserted and inhabited villages provides evidence both for evolutionary concepts of the process of nucleation, and notions that the village was formed in a single act of planning.

Low status pre-Conquest settlements do not survive as earthworks, but their sites can be located through fieldwalking, that is by collecting pottery and other artefacts from the plough soil. Systematic programmes of fieldwalking in the 1970s, especially in Northamptonshire, provided some of the clearest evidence for the date of nucleation. Scattered across the former field systems belonging to nucleated villages, fieldworkers

discovered small concentrations of pre-Conquest pottery, usually of types
dated before 850; more than twenty have been located, for example, in
the parish of Brixworth. Subsequent excavations have shown that settlements, marked by post holes and other building remains, can indeed be
found under the pottery scatters.[52] Presumably others lie undiscovered
in pastures and other inaccessible fields. The abandonment of these sites
is thought to have coincided with the growth of nucleated settlements in
the ninth or tenth centuries.

Fieldwalking in East Anglia shows different types of instability. In
central Norfolk, sites producing pottery dated before 850 were succeeded
by others, sometimes larger, belonging to the tenth and eleventh centuries, but then a further upheaval in the twelfth century sent the inhabitants
to live on the edge of commons in straggling settlements which often still
survive.[53] In other parts of East Anglia, for example in the fenland, there
were shifts of site during the pre-Conquest period, and the same is likely
to be true of western England, though here pottery before the twelfth
century is less abundant, and is not closely datable. Most programmes of
fieldwalking show that the traditional historical view of Anglo-Saxon
invaders or medieval peasants as colonisers or pioneers is largely errone-
ous. From the almost universal scatters of worked flints, at least a few
sherds of prehistoric pottery and in many cases an abundance of Romano-
British pottery, we can be sure that the medieval settlements were established within an old agrarian landscape.

Environmental archaeology, and in particular the analysis of pollen
preserved in peat deposits and bones from excavations contribute to the
wider picture of the exploitation of rural resources as background to the
history of settlement.[54] Pollen samples reflect strong regional variety in
the history of vegetation during the first millennium AD. The retreat of
cultivation and regeneration of woodland that might be expected after
400 is sometimes indicated, but often the botanical evidence shows continued agricultural activity, and in some samples the woodlands expanded
at unexpected times – in the seventh century at one site in the north-east,
and as late as the tenth century in south Oxfordshire.[55] Northern sites
suggest a pattern of expanding cultivation in the ninth, tenth and eleventh
centuries. Bone analyses of rural sites show the variations between different types of animal husbandry, with sheep predominating on many sites,
and cattle on others; the most striking discovery for the pre-Conquest
period has come from urban bone studies which indicate that sheep,
instead of being slaughtered young for their meat, were kept for a number
of years for the sake of their wool, suggesting the influence of demand
for raw materials on the agricultural economy.[56]

Other branches of archaeological research deserve at least a brief mention. Urban archaeology, long a rival to rural excavations in its demand for funding, can contribute to our understanding of rural sites, because urban styles of planning and building resemble those in many villages, and as interest grows in small towns we are confronted with the need to define more clearly the divide between urban and rural settlements. Church archaeology has a great deal to tell us about the settlements that these buildings served. The location of parish churches in relation to planned settlements in the north, where indeed churches were often not included in the layout, has suggested that planning in these cases can be dated to the twelfth century.[57]

Geography

Historical geographers have studied settlements both by large scale mapping of historical data and by small scale studies. The maps of Domesday population, ploughs and woodland, and the analysis of this material in relation to soils and topography, have given us a context for early medieval settlements.[58] Furthermore, the study of the subsequent development of the countryside has been assisted by the maps compiled from the data in the fourteenth-century lay subsidies and poll taxes.[59] The distributions reveal important elements in the English countryside which did not change – the primacy of arable farming in the midlands and south-east, for example – but also the extent to which the colonising movement of the twelfth and thirteenth centuries increased the densities of settlement in the woodlands, wetlands and uplands. However, the enduring impression must be that cultivation covered a very large area by 1086.

Perhaps the single most important contribution that geographers have been able to make has been the mapping of modern settlement forms – often taken from the nineteenth-century Ordnance Survey maps, which are our first consistent and comprehensive source of topographical information. From these maps it is possible to identify the central belt of nucleated villages, and the large areas on either side of the village region where hamlets and farmsteads predominated (Fig. 1.2).[60] Wherever medieval settlement forms have been studied from the earthworks of abandoned villages, pottery scatters, documents and early maps, it is often possible to show that the frontier in the nineteenth century between nucleated and non-nucleated settlement patterns had been in much the same position in the later middle ages.

More detailed studies have used pre-Conquest charters to explore patterns of land use and organisation, which suggest that some regional landscape types, for example the champion and woodlands of the west midlands, were already in existence long before the eleventh century.[61] The descriptions in boundary clauses of open fields, with strips, gores and headlands defining the edge of the property conveyed in the charter, have been taken to imply that the nucleated village had formed at the centre of the field system, a view supported by the close coincidence in later periods of nucleated villages and extensive open fields.[62]

Village plans have long interested historical geographers, and a succession of researchers, using mainly northern examples, has shown the regularity of many villages, and the system of measurement used in laying out the streets and tofts.[63] In many cases the orderly pattern of the village is matched by the organisation of the strips in the associated fields, both the long strips stretching across the whole village territory, a feature of east Yorkshire, and the *solskifte* system by which every furlong's strips lay in the same sequence. The date of the planning was initially supposed to be in the ninth or tenth century, but it is generally thought now to be relatively late, perhaps in the period of reconstruction after the 'Harrying of the North' in 1069–70, or more likely (especially in view of the scepticism now voiced over the severity of the destruction at that time) in the twelfth century.[64]

Changing attitudes towards field systems have reflected more general shifts in the way in which we have approached the problem of explaining change. The maps of field systems over the whole country revealed that the distribution of the regular midland field system of two or three fields had a similar distribution to that of the nucleated village, with a belt of regular fields contrasting with the irregular systems of the west and east. A historian with a strong geographical sense, Joan Thirsk, proposed in the 1960s an evolutionary model for the emergence of common fields.[65] From a starting point of small enclosed fields, the effects of partible inheritance ensured that the arable area became broken down into small strips. At the same time the extension of cultivation so reduced the area of pasture that some solution had to be found in terms of agreed rotations and communal control. Although these changes had occurred in the pre-Conquest period, it was possible to document stages in the process in the less highly developed areas in the twelfth and thirteenth centuries. Although Thirsk did not discuss in detail the implications of the theory for settlement, it was clear, in view of the connection between regular fields and nucleated settlements that she might have discovered the mechanism behind village formation, as well as the origins of the midland field systems.

However, if the extension of arable and the need to accommodate more people lay behind the common field systems of the midlands, why did the East Anglian fields which were under much greater pressure, develop in a different direction, with more individual control of land?[66] Perhaps more deliberate actions lay behind the adoption of the regular field systems, as their development coincides with the breakdown of large estates and the formation of smaller manorial territories. This suggests lords are likely to have had a hand in it; or, alternatively, perhaps the scattered strips should be seen as the deliberate creation of a community anxious to spread the risk of crop failure by giving everyone a balance of good and bad land.[67] Was the decision to reorganise the fields carried out swiftly, involving an abrupt upheaval? Opinion has swung away from evolutionary models. One famous example of a supposed progressive change, by which villages with two-field systems in the twelfth and thirteenth centuries were believed to have switched to three fields under pressure to increase the cultivated area, has been shown to have occurred rarely.[68] Once villages had adopted a field system, they clung to it, no doubt anxious to maintain yields with as much fallow as possible, and to keep the maximum number of animals on the fallow.

Place-name studies

Place-names appear to provide direct evidence for early settlement, as many were formed between the fifth and tenth centuries, and they often contain a word that can be translated as 'farm' or 'village'.[69] However, many place-names that refer to habitations – -ton, -ham, -cot, -by or -thorp are among the most common – are unlikely to refer to settlements that stood on the same site as the places now bearing these names. In some cases the name is more precise in referring to a church or mill which is unlikely to have moved. Often however the name described not a specific point on the landscape but the general character of a territory, referring to a hill, valley or marsh. 'Tun' and other names could well refer to an estate rather than a settlement. This does not deprive place-names of their value as a source, because the name can be a useful guide to the date of the occupation of a place – early in the case of names referring to British inhabitants, or containing an element deriving from a Latin or British word; or late when Norman French terms are used.

Names are also important indicators of the relationship between places: Upton stood on a height, or Weston lay to the west of a more important place; they also indicate economic functions, such as Shipton, referring to the place on an estate where sheep keeping was the main activity. We can also gain an insight into status – Mickleton ('large estate or settlement') was a place of importance, while Caldecot ('cold cottages') implies a minor hamlet in a marginal situation. Recent work on place-names has been concerned with problems of dating; relating them to the natural and man-made landscape; and with unravelling problems of ethnic influences, such as the survival of pre-English names, and the naming or renaming with a Scandinavian vocabulary after the invasions and settlement of the ninth century in northern and eastern England.[70]

Landscape history

This (sometimes known as landscape archaeology) developed in the 1970s and 1980s with the aim of overcoming the barriers between disciplines. Indeed the Society for Landscape Studies was formed out of the experiences of three researchers engaged on a survey of West Yorkshire who found that their expertise in history, archaeology and place-names produced fruitful results when they worked in a co-operative environment.

Landscape historians assume that our understanding of the past should not be constrained by barriers of space or time. To begin with space, the excavation of a single site sometimes led to the intensive study of a small area to the neglect of its surroundings. The nearby fields, woods and pastures deserve study because they provided the resources on which the inhabitants of each settlement lived, and the district within which the village territory lies will contain parallels which will help to clarify the regional characteristics of building or settlement form. Somewhere in the vicinity will be found the longer distance facilities used by the inhabitants, such as markets and religious centres. A fruitful demonstration of this approach derived from work on the landscape context of a hamlet excavated in Okehampton Park in north Devon. It was possible to show how the peasants used the nearby arable land and meadows, and also depended on the more distant pasture of Dartmoor.[71]

The refusal of the landscape historians to be confined within a particular period also extends our understanding of a place. Again to use a south-western example, recent work on Cornish moorlands shows how these supposed wastes were a valuable asset, grazed in the early middle ages as communal pastures, but later they were partly fenced off as property rights were established and farms founded, and their exploitation shifted once more when the tin deposits of the streams were worked by outsiders.[72] The moors were constantly changing in relation to the settlement of the valleys, as the balance shifted between collective and individual access to land. A much longer time span has been explored in fieldwalking research on East Anglian plough soils, where extensive modern cultivation makes it possible to reconstruct the use of land and settlement of whole parishes from prehistoric times until the present day. The interpretation of the results is enhanced by documentary research, which can reveal the extent of former greens, around which, after much instability of settlement, houses congregated in the twelfth century.[73]

An important feature of landscape history has been the reconstruction of former estates, so that developments in settlement can be related to administrative territories. A geographer, Glanville Jones, noted similarities between well documented medieval manors in Wales, and large federal estates in medieval England and applied to them the term 'multiple estate', which in spite of much criticism has remained in use ever since.[74] The ideal type of multiple estate has a number of blocks of land, often used for different purposes (grazing, grain cultivation and so on) inhabited by peasants owing services to a manorial centre. It is often argued that they have a pre-medieval origin. There is much dispute about whether these should be regarded primarily as economic or administrative units, and it is always possible that instead of a universal process of primeval estates breaking down, they may sometimes have been constructed in the early middle ages from smaller parcels. The constituent parts of estates, whatever their period of origin, are thought to have provided a territorial context for the development of settlements.

One recent achievement has been to develop techniques for analysing the modern landscape and to discover earlier elements within the pattern of roads and boundaries. In parts of Essex and Suffolk it has been possible to reveal an underlying rectilinear layout of fields.[75] These clearly predate linear features that cut across them, and in some cases they appear to be earlier than Roman roads, suggesting that the area was divided into fields in the iron age, and that continuous use of the land has preserved the ancient boundaries until recent times. Such survivals tend not to appear in much of the midland belt of nucleated villages and open fields, not least because the parliamentary enclosure hedges obliterated earlier boundaries between furlongs and fields. Oliver Rackham has proposed a distinction between the 'ancient countryside' (of East Anglia or the south-west) where boundaries survive, and the planned landscapes of the champion districts, which have undergone two reorganisations, once in the early middle ages when fields were laid out, and again in the eighteenth and early nineteenth centuries with the enclosure of the open fields.[76]

The ideal of landscape history involves adopting a broad approach to analysing a large tract of countryside in which the researcher is prepared to engage with each period of its development, and combine the data and techniques derived from every discipline. In a number of cases this has been conducted without the use of excavation – the fieldwalking and documentary studies of Norfolk villages for example, or the studies of woodland parishes in Worcestershire which have used earthwork survey, fieldwalking and documentary sources.[77] David Hall's studies of North-amptonshire field systems have combined documentary research and survey of surviving ridge and furrow with fieldwalking to develop a hypothesis that fields were laid out in the ninth century, coinciding with nucleation. His work has revealed other aspects of village territories, including the varied ways in which the lord's portion of the fields, the demesne, sometimes lay as a compact block, and was sometimes scattered through the fields.[78]

Landscape projects that have involved excavation include Raunds (Northants), where digging of a number of late pre-Conquest sites has been accompanied by plan analysis of the village of Raunds and the hamlet of West Cotton, fieldwalking to discover the pre-ninth-century settlements, and documentary research to reveal the larger estate to which Raunds once belonged.[79] The result is a remarkable hypothesis about the origins of manors and villages, with a strong emphasis on the directive role of the lord, and the importance of planning of both settlements and fields. At Wharram Percy the project began with many years of excavation, but during the last two decades the research has broadened to include the settlement plan, its non-nucleated antecedents in the middle Saxon period, and the pattern of fields and townships in the surrounding region.[80] The campaign of enquiry at Wharram continued for such a long time, and brought into the work so many specialists from a variety of disciplines that it became a proving ground for many ideas about settle-ment and landscape history. The recognition that settlements changed radically during the pre-Conquest period, and the observation that the form of a medieval village could be influenced by remaining features of the prehistoric and Romano-British periods are just two examples of influential discoveries that either began or were disseminated from the Wharram research.

Problems and questions – what is to be done?

This survey of recent work on medieval rural settlement has indicated some of the uncertainties and unresolved problems. Now some of the main outstanding questions will be posed, which will be discussed further in the following chapters. They will be presented in chronological order, dealing with the period before the nucleation of villages, the process of nucleation and the subsequent history of settlements.

Before the nucleated village

The medieval countryside inherited much from prehistoric and Romano-British cultivators, but the precise nature of that legacy is still difficult to define. Large areas of land which had been cleared, cultivated and divided into fields and estates before 400 continued in use in the post-Roman period. Some settlements, as can be seen from the burials, pottery and structures of the fifth and sixth centuries found on or near Roman sites, remained in occupation. But did any element of the management and ownership of the land and its inhabitants persist for any length of time? It is helpful to know that some estate boundaries and even field boundaries were still used, but there may have been radical changes within the territories they defined.

Two general problems relate closely to settlement history. The first concerns the decline in population which follows from current estimates that Roman Britain supported more than 5 million people, compared with a figure of about 2 million in 1086.[81] In view of the environmental and topographical evidence for woodland regeneration and the inundations on the east coast after the deterioration of the Roman drainage system, there must have been some reduction in the area under cultivation and most likely this was concentrated in the period between *c.* 450 and 600. Against this view other environmental evidence shows no retreat of cultivation,[82] and it is argued that the collapse of Roman administration and the imperial economy should not have interrupted the routines of peasant subsistence farming.

The second problem remains the much older controversy concerning the scale of Germanic immigration: some argue that only a small Anglo-Saxon elite took over the Roman province, while others believe that the changes in material culture and language can only be explained by a sizeable influx from Germany. Many cemeteries have been found containing distinctive Germanic grave goods – but it is unclear whether the people who were buried with Anglo-Saxon weapons, jewellery and pottery were necessarily migrants from across the North Sea, or their direct descendants. And how large a population was represented by groups of only a few dozen graves?[83] Early Anglo-Saxon settlements on rather marginal soils are taken as evidence that the migrants were restricted in their choice of places to live, while the native British remained on the better land, though the existence of these indigenous inhabitants remains a shadowy concept in view of the lack of many material remains attributable to them. Recent controversy has focused on the timber buildings of which evidence has been found on such sites as Chalton, West Stow and Thirlings. Are these a continuing Romano-British type of rural building or were they introduced from the continent? The latter view is now gaining ground, but even the protagonists of a large scale migration have to concede that one type of German house, the tripartite aisled long house, did not reach England, suggesting that migration may have resulted in social changes which rendered that form of building inappropriate.[84] This raises the intractable problem of whether the invaders accepted the institutions that they found, or imposed their own social structure and agricultural technology.

No fully convincing explanation has been offered for the instability of settlement of the fifth to ninth centuries. It could reflect the relative emptiness of the countryside, where a good deal of unintensive pastoral farming was practised, and new farms could be built wherever seemed convenient. Political changes may explain the shifts of high status settlements, such as the Northumbrian royal palace at Yeavering, and the same factor may apply to other sites, though we cannot be sure of the social standing of the inhabitants of a number of places, notably Cowdery's Down in Hampshire. The abandonment of some sites has been linked (without much proof) to the Danish invasions, and we do not know if incoming Danes founded new settlements or were mainly taking over existing ones. Some sites may have been moved on the orders of estate managers, or because of changes in the agricultural or commercial economy which directly affected the peasants.

Nucleation of villages

Readers will have noticed some inconsistencies in the dates given for various stages of nucleation. The earliest indications of large-scale settlement under deserted village sites is dated to the eleventh and twelfth centuries but the smaller settlements, which were abandoned, it is thought, when peasants moved into larger villages, have produced pottery no later than the ninth, though the dating is inevitably imprecise. The charter boundary clauses which refer to open field systems – which usually accompanied the compact villages – belong mainly to the tenth and eleventh centuries. The period for the building of parish churches extends from the ninth to the twelfth centuries. We cannot be sure, either, of the mechanism by which nucleation was achieved. Was it a sudden upheaval or was it spread over many years? There may have been two stages, one leading to an irregular nucleated village, with the next, after an interval as long as a couple of centuries, setting up the planned village.

The distinctive geographical distribution of settlements ought to be the key to resolving the problem of the origin of nucleation. There ought to be pronounced differences in environment (relief, soils, climate) or in social structure, which explain the differences in settlement; or perhaps economic factors were the most important, because there is a close association between villages and extensive arable cultivation, above all in regular field systems. But we cannot be certain as to why people in one district felt impelled to adopt such a method of cultivation and habitation while others did not. One model much employed in the 1960s and 1970s was based on population change. It was argued that it was the high density of people which forced them to adopt co-operative farming, but there are doubts about the coincidence between the districts of high populations and those dominated by villages.[85]

Another fashionable view attributed nucleation to the influence of lords who, anxious to improve the efficiency of their estates and to maintain a disciplined control of their tenants, forced or cajoled them into living in a planned settlement. Indeed some villages may have been created entirely by lords, as happened in the colonisation of eastern Germany.

Political factors may have played a part. It has been argued that the likely circumstances for nucleation and planning, especially when many adjacent villages have similar forms, would be a great upheaval such as the Danish settlement of around 900, or the assertion of English rule in the tenth century, or after the destruction of swathes of countryside in William the Conqueror's harrying of the north in 1069–71. The argument that close knit village communities were formed in the interests of defence, as advocated to explain some continental settlement patterns, like the movement to hill-top villages in Italy known as *incastellamento*, is less likely to have been a factor in England.[86]

Perhaps there is some connection between nucleation and the social structure of the peasant communities themselves? If the peasants were the principal actors in gathering people into a single settlement, perhaps this was a peculiarity of certain communities? Nucleated villages in the thirteenth century often contained servile peasants living on standard customary tenements while dispersed settlements are often associated with free tenants, holding lands which are not measured in standard units and traditionally assumed to be the product of twelfth- and thirteenth-century colonisation of woods and wastes. The coincidence between the timing of nucleation and the growth of towns presents another possible explanation for the formation of villages. Perhaps the planning in the countryside was based on urban models, or the growth of the market for agricultural produce changed peasant society in ways that prepared the way for new forms of rural settlement?

After nucleation

The formation of nucleated villages was evidently not a single, simple
process, and we need to understand more about the dynamics that affected
both villages and the smaller settlements of the dispersed settlement
areas. We must see to what extent villages were changed, replanned and
extended and if possible to know how or why this occurred. But our
attention in the twelfth and thirteenth centuries must focus as well on
the dispersed settlements – they too proliferated in this period, but how
can their different forms be explained? To what extent were they based
on earlier scatters of farmsteads?

The shrinkage and desertion of settlements, mainly in the fourteenth
and fifteenth centuries, has provoked more scholarly interest than any
other aspect of medieval settlement. But we still do not know why the
degree of contraction varies so much, nor whether the areas of dispersed
settlement were affected in the same way as the well-known deserted and
shrunken villages. Research into deserted settlement raises exactly the
same range of problems as settlement formation – were environmental
or social factors most important? Did the main initiatives come from the
peasants or lords? What was the chronology and geography of the process?
Indeed just as at the beginning of this chapter we saw that the modern
scientific study of settlement began with deserted villages and moved to
consider their origin, so at the end we can say that better understanding
of desertion may well provide important clues as to the beginning of the
places which lost their inhabitants in the late medieval crisis.

The east midlands research project

Having posed these questions in the study of rural settlement, how are
we to provide some answers? This book is reporting the results of a
research project devised in 1990 with the aim of approaching the study
of rural settlement in a systematic fashion, extending over a sizeable
sample of settlements. Investigations of single villages have had satisfy-
ingly detailed results, but we are often left wondering if the chosen place
was typical, or how it fitted into its region. Studies of the whole country
have given wonderful overviews, and have revealed the great diversity of
regional landscapes, but lacked specific detail.

A 'region' seemed the best scale of project, which could combine both
variety and detail. Clearly identifiable historical regions are very difficult
to find in England, and in every case those seeking to define them are
involved in debates about where to draw the boundaries, even in the
case of East Anglia which is bounded on two or three sides by the sea.
The best solution seemed to be to take a group of counties which had

some similarities, but also included varied rural landscapes. The East Anglian counties of Norfolk and Suffolk might have been a possible choice, but they lack the classic nucleated villages. The west midlands are an attractive proposition, because they have good historical documents and a mixture of terrains and settlement forms, but research into the archaeology of the crucial period 400–1200 is hampered by the lack of good datable series of pottery.

Consequently the east midlands seemed to provide a useful compromise, and the four counties of Bedfordshire, Buckinghamshire, Leicestershire and Northamptonshire were selected for investigation. They include a wide variety of soils and landscapes, from chalk hills to river valleys, and contain a large area of the undulating clay lands so characteristic of the midlands. There are large numbers of nucleated villages, as well as numerous and varied dispersed settlements, so the history of the two generic types of rural settlement could be compared side by side. And these counties have a good quantity of evidence for archaeological research: earthworks of deserted and shrunken medieval sites still survive in some quantity, and pottery of the pre-Conquest period is found in all four counties, both on excavated sites and in the plough soil. Historical sources from both public records and private archives are found in relative abundance.

A number of research projects, like the work centred on Raunds (Northants) and at Milton Keynes (Bucks), had already shown the potential of the area.[87] The counties were well known for the excellence of their archaeological services and Sites and Monuments Records, which would make the retrieval of archaeological information especially easy. The Leicestershire Museums Archaeology Unit has surveyed large numbers of medieval settlements surviving as visible earthworks,[88] and in Northamptonshire the field systems have been reconstructed from a combination of field and documentary evidence.[89] In Bedfordshire the County Archaeology Unit has methodically plotted the plans of medieval settlement remains from aerial photographs onto its Sites and Monuments Records, and carried out a series of parish surveys including details from early maps and documents.[90] And the buildings and earthworks of Northamptonshire have been catalogued by the Royal Commission on Historical Monuments.[91]

In Northamptonshire, fieldwalking exercises have produced remarkable indications of small dispersed settlements of the fifth to ninth centuries in districts later dominated by nucleated villages, and similar results have emerged from projects centred on Medbourne and the Langtons in south-east Leicestershire.[92] Excavations include those on early medieval settlements at Maxey (Northants), the village of Stratton (Beds) and Eaton Socon (historically in Bedfordshire), where eleventh-century buildings lay under a later castle.[93] Smaller early medieval sites have been found by excavation in a number of places, including Eggington (Beds).[94] Deserted medieval villages have been excavated at Faxton, Lyveden and Wythemail (Northants), and Martinsthorpe in Rutland.[95] Caldecotte, Great Linford, Tattenhoe, Westbury and other sites in north Buckinghamshire were investigated in advance of the development of Milton Keynes.[96] Historians have researched the archives of the monastic houses of Leicester, Owston and Peterborough, and there have been some notable regional studies, on the Chiltern Hills for example, and on the social structures revealed by the Hundred Rolls of 1279–80.[97]

The project involved the assembling and mapping of as much relevant information as possible. The maps formed the primary research tool for the subsequent observations and analysis. Sources used for this included the Royal Commission's National Monuments Record (NMR); the county Sites and Monuments Records (SMR); the archives of the Medieval Village Research Group (MVRG); various available soil and geological surveys; all Ordnance Survey 1:50,000 Landranger maps for the area; the Ordnance Survey first edition one inch maps for Leicestershire; and John Bryant's county maps (1826) of Bedfordshire, Buckinghamshire and Northamptonshire.

Published historical sources were used including pre-Conquest charters, Domesday Book, the Hundred Rolls, Inquisitions Post Mortem, court rolls, lay subsidy records and place-name lists. Various categories of this collated information were then mapped for each county initially at 1:250,000 and 1:50,000. The results of the analysis are reported in the succeeding chapters.

Notes

1 M. W. Beresford, 'A draft chronology of deserted village studies', *Medieval Settlement Research Group Annual Report*, 1 (1986), 18–23.

2 M. W. Beresford and J. G. Hurst (eds), *Deserted Medieval Villages* (London, Lutterworth, 1971), p. 34.

3 For details see the *Medieval Settlement Research Group Annual Report*, 1 (1986).

4 Even as late as the 1960s in some cases, as H. R. Loyn, *Anglo-Saxon England and the Norman Conquest* (London, Longmans, 1962), p. 20.

5 The best summary of the evidence is to be found in C. C. Taylor, *Village and Farmstead. A History of Rural Settlement in England* (London, George Philip, 1983), pp. 109–50.

6 B. K. Roberts, *Rural Settlement in Britain* (Folkestone, Dawson, 1977), p. 16.

7   For example, W. Rosener, *Peasants in the Middle Ages* (Cambridge, Polity Press, 1992), pp. 49–51; J.-M. Pesez, 'The emergence of the village in France and in the west', *Landscape History*, 14 (1992), 31–5.

8   F. Seebohm, *The English Village Community* (London, Longmans, 4th edn, 1905), pp. 424–36.

9   F. W. Maitland, *Domesday Book and Beyond* (Cambridge, Cambridge University Press, 1897), between pp. 16 and 17.

10   The division between public and private space is highlighted in G. Astill, 'Rural settlement: the toft and the croft', in G. Astill and A. Grant (eds), *The Countryside of Medieval England* (Oxford, Blackwell, 1988), pp. 51–4.

11   J. E. A. Joliffe, *Pre-Feudal England: the Jutes* (Oxford, Oxford University Press, 1933) was the pioneer of the approach.

12   P. H. Sawyer, *From Roman Britain to Norman England* (London, Methuen, 1978), pp. 155–6.

13   P. Stafford, *The East Midlands in the Early Middle Ages* (Leicester, Leicester University Press, 1985), pp. 29–39.

14   H. R. Loyn, *The Governance of Anglo-Saxon England* (London, Arnold, 1984), pp. 146–7.

15   J. Blair, *Minsters and Parish Churches. The Local Church in Transition, 950–1200* (Oxford, Oxford Committee for Archaeology, 1988), pp. 1–19; for a sceptical questioning of this view see E. Cambridge and D. Rollason, 'Debate: the pastoral organisation of the Anglo-Saxon church: a review of the "Minster Hypothesis"', *Early Medieval Europe*, 4 (1995), 87–104.

16   Loyn, *Anglo-Saxon England and the Norman Conquest*, pp. 195–8 reflects this view. The historiography is summarised in T. H. Aston, 'The English manor', *Past and Present*, 10 (1956), 6–13.

17   H. P. R. Finberg, 'Continuity or cataclysm?' and 'Roman and Saxon Withington', both reprinted in H. P. R. Finberg, *Lucerna: Studies of Some Problems in the Early History of England* (London, Macmillan, 1964), pp. 1–20 and 21–65; also his contribution to H. P. R. Finberg (ed.), *The Agrarian History of England and Wales, vol. 1*, pt 2 (Cambridge, Cambridge University Press, 1972), pp. 385–448; G. R. J. Jones, 'Multiple estates and early settlement', in P. H. Sawyer (ed.) *Medieval Settlement* (London, Arnold, 1976), pp. 15–40; T. H. Aston, 'The origins of the manor in England', with 'A postscript', in T. H. Aston, P. R. Coss, C. Dyer and J. Thirsk (eds), *Social Relations and Ideas* (Cambridge, Cambridge University Press, 1983), pp. 1–43.

18   C. Dyer, 'Les problèmes de la croissance agricole du haut moyen age en Angleterre', in *La croissance agricole du haut moyen age. Chronologie, modalités, géographie* (Centre Culturel de l'Abbaye de Flaran, 10e journées internationales d'histoire, Auch, 1990), pp. 120–3.

19   R. Faith, 'Demesne resources and labour rent on the manors of St. Paul's Cathedral, 1066–1222', *Economic History Review*, 47 (1994), 657–78.

20   G. Bois, *The Transformation of the Year One Thousand. The Village of Lournand from Antiquity to Feudalism* (Manchester, Manchester University Press, 1992); and critical comment by A. Verhulst, 'The decline of slavery and the economic expansion of the early middle ages', *Past and Present*, 133 (1991), 195–203.

21   P. Contamine, M. Bompaire, S. Lebecq and J.-L. Sarrazin, *L'économie médiévale* (Paris, Armand Colin, 1993), pp. 164–75.

22   Z. Razi, 'The myth of the immutable English family', *Past and Present*, 140 (1993), 3–44.

23   P. D. A. Harvey (ed.), *The Peasant Land Market in Medieval England* (Oxford, Clarendon Press, 1984), pp. 12–19.

24   C. Dyer, 'The medieval English village community and its decline', *Journal of British Studies*, 33 (1994), 407–29; R. M. Smith, 'Kin and neighbors in a thirteenth-century Suffolk community', *Journal of Family History*, 4 (1979), 219–56.

25   M. M. Postan, *The Medieval Economy and Society* (London, Weidenfeld and Nicolson, 1972), pp. 57–66.

26   For example, M. Bailey, *A Marginal Economy? The East Anglian Breckland in the Later Middle Ages* (Cambridge, Cambridge University Press, 1989).

27   B. M. S. Campbell, 'Agricultural progress in medieval England: some evidence from eastern Norfolk', *Economic History Review*, 2nd Series, 36 (1983), 24–46.

28   E. Miller (ed.), *The Agrarian History of England and Wales, vol. 3, 1348–1500* (Cambridge, Cambridge University Press, 1991), pp. 85, 113.

29   B. M. S. Campbell, J. A. Galloway, D. Keene and M. Murphy, *A Medieval Capital and its Grain Supply: Agrarian Production and Distribution in the London Region c. 1300* (Historical Geography Research Series, Institute of British Geographers, no. 30, 1993).

30   J. Thirsk, *Agrarian Regions and Agrarian History in England, 1500–1750* (London and Basingstoke, Macmillan, 1987).

31   H. C. Darby, *Domesday England* (Cambridge, Cambridge University Press, 1977); the direct comparison is made in C. Dyer, 'Documentary evidence: problems and enquiries', in Astill and Grant (eds), *Countryside of Medieval England*, pp. 14–21.

32   For example, A. Everitt, 'River and wold: reflections on the origins of regions and *pays*', *Journal of Historical Geography*, 3 (1977), 1–19; H. S. A. Fox, 'The people of the wolds in English settlement history', in M. Aston, D. Austin and C. Dyer (eds), *The Rural Settlements of Medieval England* (Oxford, Blackwell, 1989), pp. 77–101.

33   C. Phythian-Adams, 'Introduction: an agenda for English local history', in C. Phythian-Adams (ed.), *Societies, Cultures and Kinship, 1580–1850: Cultural Provinces in English Local History*, (Leicester, Leicester University Press, 1993), pp. 1–23.

34   J. G. Hurst, 'A review of archaeological research (to 1968)', in Beresford and Hurst (eds), *Deserted Medieval Villages*, pp. 93–115; J. G. Hurst, 'Rural building in England and Wales. England', in H. E. Hallam (ed.), *The Agrarian History of England and Wales, vol. 2, 1042–1350* (Cambridge, Cambridge University Press, 1988), pp. 898–915; H. E. J. Le Patourel, 'Rural building in England and Wales. England,' in Miller (ed.), *Agrarian History, vol. 3*, pp. 843–65; S. Wrathmell, *Domestic Settlement 2: Medieval Peasant Farmsteads* (Wharram: A Study of Settlement on the Yorkshire Wolds, 6, York Department of Archaeology, University of York, 1989).

35   J. G. Hurst (ed.), *Wharram: A Study of Settlement in the Yorkshire Wolds*, 1 (Society for Medieval Archaeology Monograph Series, no. 8, 1979), pp. 26–41; D. G. and J. G. Hurst, 'Excavations of two moated sites: Milton, Hampshire and Ashwell, Hertfordshire', *Journal of the British Archaeological Association*, 30 (1967), 48–86.

36   D. G. and J. G. Hurst, 'Excavations at the medieval village of Wythemail, Northamptonshire', *Medieval Archaeology*, 13 (1969), 181.

37   M. G. Jarrett, 'The deserted medieval village of West Whelpington, Northumberland: third report, part two', *Archaeologia Aeliana*, 5th Series, 16 (1988), 139–92.

38   For example, P. Rahtz, 'Upton, Gloucestershire, 1964–1968', *Transactions of the Bristol and Gloucestershire Archaeological Society*, 88 (1969), 98–103.

39   D. Austin, *The Deserted Medieval Village of Thrislington, Co. Durham: Excavations 1973–74* (Society for Medieval Archaeology, Monograph Series no. 12, 1989), pp. 164–7.

40   D. Austin, 'Dartmoor and the upland village of the south-west of England', in D. Hooke (ed.), *Medieval Villages* (Oxford University Committee for Archaeology, Monograph no. 5, 1986), pp. 71–9; D. Austin and M. J. C. Walker, 'A new landscape context for Houndtor, Devon', *Medieval Archaeology*, 29 (1985), 147–52; G. Beresford, 'Three deserted medieval settlements on Dartmoor', *Medieval Archaeology*, 32 (1988), 175–83. Another hamlet with evidence for the twelfth century and no earlier is described in P. A. Barker, 'The deserted medieval hamlet of Braggington', *Transactions of the Shropshire Archaeological Society*, 58 (1966), 122–39.

41   J. G. Hurst, 'The Wharram research project: results to 1983', *Medieval Archaeology*, 28 (1984), 77–111.

42   C. A. Ralegh Radford, 'The Saxon house: a review and some parallels', *Medieval Archaeology*, 1 (1957), 27–38; P. A. Rahtz, 'Buildings and rural settlement', in D. M. Wilson (ed.), *The Archaeology of Anglo-Saxon England* (Cambridge, Cambridge University Press, 1976), pp. 49–98. A recent database has used a sample of 267 pre-Conquest timber buildings: A. and G. Marshall, 'A survey and analysis of the buildings of early and middle Anglo-Saxon England', *Medieval Archaeology*, 35 (1991), 29–43.

43   S. West, *West Stow: the Anglo-Saxon Village* (East Anglian Archaeology, 24, 1985).

44   H. Hamerow, 'Settlement mobility and the "middle Saxon shift"; rural settlement and settlement patterns in Anglo-Saxon England', *Anglo-Saxon England*, 20 (1990), 1–17; D. Powlesland, 'An interim report on the Anglo-Saxon village at West Heslerton, North Yorkshire', *Medieval Settlement Research Group Annual Report*, 5 (1990), 36–40.

45   A. Goodier, 'The formation of boundaries in Anglo-Saxon England: a statistical study', *Medieval Archaeology*, 28 (1984), 1–21; P. Rahtz, T. Dickinson and L. Watts (eds), *Anglo-Saxon Cemeteries* (British Archaeological Report, British Series, 82, 1980).

46   The more complete and informative gazetteers are for Northamptonshire and Oxfordshire: K. J. Allison, M. W. Beresford, J. G. Hurst *et al.*, *The Deserted Medieval Villages of Oxfordshire* (University of Leicester Department of English Local History, Occasional Papers, 1st Series, 17, 1965); K. J. Allison, M. W. Beresford, J. G. Hurst *et al.*, *The Deserted Medieval Villages of Northamptonshire* (University of Leicester Department of English Local History, Occasional Papers, 1st Series, 18, 1966).

47   C. J. Bond, 'Medieval Oxfordshire villages and their topography: a preliminary discussion', in Hooke (ed.), *Medieval Villages*, pp. 101–23.

48   C. Dyer, *Hanbury: Settlement and Society in a Woodland Landscape* (University

of Leicester Department of English Local History, Occasional Papers, 4th Series, 4, 1991), p. 53.

49 F. A. Aberg (ed.), *Medieval Moated Sites* (Council for British Archaeology Research Reports, 17, 1978), pp. 1–4.

50 Notably in the volumes covering the counties of Cambridgeshire, Dorset and Northamptonshire; and most recently in P. L. Everson, C. C. Taylor and C. J. Dunn, *Change and Continuity: Rural Settlement in North-West Lincolnshire* (Royal Commission on the Historical Monuments of England, London, HMSO, 1991).

51 This type was first described in C. C. Taylor, 'Polyfocal settlement and the English village', *Medieval Archaeology*, 21 (1977), 189–93.

52 G. Foard, 'Systematic fieldwalking and the investigation of Saxon settlement in Northamptonshire', *World Archaeology*, 9 (1978), 357–74; D. N. Hall and P. W. Martin, 'Brixworth, Northamptonshire: an intensive field survey', *Journal of the British Archaeological Association*, 132 (1979), 1–6; M. Shaw, 'The discovery of Saxon sites below fieldwalking scatters: settlement evidence at Brixworth and Upton, Northamptonshire', *Northamptonshire Archaeology*, 25 (1993/4), 77–92.

53 For example, A. Davison, *The Evolution of Settlement in Three Parishes in South-East Norfolk*, (East Anglian Archaeology, 49, 1990); R. J. Silvester, 'The Fenland project in retrospect' (East Anglian Archaeology, 50, 1993), pp. 24–39.

54 The evidence is summarised in M. Bell, 'Environmental archaeology as an index of continuity and change in the medieval landscape', in Aston *et al.* (eds), *Rural Settlements*, pp. 269–86; C. Fenton-Thomas, 'Pollen analysis as an aid to the reconstruction of patterns of land-use and settlement in the Tyne-Tees region during the first millenium BC and AD', *Durham Archaeological Journal*, 8 (1992), 51–62; J. Rackham (ed.), *Environment and Economy in Anglo-Saxon England* (C. B. A. Research Report, no. 89, 1994).

55 S. P. Day, 'Post-glacial vegetational history of the Oxford region', *New Phytologist*, 119 (1991), 445–70.

56 J. Bourdillon, 'Countryside and town: the animal resources of Saxon Southampton, in D. Hooke (ed.), *Anglo-Saxon Settlements* (Oxford, Blackwell, 1988), pp. 176–96; P. Crabtree, *West Stow: Early Anglo-Saxon Animal Husbandry* (East Anglian Archaeology, 47, 1990).

57 R. Morris, *Churches in the Landscape* (London, Dent, 1989), pp. 245–6.

58 The results of the Domesday geography project are summarised in Darby, *Domesday England*.

59 For example, R. E. Glasscock, 'England circa 1334', and A. R. H. Baker, 'Changes in the later middle ages', in H. C. Darby (ed.), *A New Historical Geography of England before 1600* (Cambridge, Cambridge University Press, 1973), pp. 136–247.

60 Roberts, *Rural Settlement*, pp. 15–17.

61 D. Hooke, *The Anglo-Saxon Landscape: the Kingdom of the Hwicce* (Manchester, Manchester University Press, 1985), pp. 154–226.

62 D. Hooke, 'Open-field agriculture – the evidence from pre-conquest charters of the west midlands', in T. Rowley (ed.), *The Origins of Open Field Agriculture* (London, Croom Helm, 1981), pp. 39–63.

63 P. Allerston, 'English village development', *Transactions of the Institute of British Geographers*, 51 (1970), 95–109; B. K. Roberts, 'Village plans in Co.

Durham: a preliminary statement', *Medieval Archaeology*, 16 (1972), 33–56; J. A. Sheppard, 'Metrological analysis of regular village plans in Yorkshire', *Agricultural History Review*, 22 (1974), 118–35; M. Harvey, 'Regular field and tenurial arrangments in Holderness, Yorkshire', *Journal of Historical Geography*, 6 (1980), 3–16; B. K. Roberts, *The Making of the English Village* (London, Longmans, 1987); L. H. Campay, 'Medieval village plans in County Durham: an analysis of reconstructed plans based on medieval documentary sources', *Northern History*, 25 (1989), 60–87.

64 D. M. Palliser, 'Domesday Book and the "Harrying of the North"', *Northern History*, 29 (1993), 1–23.

65 J. Thirsk, 'The common fields', *Past and Present*, 29 (1964), 1–25.

66 For this specific criticism see B. M. S. Campbell, 'The regional uniqueness of English field systems? Some evidence from eastern Norfolk', *Agricultural History Review*, 29 (1981), 16–28; B. Campbell, 'Population change and the genesis of common fields on a Norfolk manor', *Economic History Review*, 2nd series, 33 (1980), 174–92; the literature on field systems offering modifications to the Thirsk hypothesis includes Rowley (ed.), *Origins*; C. Dahlmann, *The Open Fields and Beyond* (Cambridge, Cambridge University Press, 1980); R. A. Dodgshon, *The Origin of British Field Systems: An Interpretation* (London, Academic Press, 1980).

67 D. McCloskey, 'English open fields as behavior towards risk', *Research in Economic History*, 1 (1976), 124–70.

68 H. S. A. Fox, 'The alleged transformation from two-field to three-field systems in medieval England', *Economic History Review*, 2nd series, 39 (1986), 526–48.

69 M. Gelling, *Signposts to the Past* (London, Dent, 1978) and M. Gelling, *Place-Names in the Landscape* (London, Dent, 1984).

70 For example, G. Fellows-Jensen, *Scandinavian Settlement Names in the East Midlands* (Copenhagen, Akademisk Forlag, 1978); C. D. Morris, 'Aspects of Scandinavian settlement in northern England: a review', *Northern History*, 20 (1984), 1–22.

71 D. Austin, R. H. Daggett and M. J. C. Walker, 'Farms and fields in Okehampton Park, Devon: the problems of studying medieval landscapes', *Landscape History*, 2 (1980), 39–58.

72 D. Austin, G. A. M. Gerrard and T. A. P. Greeves, 'Tin and agriculture in the middle ages and beyond: landscape archaeology in St Neots parish, Cornwall', *Cornish Archaeology*, 28 (1989), 5–251.

73 Davison, *Evolution of Settlement*; P. Rutledge, 'Colkirk: a north Norfolk settlement pattern', *Norfolk Archaeology*, 41 (1990), 15–34.

74 G. R. J. Jones, 'Multiple estates and early settlement' in Sawyer (ed.), *Medieval Settlement*, pp. 15–40. A full list of references to Jones's writing, and a criticism of the concept, is in N. Gregson, 'The multiple estate model: some critical questions', *Journal of Historical Geography*, 11 (1986), 352–63.

75 For example, T. Williamson, 'Settlement chronology and regional landscapes: the evidence from the claylands of East Anglia and Essex', in Hooke (ed.), *Anglo-Saxon Settlements*, pp. 166–7; W. Rodwell, 'Relict landscapes in Essex', in H. C. Bowen and P. J. Fowler (eds), *Early Land Allotment in the British Isles* (British Archaeological Reports, 48, 1978), pp. 89–98.

76 O. Rackham, *The History of the Countryside* (London, Dent, 1986), pp. 4–5.

77   C. Dyer, 'Dispersed settlements in medieval England. A case study of Pen-
      dock, Worcestershire', in C. Dyer, *Everyday Life in Medieval England* (London,
      Hambledon, 1994), pp. 147–76.

78   For example, D. Hall, 'Late Saxon topography and early medieval estates',
      in Hooke (ed.), *Medieval Villages*, pp. 61–9; D. Hall, 'The late Saxon country-
      side: village and fields', in Hooke (ed.), *Anglo-Saxon Settlements*, pp. 99–122;
      D. Hall, 'Fieldwork and the documentary evidence for the layout and organ-
      isation of early medieval estates in the English midlands', in K. Biddick
      (ed.), *Archaeological Approaches to Medieval Europe* (Kalamazoo, Michigan,
      Medieval Institute Publications, Western Michigan University, 1984),
      pp. 44–68; D. Hall, 'Field systems and township structure', in Aston *et al.*
      (eds), *Rural Settlements*, pp. 191–205.

79   G. Cadman, 'Raunds, 1977–1983: an excavation summary', *Medieval Archae-
      ology*, 27 (1983), 107–22; G. Cadman and G. Foard, 'Raunds, manorial and
      village origins', in M. Faull (ed.), *Studies in Late Anglo-Saxon Settlement* (Ox-
      ford, Oxford University Department for External Studies, 1984), pp. 81–100.

80   M. W. Beresford and J. G. Hurst, *Wharram Percy* (London, Batsford and
      English Heritage, 1990).

81   P. Salway, *Roman Britain* (Oxford, Oxford University Press, 1981), p. 544.

82   See note 54 above.

83   The controversy is summarised in H. Hamerow, 'Migration theory and the
      migration period', in B. Vyner (ed.), *Building on the Past. Papers Celebrating
      150 Years of the Royal Archaeological Institute* (London, Royal Archaeological
      Institute, 1994), pp. 164–77; she refers to the most recent literature, such
      as N. J. Higham, *Rome, Britain and the Anglo-Saxons* (London, Seaby, 1992),
      which denies mass migration.

84   Hamerow, 'Migration theory', pp. 169–73.

85   T. Williamson, 'Explaining regional landscapes: woodland and champion
      in southern and eastern England', *Landscape History*, 10 (1988), 5–13.

86   L. Génicot, *Rural Communities in the Medieval West* (Baltimore, Johns Hopkins
      Press, 1990), p. 10.

87   Cadman, 'Raunds, 1977–1983'; Cadman and Foard, 'Raunds: manorial and
      village origins'; G. Foard, 'The administrative organisation of Northamp-
      tonshire in the Saxon period', *Anglo-Saxon Studies in Archaeology and History*,
      4 (1985), 185–222; D. Windell, A. Chapman and J. Woodiwiss, *From Barrows
      to By-pass* (Northampton, Northamptonshire Archaeological Unit, 1990);
      R. Croft and D. Mynard, *The Changing Landscape of Milton Keynes* (Aylesbury,
      Buckinghamshire Archaeological Society Monograph Series no. 5, 1993).

88   R. F. Hartley, *The Mediaeval Earthworks of Rutland* (Leicester, Leicestershire
      Museums, Art Galleries and Records Service Archaeological Reports Series,
      7, 1983); R. F. Hartley, *The Medieval Earthworks of North-East Leicestershire*
      (Leicester, Leicestershire Museums, Art Galleries and Records Service
      Archaeological Reports Series, 88, 1987); R. F. Hartley, *The Medieval Earth-
      works of Central Leicestershire* (Leicester, Leicestershire Museums, Arts and
      Records Service Archaeological Reports Series, 103, 1989).

89   D. N. Hall, *The Open Fields of Northamptonshire* (Northampton, Northamp-
      tonshire Heritage, 1994); and numerous studies drawing on individual
      Northamptonshire parishes, for example, D. Hall, 'Field systems and town-
      ship structure', in Aston *et al.* (eds), *Rural Settlements*, pp. 191–205.

90 Including the parishes of Cardington, Chalgrave, Cranfield, Hockcliffe, Kempston and Sharpenhoe.

91 Royal Commission on Historical Monuments, England, *An Inventory of the Historic Monuments in the County of Northampton* (London, Her Majesty's Stationery Office, 1975–82).

92 See the works cited in note 52 above, and P. Liddle, 'The Medbourne area survey', in M. Parker Pearson and R. T. Schadla-Hall (eds), *Looking at the Land – Archaeological Landscapes in Eastern England* (Leicestershire Museums, Art Galleries and Record Services, 1994), pp. 34–6.

93 P. V. Addyman, 'A dark-age settlement at Maxey, Northamptonshire', *Medieval Archaeology*, 8 (1964), 20–73; B. S. Nenk *et al.*, 'Medieval Britain and Ireland in 1991', *Medieval Archaeology*, 36 (1992), 193–4; P. V. Addyman, 'Late Saxon settlement in the St. Neots area: I. The Saxon settlement and Norman castle at Eaton Socon, Bedfordshire', *Proceedings of the Cambridgeshire Antiquarian Society*, 58 (1965), 48–50.

94 Information from Sites and Monuments Record.

95 D. M. Wilson and D. G. Hurst, 'Medieval Britain in 1966', *Medieval Archaeology*, 11 (1967), 307–9, and in subsequent years; J. M. Steane and G. F. Bryant, 'Excavations at the deserted medieval settlement at Lyveden', *Journal of the Northampton Museums and Art Gallery*, 12 (1975); Hurst and Hurst, 'Excavations at the medieval village of Wythemail', 167–203; J. S. Wacher, 'Excavations at Martinsthorpe, Rutland, 1960', *Transactions of the Leicestershire Archaeological Society*, 39 (1963–4), 1–19.

96 D. Mynard and R. Zeepvat, *Great Linford* (Aylesbury, Buckinghamshire Archaeological Society Monograph Series, no. 3, 1991); R. J. Zeepvat, J. S. Roberts and N. A. King, *Caldecotte* (Aylesbury, Buckinghamshire Archaeological Society Monograph Series, no. 9, 1994); D. C. Mynard, *Excavations on Medieval Sites in Milton Keynes* (Aylesbury, Buckinghamshire Archaeological Society Monograph Series, no. 6, 1994); R. Ivens, P. Busby and N. Shepherd, *Tattenhoe and Westbury* (Aylesbury, Buckinghamshire Archeological Society Monograph Series, No. 8, 1995).

97 R. H. Hilton, *The Economic Development of some Leicestershire Estates in the 14th and 15th Centuries* (London, Oxford University Press, 1947); E. J. King, *Peterborough Abbey, 1086–1310* (Cambridge, Cambridge University Press, 1973); D. Roden, 'Studies in Chiltern Field Systems' (unpublished Ph.D. thesis, University of London, 1965); E. A. Kosminsky, *Studies in the Agrarian History of England in the Thirteenth Century* (Oxford, Blackwell, 1956).

2

The east midlands counties: an introduction

This chapter provides an introduction to the counties selected for investigation, and is divided into three parts. The first provides an overview of the study area by analysing its various geographical divisions in terms of terrain, soils and their present appearance and use. The second part gives a brief account of the main historical events and developments from later prehistory until the twelfth century, especially in local administration. The third turns to the main focus of the study, the settlement pattern, as it is depicted on early nineteenth-century maps, the first comprehensive and detailed sources for the form of villages, hamlets and farmsteads.

The region and its physical landscape

Our research is concerned with the counties of Buckinghamshire, Bedfordshire, Northamptonshire and Leicestershire, including Rutland, long separate from Leicestershire, and the Soke of Peterborough, historically part of Northamptonshire although now in Cambridgeshire. Stretching from the River Thames in the south as far north as the Trent, this area includes a wide range of landscape types (Fig. 2.1). The four counties lie mainly within the 'midlands', but in terms of both aspect and drainage, the chalkland Chiltern regions of both Buckinghamshire and Bedfordshire really belong to southern England.[1]

We must begin our examination of the region with its physical landscape, because it is the surface on which human activity is inscribed. Settlements are influenced by the soils available for agriculture, and decisions about their siting often take into account the local terrain. In the past a deterministic view has perhaps exaggerated the importance of topography and soil, presuming that nucleated settlement would appear on the better land, while the poorer soils would be associated with dispersed settlement. Even if we now need to modify such a dogmatic view, no study of settlement can ignore the geology and soils on which people lived and farmed.

The natural landscape was formed from the underlying structure of geological formations, moulded by human activity. Solid geological deposits (bedrock), eroded and overlain by drift deposits (laid down by geomorphological processes such as glaciation and alluviation) created the terrain of hills and valleys. The types of soil, derived partly from underlying geological material, and changed by climate, together with vegetation and previous human activity, influence the suitability and capacity of the land for agricultural production.[2] Layers of solid bedrock extend across central England, and dip to the south-east. The study area spans a number of such layers, from Upper Carboniferous millstone grit which outcrops in north-west Leicestershire, to much more recent Tertiary London clay in the Thames valley (Fig. 2.2). These formations, however, lie at the extremities of the area and intrude into it only slightly. Of more significance are

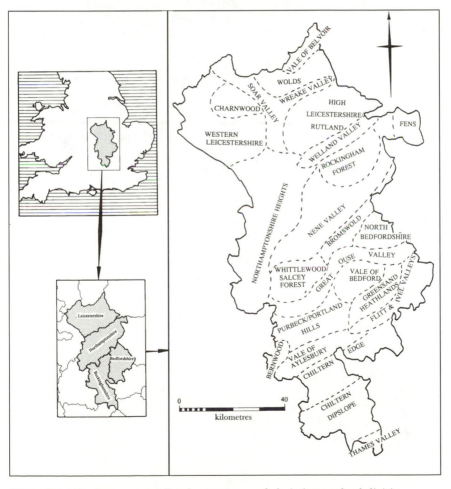

Figure 2.1 The four east midland counties, and their internal subdivisions.

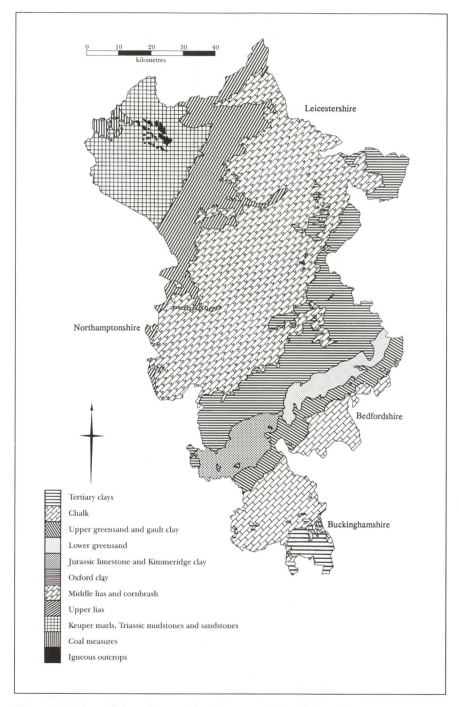

Figure 2.2 The solid geology of the four east midland counties.

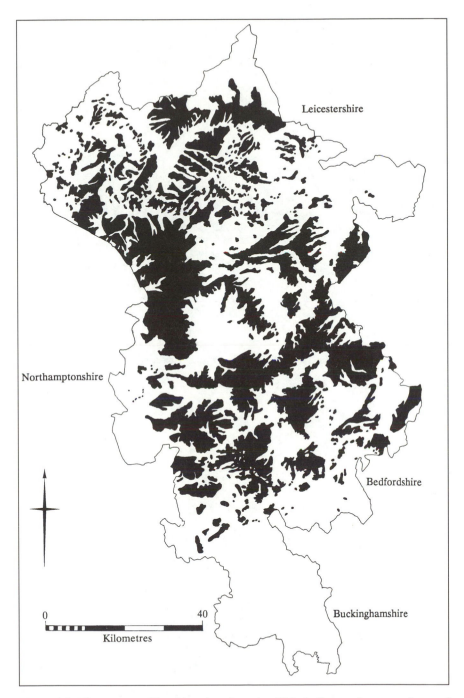

Figure 2.3 The extent of boulder clay deposits. This indicates the area of one of the most important of the soil types of the four counties.

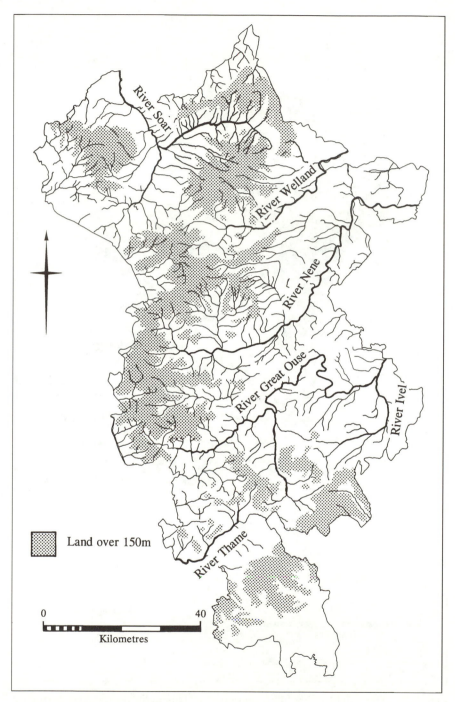

Figure 2.4 Relief and drainage.

the intervening successive beds of mudstones, limestones, clays and chalks, which are overlain by glacial drift formations, eroded by rivers, and exploited by human populations to produce much of the now visible topographical variety (Figs 2.3, 2.4).[3] This variety is nowhere extreme; indeed the overall impression gained by casual observers making their way rapidly across the region would be of undulating rural uniformity, interrupted only by the desolate flat levels of the Fens around Peterborough or the intrusive ancient rocky outcrops of Charnwood in north-west Leicestershire. However, away from the main roads, a more detailed examination reveals small-scale yet significant variations.

The Chilterns

The southernmost part of the study area is mostly on chalk and greensand, an elevated region which rises to more than 200m (650ft) OD. These are the Chiltern Hills which extend across the southernmost third of Buckinghamshire and a small part of south Bedfordshire around Luton. The district is extensively wooded, with small intimate valleys. When cleared of natural beech woodland, the Chiltern soils are predominantly thin, freely draining, friable and easy to cultivate. They lend themselves to short-term or non-intensive arable, although they fail in the face of long-term or intensive cultivation unless extensively and thoroughly fertilised. Where the chalk is overlain by glacial deposits of clay-with-flints, however, the resulting stony soils are difficult to work, and large areas remain wooded to the present day. The Chilterns are drained by several rivers which flow south into the Thames, which historically formed the county boundary of Buckinghamshire at its southern tip. Much of the district lacks easily available sources of water, as there are few streams or rivers, and consequently those that do exist appear to have been attractive to settlement.

To the north, the Chilterns are edged by a band of greensand which bisects the two counties along a south-west/north-east line south of Aylesbury and north of Luton. This ridge, the Chiltern Edge, towers 150m (500ft) above the countryside to the north, and it is the undulating densely wooded line of this escarpment rising above the claylands which provides the only really striking topographical contrast in the whole of the south of the study area. North of this escarpment the landscape drops sharply into the Vale of Aylesbury.

The southern claylands

In the Vale of Aylesbury, the softer contours of the underlying Jurassic clays differ sharply from the wooded slopes of the younger Cretaceous

Chiltern chalk and greensand, and this contrast is reflected in almost every aspect of the historic landscape. The major river is the Thame which flows south-west along a wide fertile valley at the foot of the greensand ridge, ultimately to join up with the Thames at Dorchester-on-Thames.

The claylands of the Vale of Aylesbury were naturally covered by dense oak and ash forest. When cleared they tend to form heavy soils which are fertile but difficult to plough, and which become waterlogged in winter and crack in dry summers. Scarpfoot springs and a network of streams have however long attracted settlement. Recently the district has favoured a predominantly pastoral rural economy of dairy farming and sheep rearing: the Vale of Aylesbury was well-known for its livestock in the nineteenth century, and, of course, famed for the quality of its eponymous ducks.

In the north of the Vale of Aylesbury the bedrock geology is subject to some confusion as islands of limestones and greensand survive inter-mittently on top of the Jurassic clays, giving the region a hilly, varied character known as the Purbeck and Portland hills. Consequently, parts of this area contain soils that are lighter, sometimes sandy and more freely draining than others to the north and south. In other places, however, glacial deposits of boulder clay produce poorly drained soils. Although fertile, they are very difficult to work and even with modern farming methods are best suited to pasture, ideally aided by artificial drainage.

Further east, the solid formations of the Jurassic (Oxford) clay in the Vale of Bedford are only occasionally overlain by glacial boulder clay, producing soils which are generally very heavy and poorly draining. Without human intervention they will support, or revert to, oak and ash woodland, and when cleared are generally more suited to pasture than arable.

The Bedfordshire greensand heathlands

In Bedfordshire, an extensive area of exposed lower greensand is present between the gault clay of the Vale of Aylesbury and the Oxford clay of the Vale of Bedford. The greensands are drained by the River Flitt and numerous small tributary streams which have carved out small, sharp valleys. Until recently these sandy soils were covered by extensive wood-land interspersed with large open heaths, and even today it still appears marginal and underexploited. In earlier times it may have been more attractive to cultivators as the sandy deposits produce soils which are easy to work and are rendered fertile for a short time by the organic material from the former woodland immediately after clearance.

The Ouse valley

The northern parts of both Buckinghamshire and Bedfordshire are dominated by the wide meandering valley of the River Great Ouse, which rises in Buckinghamshire before flowing sedately north-east through Bedfordshire, ultimately to the North Sea. The river's function as a major communication route has helped to make it a magnet for settlement. The river flows along the interface between the Oxford clays which underlie central Buckinghamshire and Bedfordshire and the earlier (Middle Jurassic) oolitic limestone formations which characterise much of central Northamptonshire. The river has eroded much of the heavy clay and laid down spreads of gravel interspersed with glacially derived gravels as much as 4km (2.5 miles) wide, and bands of alluvium.

The valley of the River Ivel, a tributary of the Great Ouse which flows north through eastern Bedfordshire, likewise contains widespread deposits of gravels. In these valleys the rivers have helped to create loamy soils which are fertile, easily worked and maintain a good texture when ploughed. However, they tend to dry out when springtime rainfall is limited and are prone to flooding and poor drainage. Today they are regarded as prime land and are used extensively for market gardening.

The Ouse/Nene watershed

An extensive zone of glacial boulder clay overlying the northernmost extent of the Oxford clay, beyond the Ouse valley, occupies much of north Bedfordshire, including Bromswold. Clay soils are typically fertile, but heavy and difficult to work. The hilly and rather exposed terrain makes north Bedfordshire less attractive to settlement than the nearby Ouse valley. Furthermore, although the soil can be highly productive in years when dry autumns and hard winters break up the clods after ploughing, wet autumns and winters can make it virtually unmanageable without modern machinery and drainage. Although this area is best suited to pasture, it is now extensively cultivated for cereals, but retains traces of woodland which were formerly more extensive. Further west, in north Buckinghamshire and south Northamptonshire, the historic forests of Whittlewood and Salcey lie immediately north of the Ouse valley. Here Middle Jurassic oolite and cornbrash are intermittently overlain with boulder clay. This has produced an intimate hilly landscape which today supports a mixed agricultural economy with some areas of extensive woodland.

The Nene valley

The low-lying, fertile valleys of the River Nene and its tributaries form the dominant natural feature across the centre and east of Northamptonshire.

A lesser river than the Ouse, the Nene's tributary streams form a more widespread network of connected valleys because the underlying oolitic limestones are more easily eroded. Boulder clay sometimes lies over the limestone, but in the valleys where this has been eroded there are extensive deposits of alluvium and gravel. The resulting soils are fertile, easily cultivated and well drained, and have attracted extensive settlement over a long period. The contrasting forest of Rockingham which occupies most of the area around Corby between the valleys of the Nene and the Welland is on higher ground than the adjacent river valley (though still below 150m, or 500ft), and is dominated by boulder clay.

The Fens

In the Soke of Peterborough, historically part of Northamptonshire, the land drops as low as 2m (6ft) OD. This remorselessly flat landscape, which without human intervention would be permanently marshy and regularly flooded, has been reclaimed by the construction of drains and dykes in a process begun by the Romans. After inundation in the post-Roman period, it was only effectively and permanently converted to agricultural use in the twelfth and thirteenth centuries. Now this highly fertile land is used extensively for vegetable crops. However, with the advent of effective drainage, the naturally waterlogged peat soil dries, shrinks and blows away causing the already low-lying land to drop still further, making defence from flooding still more difficult.

The Northampton Heights

The Northampton Heights rise above 150m (500ft) OD north-west of the Nene valley, forming an arc of higher land extending to the west and south. Only at the far southern tip of the county does the land start to dip again. The extensive lias deposits of the Heights are overlain in places by intermittent deposits of boulder clay. The resulting mixed soils, though fertile, are sometimes heavy, poorly drained and prone to waterlogging. Pasture now predominates in the district, but extensive ridge and furrow attests to its extensive use as arable in the middle ages.

The Soar valley

The centre of Leicestershire is dominated by the Soar Valley, and indeed much of the old county (minus Rutland) coincides with the catchment area of the upper reaches of this river which flows north into the Trent. The valley of the Soar and its main tributaries form a wide vale occupying the junction between the Jurassic lias formations to the east and the earlier Triassic mudstones to the west. The glacial boulder clay that once overlay them has been eroded by numerous small streams, and in the larger valleys alluvium and gravels have been laid down in river terraces. Fertile and easily ploughed land is found on the valley slopes, and as with other major river valleys, it has long proved attractive to settlement.

Western Leicestershire

To the north-west of the Soar valley lies the distinctive district of Charnwood. Bardon Hill in its centre rises to a height of 278m (900ft) OD, the highest point in our area of study, and forms part of an outcrop of older, harder rock formations. Charnwood is intersected by sharply defined stream valleys, and around Bardon Hill the combination of rough pasture and exposed outcrops of igneous rock give the landscape a wild moorland quality. Poor and stony soils predominate, with better agricultural land available only in the valleys. To the west of Charnwood the Leicester coalfields have been exploited since at least the thirteenth century; and the area is also a good source of clay. Today's landscape is dominated by mining and industrial settlements, obscuring medieval occupation which can only be identified with difficulty.

South-west of Charnwood, a low-lying area extends to the county boundary along Watling Street. Boulder clay deposits in this area are considerably less extensive than in the Soar valley, and around Hinckley they are overlain by sand and gravel. In this area, mudstones, marls and sandstones produce soils which vary in texture and drainage; the mixed quality of the land includes some quite good arable. Further east, along the county boundary, the elevated plateau around Lutterworth, much overlain by thick boulder clay, has superficial deposits of gravel and sand which have also produced more manageable soils.[4]

Eastern Leicestershire

In the east of the county the undulating plateau of the wolds occupies the district between the Wreake valley and the Vale of Belvoir; it mostly lies above 125m (400ft) OD and is covered with extensive tracts of boulder clay. The district has long been regarded as barren and difficult; cereal crops can be grown in some parts, but they require careful management. The Vale of Belvoir itself occupies the northernmost tip of the study area, and is notably free of boulder clay. To the south-east, High Leicestershire (including Rutland) lies on the watershed between the Welland and the Soar. Similar to the wolds north of the Wreake, it forms part of the same block of elevated Lower Jurassic lias which also includes the Northampton Heights to the south. It now has little arable land and sparse settlement, and is used extensively for sheep rearing. However, the earthworks of deserted medieval villages and ridge and furrow indicate that it has supported dense settlement and extensive cultivation.

Political history and organisation

The iron age and Roman period

Our knowledge of the political organisation of the late iron age in the east midlands derives from the fact that the provinces *(civitates)* of the Roman administration were based on the tribal territories current at the time of the conquest.[5] From the mid-first century AD onwards, the Roman government imposed an administrative structure necessary for a highly developed and bureaucratic state.[6] The area studied here lay mostly within the territories of the Catuvellauni and the Corieltauvi (once known as the Coritani).[7] The Catuvellaunian *civitas*, centred on *Verulamium* (St Albans, Hertfordshire) included most of Bedfordshire and Buckinghamshire and part of Northamptonshire, while the *civitas* of the Corieltauvi, based on *Ratae* (Leicester), seems to have included Leicestershire and northern Northamptonshire.

If the British *civitates* resembled Roman administration on the continent, there may have been a lower tier of government consisting of a network of sub-divisions *(pagi)* or urban communities *(vici)*, with associated territories.[8] *Durobrivae* (Water Newton) on the border of Northamptonshire and Huntingdonshire is known to have been a *vicus*,[9] and it has even been suggested that it could have been another *civitas* capital of late creation. Any territory linked with it would have extended into the later Soke of Peterborough. Smaller towns may also have had some powers of self government, and some roadside settlements enjoyed official status as the sites of official post stations *(mansiones)*, as at Great Casterton (Rutland) and Towcester (Northants).[10]

The fifth to the ninth centuries

There is a great deal of debate about the scale of the germanic migration in the fifth and sixth centuries, some insisting upon the influx of large numbers of migrants who brought about a transformation of language and culture, and others seeing the process as limited to a political takeover of a predominantly British population. There can be no doubt that the period saw the establishment of a ruling elite of Anglo-Saxon origin over much of the former Roman province, though a British enclave may have survived in the Chilterns in the century or two after 400.[11] The earliest evidence of political organisation in the post-Roman era relates to the

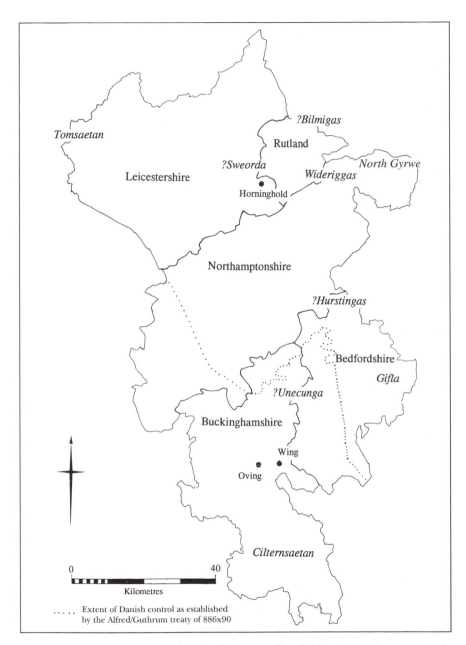

Figure 2.5 Early political divisions and later medieval shires. This shows the likely location of the groupings of people recorded in the seventh century, or whose presence can be deduced from later documents and place-names. Also marked is the boundary of the Danelaw agreed at the end of the ninth century, and the shires established in the tenth and eleventh.

sixth and seventh centuries and portrays considerable fragmentation, particularly in the east midlands.

Although the principal Anglo-Saxon kingdoms had emerged by this time, much of the east midlands seems not to have been included within any of them. Evidence for political geography comes from the Tribal Hidage, which lists the kingdoms and peoples in the seventh century and provides assessments in hides which indicate their size.[12] As well as enumerating the principal kingdoms south of the Humber it also contains the names of a number of separate, lesser political groupings, most of which can be located in the east and southern midlands, and which from other evidence appear to be collectively identifiable as the Middle Angles.[13] A number of these groupings can be identified as lying wholly or partly within the study area. These include the *Cilternsaetan* in the Chilterns, the *Gifla* in the Ivel valley in Bedfordshire, the *Wideriggas* around Wittering (Northants) and the *North Gyrwe* in the Soke of Peterborough (Fig. 2.5).

Other sources also provide evidence for similar groups, for example the *Tomsaetan*, who impinged on western Leicestershire, and appear in a ninth-century charter.[14] Others may be identifiable from place-names reminiscent of those in the Tribal Hidage, such as Wing meaning 'Weohthun's people' and Oving, 'Ufa's people' (both Bucks) or Horninghold (Leics).[15]

These groups seem to have had only a short life, and in most cases the Tribal Hidage provides the only record of their existence. Although they are identifiable with specific areas they appear to have been defined by extended kinship and personal association.[16] This social basis of their organisation might account for their fleeting appearance in the sources. At the time of the Tribal Hidage they obviously had some level of autonomy, and from sources like Bede some are known to have had their own leaders described as *principes* or ealdormen.[17] But these terms, and the designation of such groupings as *regiones* or *provinciae*, suggests subordination to a kingdom. Some are known to have been subdivisions of larger groupings, such as the territory of the *Tomsaetan* which was clearly an integral part of Mercia.

In the seventh century the independence of small groupings of people was already under threat from larger kingdoms, especially Mercia.[18] The appointment in the mid-seventh century by Penda of Mercia of his son Peada as king of the Middle Angles suggests the creation of a client kingdom uniting the smaller, disparate groupings under Mercian control.[19] However its status as a separate kingdom did not last, and in the eighth and ninth centuries the east midlands was absorbed fully into the

Mercian kingdom, though its identity may have been perpetuated as the province of an ealdorman.[20]

Danish influences

The political geography of the east midlands, as of the rest of northern and eastern England, was altered again in the late ninth century by the Danes.[21] The greater part of the study area came under their control, reaching as far west as Watling Street by the beginning of the tenth century. As with the Anglo-Saxon 'invasion' before it, the Danish takeover has also traditionally been seen as a mass folk migration displacing an existing population. However there is little archaeological evidence for Scandinavian settlement, and it has been suggested that the special character of the Danelaw may have been due to the influence of only a small number of conquering overlords.[22]

An indication of an extensive Danish migration has been seen in the Scandinavian vocabulary and language of many of the place-names of the area.[23] However, it has been pointed out that names such as the numerous 'Grimston hybrids', in which a Scandinavian personal name is combined with an English habitative term, may derive from a change of lords rather than from a change of whole populations, *Grim's tun* implying a Scandinavian lord of a place retaining an Anglo-Saxon word for 'estate' or 'settlement'. Nevertheless the presence of some pure Scandinavian names seems to suggest that Scandinavian language was in general use in their vicinity. Even these, however, need not indicate the presence of people who actually came from Scandinavia, although they do suggest a high level of Scandinavian influence. The patchiness of that influence is suggested by the uneven distribution of these place-names. Scandinavian place-names are concentrated almost entirely in the north-east, and above all in eastern Leicestershire, especially in the Wreake valley. Further south they are much more sparse, and are almost entirely absent from Bedfordshire and Buckinghamshire, where a few belong to the 'Grimston hybrid' type.

The ninth to the eleventh centuries

With the defeat of Mercia and the loss of a large swathe of its territory to the Danes, remaining English parts of the midlands came increasingly under the authority of the kings of Wessex. In the early decades of the tenth century persistent pressure from the West Saxons also brought the Danish areas of the east midlands and East Anglia under their control, after which the kings of Wessex dominated all of England south of the Humber. The unity imposed by the West Saxon kings on England did not automatically produce an integrated polity. Both former Mercia and the previously Danish areas maintained their identities under West Saxon rule, and initially may even have retained some level of autonomy.[24] In particular, Mercia, and above all the Danish regions, long continued to be recognised as areas of distinct legal custom and practice, known as the Mercian Law and the Danelaw.

While the Mercian and West Saxon law differed only slightly, the Danelaw was much more distinct.[25] For example Scandinavian practices were employed in the transfer of land in eastern Northamptonshire in the late tenth century.[26] In the tenth century, divisions appear within the Danelaw itself, with distinct areas with their own legal custom, such as the territory of the Five Boroughs, amongst which Leicester and Stamford were included (along with Derby, Nottingham and Lincoln). The legal peculiarities of the Danelaw were still remembered after the Norman Conquest, though by the twelfth century all four counties of the study area were considered to belong to the Danelaw, despite the fact that some parts, particularly southern Buckinghamshire, had always remained under English control.[27]

With the unification of England under West Saxon rule in the tenth century came the development of a system of local administration based on three tiers: the shires, hundreds (called wapentakes in Leicestershire) and vills. The earliest traces of any of the east midland shires lie in the period of Danish control when central towns, such as Leicester, appear to have been established as key strongholds exercising control over their surrounding districts. However no shires, named as such, appear in the historical record until the early eleventh century.[28] Therefore it has been suggested that while they may have existed in embryo in the first decades of the tenth century as administrative districts based on a royal *burh*, the shire system may have emerged fully only around 1000, perhaps under the stimulus of the financial and military response to renewed Danish incursions.[29]

The tiny shire of Rutland represents something of an anomaly. It does not appear fully as a shire in its own right until after Domesday Book, and although it is included as a separate entity in that survey, only about half of its later area is surveyed as 'Rutland', and it seems to have been considered to belong to Nottinghamshire. The rest was included in Northamptonshire and Lincolnshire. One explanation of its existence is that it originated as a territory of the *burh* of Stamford, while another links its origins to its claimed status as dower land of the queen, which may have made it a royal franchise lying outside the normal shire system.[30]

The administrative unit of the hundred is first mentioned in laws of the mid-tenth century, and its origins have been linked to attempts to maintain more effective public order, first traceable in the legislation of Edward the Elder.[31] Hundreds within the study area appear in two documents of the second half of the tenth century, dealing with the estates of Peterborough Abbey in eastern Northamptonshire, but their names and extents are not fully recorded until Domesday Book.[32] From the Leicestershire Survey of the early twelfth century a second level of hundredal organisation emerges in addition to that recorded in Domesday Book.[33] These were smaller units known as 'hundreds', which were grouped together to make 'wapentakes', the major administrative units equivalent to hundreds elsewhere. In fact the existence of more than one level of hundredal units was a feature of other parts of the study area too. In Buckinghamshire the smaller hundreds of Domesday were often grouped into threes, a convention reminiscent of the 'shipsokes' known in some other counties, while groups of hundreds are also found in parts of Northamptonshire.[34]

At the lowest level of the late Anglo-Saxon administrative structure lay the vill. Local territories similar in size to the vill of the later middle ages are first found in charters, the earliest of which date from the seventh and eighth centuries. However these early documents transferring property rarely include boundary clauses, and when they do they provide only vague descriptions.[35] In charters from the late ninth century onwards, however, the territories conveyed are described more precisely in boundary clauses. Some of the conventions used in describing these territories indicate their communal characteristics. For example the charter of 969 dealing with Aspley Guise (Beds) refers to the surrounding lands as those of '*Crancfeldinga*', '*Woburninga*', '*Mercstuninga*' and '*Wafanduninga*'; meaning those of 'the people of Cranfield', 'the people of Woburn', 'the people of Marston' and 'the people of Wavendon', suggesting the collective nature of these vills and their clearly defined boundaries.[36]

The late Anglo-Saxon period saw significant developments in the governmental functions of the vill. Law codes of the tenth century make it clear that these communities were taking over roles of legal accountability and mutual responsibility that in previous centuries had been performed by other bodies such as kin groups.[37] We can see, therefore, that the kings of Wessex instituted in the east midlands a hierarchy of administrative structures which provided them with an effective system of government, capable of imposing law and order, and of raising military service and taxation. In many respects it was this system that provided the framework for government for the rest of the middle ages.[38]

The organisation of the church was also going through changes at this time, no doubt allied to those in the secular sphere. A network of dioceses had been created in the seventh and eighth centuries based on then existing political divisions. Much of the study area was included in the diocese of the Middle Angles with a see founded at Leicester in 679, and apparently refounded in 737.[39] However the diocesan organisation of the area was disrupted by the Danish invasions of the late ninth century, and the succession of bishops of Leicester came to an end. Eventually the area was brought under the authority of the bishop of Dorchester-on-Thames in the tenth century, who administered a diocese which extended from the Thames to the Humber.[40] This see was ultimately transferred to Lincoln after the Norman Conquest.

Prior to the tenth century a few churches already fulfilled a pastoral role, such as the monastery at Breedon-on-the-Hill (Leics), which was founded 'to bring baptism to the area around' in the late seventh century.[41] Churches such as these, the 'old minsters', have been identified as the earliest 'parish' churches. Indeed it has been argued that there was a network of these, providing pastoral care in a 'proto-parochial' system, which had been established in the seventh and eighth centuries. In the tenth century local churches proliferated, with much smaller areas under their care representing the beginning of the parochial system proper.[42]

By the end of the twelfth century there existed in the east midlands a fully fledged system of ecclesiastical organisation, having a similar hierarchy to the secular administration. The diocese was divided into archdeaconries often based on the shires; and within them rural deaneries matched the hundreds, made up in turn by parishes that often coincided with the vills.[43]

Lords and lordship

Although the king's authority, exercised through a well organised system of local government, and bolstered by the support of the church, was greater in England than any other part of Europe in the tenth and eleventh centuries, lordship also provided an important source of power and protection. To some extent lords acted as the allies and agents of the crown, and received patronage from the king. Successive conquests of the tenth and eleventh centuries enabled kings to develop extensive authority in matters of landholding through the ensuing redistributions of land, above all after the Norman Conquest. In the study area, as elsewhere in England, by 1086 there had been an almost complete replacement of the Anglo-Saxon lords by a new Norman elite, the tenure of whose lands was closely dependent on the will of the king.[44]

For the inhabitants of rural settlements the main importance of lordship lay in the exercise of social and economic control by the aristocracy through the manor. Domesday Book shows that by the end of the Anglo-Saxon period, the manor had become a universal institution, generating incomes for lords that are reflected in Domesday valuations. By this time also a well established church landlord, Peterborough Abbey, wielded extensive powers of private jurisdiction in its soke, the two hundreds of Nassaburgh in eastern Northamptonshire.[45]

Forests, commons and communalism

Royal forests were created in some localities in the post-Conquest period, imposing another layer of royal jurisdiction, ostensibly to preserve game. There were six of these in the four counties by the thirteenth century. The forest of Rutland (otherwise Leighfield) covered Rutland and parts of eastern Leicestershire; Rockingham lay in north central Northamptonshire; the forests of Whittlewood and Salcey occupied the border between Northamptonshire and Buckinghamshire; the forest of Bernwood extended across west Buckinghamshire into eastern Oxfordshire; and a small part of the forest of Windsor stretched across the Thames from Berkshire into the far south of Buckinghamshire. Although royal forests attained a formal legal status only after the Norman Conquest, some were already recognised as distinct districts in the pre-Conquest period, such as Bernwood, mentioned in the Anglo-Saxon Chronicle in the early tenth century.[46] These areas are likely to have been distinguished both by containing much dense woodland and by the presence of royal estates and residences, as are known in the tenth and eleventh centuries in Rockingham, Whittlewood and Bernwood.[47]

Wastes and woods, including royal forests, were generally used as commons by large groups of people.[48] A waste that did not later become royal forest, Leicester Forest, was named as *Hereswode* and described as 'the woodland of the whole Sheriffdom' in Domesday.[49] Clearly this wood was thought to belong to the whole county, and although *here* is often ascribed the specific sense 'army', the term also had the broader connotation of 'the people'. The public character of wastes seems to have been ancient, as suggested by names linking them with early tribal groups like 'Gyrwan fenne'; the fen of the *Gyrwe* (a people of the Tribal Hidage that impinged on eastern Northamptonshire).[50] The phenomenon also seems implicit in a number of place-names, such as Markfield ('the open land of the Mercians'), on the fringes of Charnwood in western Leicestershire, and Horninghold ('the wold of the Horningas', an otherwise unknown group) in eastern Leicestershire. Royal authority could be established over the forests because public assets increasingly came to belong to the king, and might ultimately be appropriated for his own profit.[51]

Early narrative sources and place-names give the impression that a great deal of the study area lay uncultivated and under wood and waste in the pre-Conquest period, suggesting a process of clearance in the century or two immediately before Domesday. For example, Bromswold is mentioned in the legend of Hereward the Wake as the wooded area where the hero is supposed to have taken refuge from the Normans in the aftermath of his revolt;[52] its considerable extent in earlier centuries is indicated by the occurrence of its name in several place-names in and around the border of Northamptonshire with Bedfordshire and Huntingdonshire,[53] though little wood is recorded here in 1086.

By the later middle ages communities shared rights to land only to a limited extent, and though intercommoning between many pairs or small groups of communities long survived, increasingly each village had its own area of common pasture or wood, which it defended against encroachment by outsiders.[54] As woods and wastes diminished through clearance, local communities became increasingly focused within their own well-defined territories, though in the districts with extensive woods and common pastures, the size of parishes tended to be larger than those of the predominantly arable villages.

The pattern of settlement in the nineteenth century

The varied pattern of medieval settlement across the east midlands is still visible, even in the late twentieth-century landscape, after many recent changes. The origins of the pattern and layout of most settlements, however, lie in earlier centuries, and a central aim of our enquiry is to identify and record the form of all settlements in the region, as a first step towards understanding their development. The earliest consistent and comprehensive evidence for the pattern of rural settlement in the east midlands comes from county maps dating to the early nineteenth century. The maps used in this project are that prepared by the Ordnance Survey (at one inch to the mile, 1:63,360) for Leicestershire and those produced by map-maker John Bryant in 1826 for the other three counties.[55] The Bryant maps were printed at a scale of slightly more than one inch to the mile.

Five basic forms were identified and used, singly or combined together, to define the notional physical layout of each settlement on the maps, which were then recorded on the project database and mapped using simple symbols. This classification focused on the distinctions between agglomerative and linear plans, and regular and irregular plans. It represents a simplification of Roberts's classificatory system, conflating various of those categories into their group types,[56] updated particularly to take into account recent work on dispersed settlements. The types are as follows:

1 nucleated clusters: these are agglomerated settlements where more than five dwellings or farmsteads are grouped together at a single point in a compact grid, radial or cluster plan, sometimes around a green, market place or other focus (Fig. 2.6).

2 nucleated regular streets or rows: these are linear settlements which are arranged contiguously along a straight street or green with boundaries which lie at right angles to the street. The plots are usually all of equal length, and often of equal width (Fig. 2.7).

3 interrupted or irregular rows: these are dispersed settlements where tofts are strung out along lanes, usually separated from their neighbours by small arable or pasture fields and often winding for a kilometre (0.6 mile) or more (Fig. 2.8).[57]

4 common-edge settlements: these forms of dispersed settlements are similar to the previous group but here the tofts are perched on the edges of tracts of common or heath land, often close to the margins of parishes or townships.

5 small farmstead clusters: these include single farms and clusters of less than five tofts (Fig. 2.9).

Clearly, an indefinitely large number of different settlement layouts could potentially be formed from combinations of these types. No two settlements will ever display identical plans. This system identifies broad similarities and differences in plan structure, either of whole settlements or of individual elements within settlements. It provides a set of categories which is based purely on spatial organisation as recorded in the early nineteenth century.

Buckinghamshire

The distribution of nucleated and dispersed settlements in Buckinghamshire highlights the difference between the Chilterns (in the south) and the rest of the county (Figs 2.10, 2.11). The Chilterns were still extensively wooded in the early nineteenth century; only towards the Thames valley, between Taplow and Colnbrook, where the settlement pattern was characterised mainly by short irregular rows, did the landscape contain less woodland. Most settlements to the south-west of the Chiltern dipslope took the form of single farmsteads, which were sited at quite regular

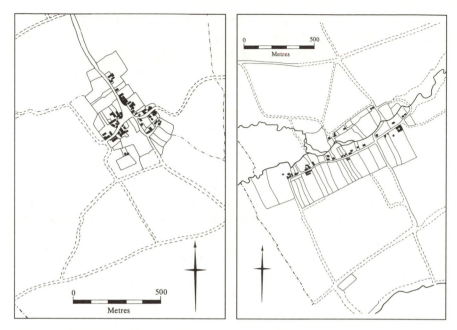

Figure 2.6 A nucleated cluster, Tebworth in Chalgrave, Bedfordshire, *c*. 1800.

Figure 2.7 A nucleated regular row, Harrowden, Bedfordshire, in 1794.

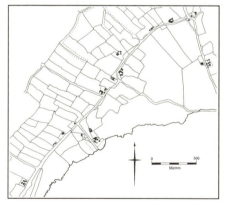

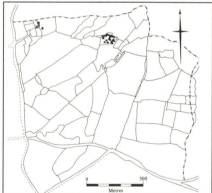

Figure 2.8 An interrupted row, Kempston West End, Bedfordshire, 1804.

Figure 2.9 Isolated farmsteads in Chalgrave, Bedfordshire, *c*. 1800.

intervals across the landscape. To the south-east the settlement pattern included a greater variety of types. It was however still essentially dispersed, consisting mostly of interrupted rows or single farmsteads, the latter tending to cluster loosely together. The dividing line between interrupted rows and single farmsteads can sometimes only be drawn with difficulty, but the two types are likely to have had a similar organisation and development. Many of the irregular rows lay along roads which are oriented north–south, which probably marked early routes linking the woodland to the arable regions, as can be seen in the Warwickshire Arden or the Weald of Kent. Little common land remained in this area in 1826.

In contrast, further north on the Chiltern Edge extensive tracts of common land still survived in the early nineteenth century. These were often located close to or across parish boundaries, such as at Kingshill, where the common was divided between the parishes of Hughenden, Great Missenden and Hazelmere; at Naphill, divided between The Lee and Great Missenden; or at Holmer Green, between Little Missenden, Amersham and Penn. Settlement was arranged along the fringes of these commons or heaths, such as at Wycombe Heath or Hailey Common, but an exception to this pattern is found at Prestwood, where a ring of settlement surrounding an area of regularly shaped common land lies squarely within the centre of the parish of Great Missenden. Despite the superficially random and sprawling appearance of the settlements in this part of the county, closer examination reveals a degree of regularity: the arrangement of interrupted row or common-edge settlements and single farmsteads seems almost standardised, with individual tofts set at regular intervals. At the northern extremity of the Chilterns, the gault clay was characterised by long irregular rows similar to the common-edge settlements to the south. But this district lacked common land in 1826, which may reflect the medieval situation. Irregular row and common-edge settlements may have had similar origins as people established themselves along road sides or on the edge of woodland (Fig. 2.12).

The nineteenth-century pattern clearly reflects the dispersed settlement of the medieval period recorded in documents, with numerous individually named farmsteads and cottages. Many of the small farmstead clusters were first recorded in the twelfth and thirteenth centuries. In addition, many of the larger dispersed settlements have two or more names referring to different sections of the settlement: in some cases different names refer to the same part of the settlement because place-names have changed. However some of the dispersed settlement is likely to have had a modern origin. For example, the 1826 map apparently shows common land on the Chiltern Edge in process of being encroached by small homesteads.

North of the Chilterns the settlement pattern changed abruptly: only in the forest of Bernwood in the west of the county did settlement continue to be entirely dispersed, forming irregular rows or lying around

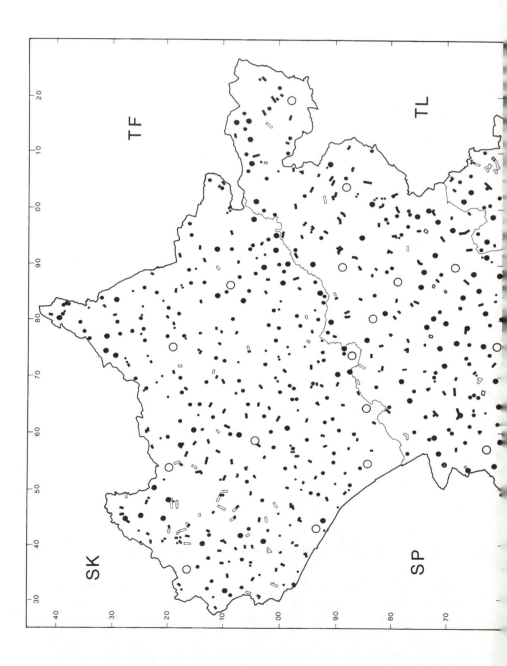

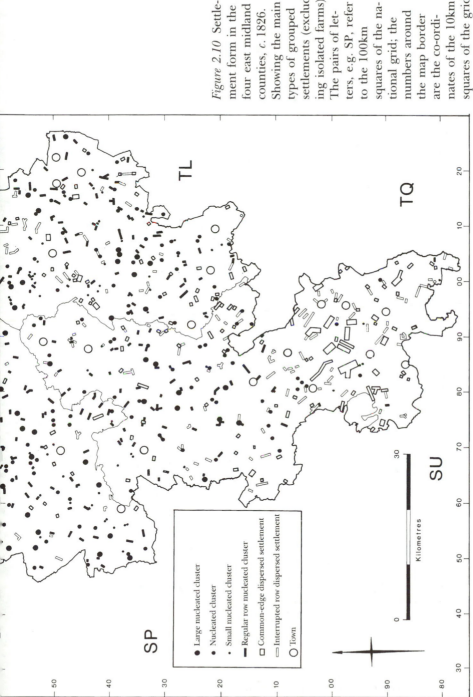

Figure 2.10 Settlement form in the four east midland counties, *c.* 1826. Showing the main types of grouped settlements (excluding isolated farms). The pairs of letters, e.g. SP, refer to the 100km squares of the national grid; the numbers around the map border are the co-ordinates of the 10km squares of the grid.

Legend:
- ● Large nucleated cluster
- • Nucleated cluster
- · Small nucleated cluster
- ▬ Regular row nucleated cluster
- □ Common-edge dispersed settlement
- ▭ Interrupted row dispersed settlement
- ○ Town

Kilometres
0   30

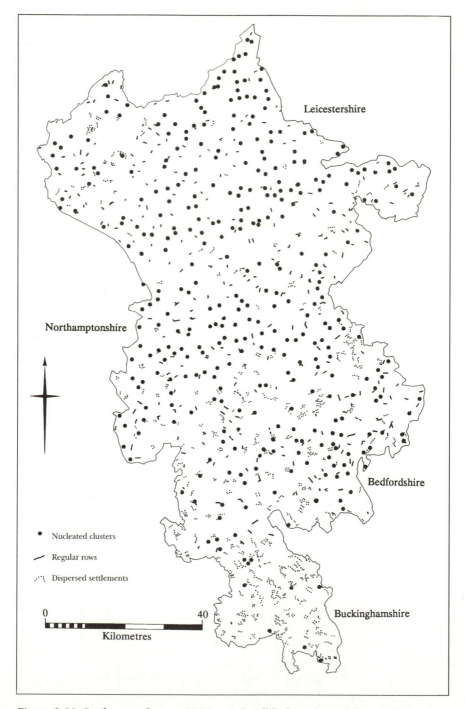

Figure 2.11 Settlement form *c.* 1826 – a simplified version of figure 2.10.

commons or large irregular greens such as at Oakley, Boarstall, Brill and Chilton, but this area of dispersal was much more limited than that of the Chilterns. Nucleated settlements predominated in the Thame valley, with a single large settlement in each township (Fig. 2.13). Their form, however, varied a great deal and consisted of regular rows such as at Bierton, or compact clusters such as at Stone and Cuddington; others, such as at Haddenham and Westlington had a widely spaced but fairly regular structure, suggesting that they had been planned around a small area of common land. Some, such as Aston Sandford and Ford had a very irregular dispersed form, and others such as Kingsey comprised little more than a row of farmsteads. Many of the townships were very small, as little as two or three hundred hectares (500–750 acres) in some cases, and most have now been amalgamated into larger parishes. These contrast with the vast parishes of the Chilterns.

A mixed pattern continued further north: only the area between Buckingham, Bletchley and Stewkley appears to have been largely devoid of any type of dispersed settlement. Elsewhere some nucleated settlements such as Quainton and Waddesdon formed compact clusters while others, such as Mursley and Stewkley, were regular rows: here no single form dominated. Other settlements had elements of both rows and clusters, such as Newton Longville or Drayton Parslow. Many nucleated settlements also had irregular dispersed elements loosely attached to the settlement core as at Steeple Claydon, Thornborough or Sherington. Mixed settlement forms were also characteristic of both the Great Ouse valley and on the fringes of Whittlewood Forest. A relatively small number of nucleated settlements occurred in the valley itself. This is surprising, as elsewhere a high proportion of nucleated forms tended to occur near rivers. In fact a number of places in the Buckinghamshire Great Ouse valley such as Gayhurst or Haversham were small and irregular in form and only a few such as Maids Moreton and Emberton displayed a regular row layout typical of river valleys. Perhaps nearby Whittlewood Forest was influencing these settlements; certainly woodland place-names, like Gayhurst, are found among valley settlements. Dispersed settlement is generally common in woodland, although again Whittlewood is somewhat an exception, as its settlements were, in fact, quite mixed in form.

Bedfordshire

Bedfordshire lacks the strong topographical contrast of Buckinghamshire: it is a superficially homogeneous county in terms of its natural landscape, but displayed considerable variety in its settlement pattern.

Several distinct zones of dispersed settlement existed in the heavy

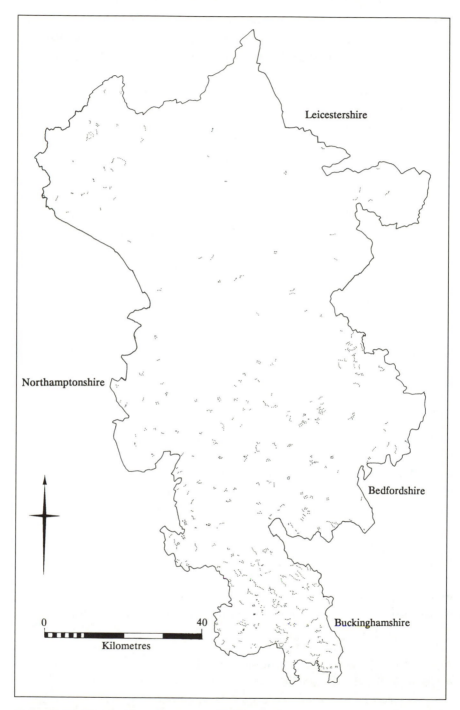

Figure 2.12 Dispersed settlements, *c.* 1826.

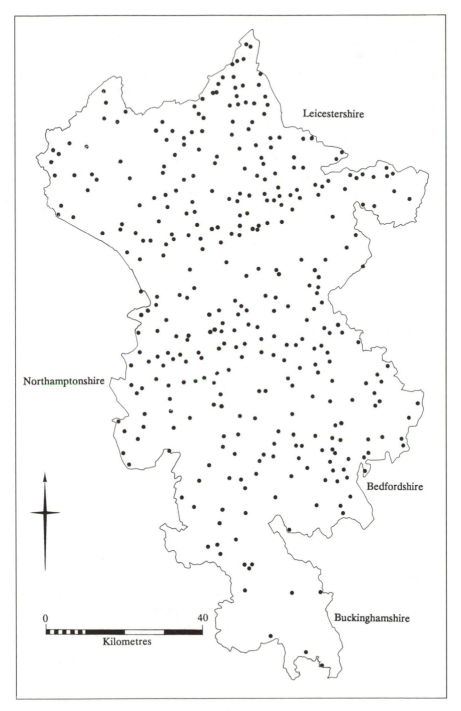

Figure 2.13 Nucleated cluster settlements, *c.* 1826.

claylands both to the north and to the south of Bedford itself. Although the settlement patterns in both districts were highly scattered, and though they had similar topography and land use, they differed in other ways: in the north, interrupted rows and isolated farmsteads predominated, at such places as Thurleigh, Bolnhurst, Colmworth, Wilden and Ravensden. Despite their straggling appearance, these displayed some degree of regularity in their siting and layout. If we examine the nineteenth-century maps in the light of archaeological and documentary evidence for the middle ages, we can identify a clearly defined hierarchy, with larger settlements carrying the names of Domesday holdings sited centrally within parishes and displaying little or no sign of shrinkage, and much smaller subsidiary settlements, mostly undocumented and frequently deserted or very shrunken, sited towards the periphery of parishes.

South of the Ouse in the Vale of Bedford, on the other hand, more variety of form was displayed, with some small clusters (e.g., Stagsden, Lidlington), short regular rows (e.g., Upper and Lower Shelton, Millbrook), interrupted rows (e.g., Kempston Box End), common-edge settlements (e.g., Cranfield, Wootton) and numerous isolated farmsteads. Again reference to earlier evidence shows several medieval settlements in each parish, with a high incidence of fission of dispersed elements into smaller named units, often called 'ends'. Woodland is recorded in the names of many settlements (e.g., Bolnhurst), and provides another example of the common coincidence of dispersed settlement and woodland landscapes.

Dispersed settlement forms also commonly occurred across much of the rest of the south of the county, although here mixed with nucleations. The heavily wooded greensand heathland, drained by the River Flitt, had a rich mixture of settlement types ranging from large polyfocal villages (e.g., Westoning, Harlington, Woburn), through regular rows (e.g., Silsoe, Barton-in-the-Clay, Husborne Crawley), interrupted rows (e.g., Eversholt), common-edge settlement (e.g., Heath and Reach) to numerous single farmsteads. Highly dispersed parishes such as Eversholt lay next door to others such as Steppingley and Tingrith, which contained a single nucleated settlement. The polyfocal villages tended to have a rather confused layout, within which earlier, dispersed elements seem to have fused to make a single larger settlement by the early nineteenth century.

Generally, nucleations in Bedfordshire were concentrated in the northwest (e.g., Riseley, Melchbourne, Yelden, Shelton, Swineshead), where regular clusters predominated (Fig. 2.13). In the broad river valleys of the Ouse and the Ivel in the north and the east are found a mixture of clusters (e.g., Pavenham, Roxton, Harrold, Great Barford) and regular rows (e.g., Langford, Cople, Willington, Elstow), but the latter type is more common. Many of these parishes have regular shapes, either forming an approximate square focused on a tributary streamlet (in north-west Bedfordshire), or a narrow block or strip extending up from the river terrace of the Ouse and Ivel onto the clay valley sides. Regularity of layout in both settlements and parishes suggests planning, particularly in the nucleated clusters of the north-western claylands, which differed markedly from the large polyfocal market villages of the greensand heathland and Flitt valley, which had little sign of regular plans and may have developed through organic growth and fusion, though no doubt the foundations of the markets injected an element of planning.

Northamptonshire

This was a county of mainly nucleated settlements, particularly frequent in the Nene valley, the Northampton Heights and, to a lesser degree, the Welland valley. Regular row settlements were predictably common in the river valleys, but more unexpectedly this form dominated in the forest of Rockingham (Fig. 2.14). Conversely, regular rows were notably absent from both the vicinity of Brixworth and to the south of Kettering, in river valleys where they might be expected. The medieval origin of the regular plans visible on the nineteenth-century maps can be demonstrated from the earthworks of deserted or very shrunken settlements, particularly on the Northampton Heights, which preserve in fossilised form the layout of villages in their final phase of medieval occupation.

An analysis of the larger nucleated clusters reveals apparent differences in their structure which may give a clue to their early development.[58] Some of the very compact and regular clusters seem likely to have been planned at an early stage. Large polyfocal settlements, on the other hand, may fall into two categories. Firstly, some may have developed from an early settlement nucleus, with extensions, planned or otherwise, which had subordinate names such as 'end' or 'cote'. They appear to have grown to a point of fission which then gave rise to these separate named parts. Others, secondly, were formed from a cluster of originally discrete units which later fused as the constituent settlements grew to fill in the gaps.

Its plan alone cannot tell us certainly whether a settlement has experienced fission or fusion, and we will only know when the settlements have been subjected to more detailed historical and archaeological research. The clusters apparently of the second type seem to occur most frequently on the Northampton Heights and in the Nene valley close to Bromswold. While their development into large nucleations may be at least partly due to post-medieval expansion, there must surely be some significance in

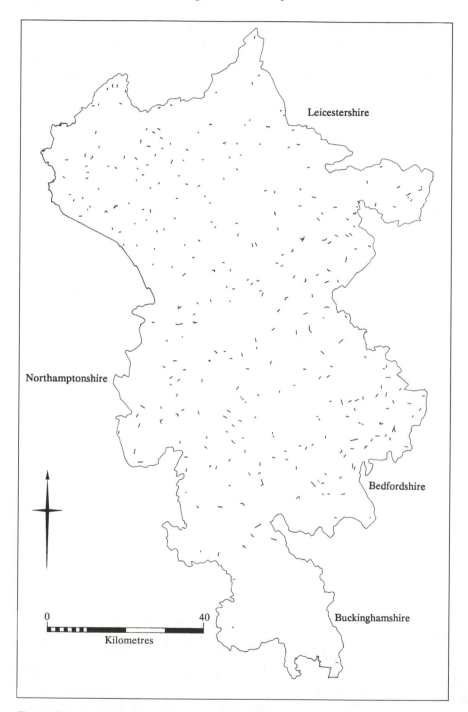

Figure 2.14 Regular row settlements, *c.* 1826.

their location near to some of the relatively few patches of dispersed settlement in the county. Perhaps these indicate that a dispersed settlement pattern underlay the later nucleations, particularly on the Northampton Heights, and the move from dispersed to nucleated settlement occurred here later. Alternatively, the force for change varied in intensity, and hence obliterated the preceding pattern completely in some places, while traces of it survived elsewhere.

Dispersed settlement in Northamptonshire was confined to only a few localities. Its appearance in the royal forests of Whittlewood and Salcey in the south of the county accords with the widely recognised coincidence between woodland landscapes and dispersed settlement, but even here considerable numbers of regular row settlements, and even one or two small clusters are found. Also contradicting this common assumption is the forest of Rockingham where, with the exception of the medieval pottery manufacturing centre of Lyveden, settlement was nucleated, in the form of regular rows. Other cases of dispersed settlement in Northamptonshire correlate less easily with landscapes: in particular around Chipping Warden in the west of the county a number of irregular rows and common-edge settlements (e.g., Chipping Warden, Aston le Walls, Appletree) contrast with nucleated parishes to the north and west (e.g., Culworth, Woodford, Byfield). There was also a scatter of partly or wholly dispersed settlements around Daventry and south-west of Desborough, both in the Northampton Heights.

Single medieval farmsteads are rare in Northamptonshire. As we know from historical evidence that most of the county's villages were associated with regular 'midland' field systems in the later middle ages, it seems likely that the bulk of the households would be located in the central settlement of the township or parish. The large number of single farms which extended east and north of Daventry in the early nineteenth century were of post-medieval origin. Other nineteenth-century farms in the far south-west of the county are found from archaeological fieldwork to be associated with earthworks of former larger settlements. Only a few sites, in the south and north-east of the county, and in the Northampton Heights, may be of medieval origin and have never been larger than farmsteads. The Soke of Peterborough had several isolated farmsteads, some moated, which are recorded in the middle ages.

Leicestershire and Rutland

The settlement pattern of Leicestershire resembles that of Northamptonshire, in that nucleated settlement forms predominated, particularly in the east of the county. The Vale of Belvoir, the wolds, High Leicestershire and Rutland all showed many nucleations, with a single settlement lying within each township. Compact clusters occurred most frequently, particularly in Rutland and the Vale of Belvoir. Many of these settlements displayed a very regular plan, the medieval origin of which is suggested by the similar regularity of those shrunken sites where surveys have been made of the earthworks.[59] Over much of the county, parishes of relatively uniform size often had settlements located centrally within them. Subsidiary settlements are rarely recorded on the nineteenth-century maps or in archaeological or historical sources. Dispersed settlements or single farmsteads were notably absent: most of the handful of sites where the settlement pattern in the early nineteenth century did appear less regular (e.g., Burley and Upper Hambleton, both in Rutland) are associated with earthworks indicating that in the middle ages they had once been regular rows.

An exception to this pattern can be found in the slightly higher ground around Tilton, where at Halstead an interrupted row has no recorded evidence of shrinkage, and at Brook Farm in Launde, recorded in the twelfth century, which lacks evidence for previous more extensive settlement. Another exception is the dispersed hamlet of Pickworth which has little evidence for an antecedent village, and to which is attached a small subsidiary settlement, Top Pickworth, *c*. 800m (½ mile) to the south-west.[60]

In contrast to the numerous compact clusters in the east of the county, regular rows interspersed with fewer clustered nucleations predominated in the main valleys of the rivers Soar, Wreake and Sence, and of the Rothley Brook. These settlements were generally regularly spaced along either side of the valley floor. Some very long rows extended for as much as a kilometre (0.6 mile), such as those between Leicester and Loughborough at Mountsorrel, Swithland, Newtown Linford and Woodhouse Eaves. Parishes, in accordance with the classic riverine pattern, had boundaries designed to include a combination of all land types from meadows on the valley floor to higher ground near the watershed.

Further west in Leicestershire greater variety is found with a higher proportion of dispersed settlements, and this cannot be attributed solely to the irregular and piecemeal development of the modern coal industry. In south-west Leicestershire, adjacent to the Northampton Heights, compact clusters were rather more numerous than regular rows in a mixed settlement pattern. Few single farmsteads were recorded, with the exception of a dense scatter in the southernmost extremity of the county, between Husbands Bosworth and Lutterworth. Further north-west is a very confused settlement pattern, in which irregular rows were combined with very small regular rows and interspersed with strings of single farmsteads and occasional small clusters. Different again, around Ashby de la Zouch in the westernmost part of the county, was a district of larger clustered nucleations each sited within regularly sized parishes. Many of these settlements had a less regular plan than those in the east of the county, and many (such as Appleby Magna and Oakthorpe) contained smaller appendant elements. Small unnamed settlements, most of which have vanished in the last 150 years, sometimes lay on parish boundaries, often at points where several parishes meet.

Immediately to the north, Charnwood contained many isolated farmsteads of probable post-medieval origin. Around the fringes, a ring of densely distributed farmsteads included several with names recorded in the twelfth or thirteenth centuries. Still further away from the wooded, hilly centre (which was largely devoid of settlements) irregular rows, farmsteads and tiny regular streets and clusters formed long chains. One complex polyfocal settlement included Newbold, Outwoods, Coleorton Moor, Limby, Swannington, Peggs Green and Griffydam. These separate elements are difficult to untangle within a settlement sprawl which extended across more than six square kilometres (2½ square miles) around a point where six parishes met. Much of this clearly developed after the middle ages judging from the names, and from their siting on what may have been waste land with grazing rights. The medieval settlement pattern was probably limited to single farmsteads abutting or encroaching onto common pasture.

Summary

Comparisons of the results of this mapping of early nineteenth-century settlement patterns with the plans derived from survey, aerial photography and fieldwalking of deserted and shrunken medieval settlements, which may be assumed to preserve the later medieval plan free of subsequent alterations, suggest that the settlement forms observed on the modern maps reflect broadly the medieval settlement plans. This observation can be made with most assurance in the areas of nucleated settlements where completely deserted village sites are available for comparison with their neighbours which have survived.

The detailed mapping of later settlements, if combined with archaeological and historical information, provides us with evidence for the distribution of settlement types and, combined with information about the township or parish boundaries, can reveal something of the relationship between settlements and their territories. The maps, though late in date, provide a secure point from which to start analysis of the mechanics of change in the landscape, and to formulate hypotheses which can be tested against other evidence.

In drawing some preliminary conclusions about the east midlands, the identification of eastern Leicestershire as a land of nucleated villages or the Chilterns as an area of dispersal is not at all new. But, as we have seen from the details of settlement zones in each county, the division into 'dispersed' and 'nucleated', while representing a general truth, is inadequate to express the rich variety of the patterns. Applied too rigidly the antithesis of 'dispersed' versus 'nucleated' could be an obstacle to explaining the origins or evolution of this settlement pattern: all 'nucleated' settlements need not be the end product of the same process, just as many 'dispersed' settlements are likely to have originated in different ways. The variety of settlement is clearly the product of complex influences and forces.

Having seen the nature of our study area and its settlement pattern, and surveyed its history, we can turn to give an account of its evolution from later prehistory, and to observe the development of its settlement and landscape in the middle ages.

Notes

1   See B. K. Roberts, 'Rural settlement and regional contrasts: questions of continuity and colonisation', *Rural History*, 1 (1991), 51–72.

2   Changes in altitude are one factor, the proximity of a permanent source of water is another. Perhaps the most important, however, are the variations in soil productivity and manageability. Sources for geological information are the Ordnance Survey 1:50,000 geological maps; also M. Reed, *The Buckinghamshire Landscape* (London, Hodder and Stoughton, 1979); P. Bigmore, *The Bedfordshire and Huntingdonshire Landscape* (London, Hodder and Stoughton, 1979); J. Steane, *The Northamptonshire Landscape* (London, Hodder and Stoughton, 1974); G. H. Dury, *The East Midlands and the Peak* (Edinburgh, Nelson, 1963).

3   The ease with which soils can be ploughed, their ability to form an even-textured, well-drained tilth after ploughing, or the length of time for which they maintain their fertility, determines the suitability of different land for different agricultural purposes. However, any discussion of soil types as a prelude to an examination of the evolution of the medieval settlement pattern is limited by the fact that modern surveys can only record presently existing soils. Previous land use itself affects the developing character of soils so that local variations in modern soil profiles may not be exactly the same as those of the preceding two millennia.

4   R. J. Rice, 'Geomorphology', in N. Pye (ed.), *Leicester and its Region* (Leicester, Leicester University Press, 1972), pp. 59–83.

5   P. Salway, *Roman Britain* (Oxford, Oxford University Press, 1981), p. 111.

6   M. Todd, *The Coritani*, 2nd edn (Stroud, Alan Sutton, 1991), pp. 11–12.

7 K. Branigan, *The Catuvellauni* (Gloucester, Alan Sutton, 1985), pp. 26–30; Todd, *Coritani*, pp. 11–19.
8 Salway, *Roman Britain*, p. 535.
9 B. C. Burnham and J. Wacher, *The Small Towns of Roman Britain* (London, Batsford, 1990), pp. 89–91.
10 Burnham and Wacher, *Small Towns*, pp. 130, 155.
11 N. J. Higham, *Rome, Britain and the Anglo-Saxons* (London, Seaby, 1992) for a view espousing minimal migration, and H. Hamerow, 'Migration theory and the migration period', in B. Vyner (ed.), *Building on the Past: Papers Celebrating 150 Years of the Royal Archaeological Institute* (London, Royal Archaeological Institute, 1994), pp. 164–77 for the argument for extensive migration. On the continuation of British rule K. R. Dark, *Civitas to Kingdom: British Political Continuity, 300–800* (Leicester, Leicester University Press, 1994), pp. 86–9
12 W. Davies and H. Vierck, 'The contexts of Tribal Hidage: social aggregates and settlement patterns', *Frühmittelalterliche Studien*, 8 (1974), 223–93.
13 W. Davies, 'Middle Anglia and the Middle Angles', *Midland History*, 2 (1973), 18–20.
14 The area of the Tomsaetan is known to have included Breedon-on-the-Hill: W. de G. Birch (ed.), *Cartularium Saxonicum* (London, Whiting, 1885–93), no. 454 (henceforth *BCS*); P. H. Sawyer, *Anglo-Saxon Charters* (London, Royal Historical Society, 1968), no. 197 (henceforth *S.*).
15 A. Mawer and F. M. Stenton (eds), *The Place-Names of Buckinghamshire* (English Place-Name Society, 2, Cambridge University Press, 1925), pp. 86–7 and 107; B. Cox, *The Place-Names of Leicestershire and Rutland* (unpublished Ph.D. thesis, University of Nottingham, 1971), pp. 230–1.
16 Davies and Vierck, 'Tribal Hidage', 228, 279.
17 For Tondbert, prince of the South Gyrwe, see C. Plummer (ed.), *Venerabilis Baedae Opera Historica, vol. 1* (Oxford, Oxford University Press, 1896), p. 243; and for *principes* of the Tomsaetan, see *BCS*, 454.
18 For indications of West Saxon influence and also the reference to the capture of Aylesbury: D. Whitelock, D. C. Douglas and S. I. Tucker (eds), *The Anglo-Saxon Chronicle* (London, Eyre and Spottiswoode, 1961), p. 13.
19 Davies, 'Middle Anglia', 18–20; and also D. Dumville, 'Essex, Middle Anglia, and the expansion of Mercia in the south-east midlands', in S. Bassett (ed.), *The Origins of Anglo-Saxon Kingdoms* (Leicester, Leicester University Press, 1989), pp. 123–40.
20 That the area was part of the Mercian kingdom in the eighth and ninth centuries is suggested by references in chronicles. See for instance, A. Campbell (ed.), *The Chronicle of Aethelweard* (London, Nelson, 1963), p. 51, which suggests that the area to the west of Stamford was considered Mercian in the early tenth century. Moreover it is found that Mercian rulers were making grants of land within the area without any intermediary (e.g., at Wotton Underwood in Buckinghamshire, *S.*, 204 and Monks Risborough, Buckinghamshire, *S.*, 367) and were also holding assemblies at places more or less throughout the area: Glen, Gumley and Croft in Leicestershire, Irthlingborough in Northamptonshire and Princes Risborough in Buckinghamshire, *BCS*, 455, 140, 210, 416, 1334 and 552 respectively and comments in *S.*, 1272, 90, 109, 1184 and 219.

21 For the basic accepted narrative of this period see F. M. Stenton, *Anglo-Saxon England*, 3rd edn (Oxford, Oxford University Press, 1971), pp. 239–76, 320–63.

22 D. M. Wilson, 'The Scandinavians in England', in D. M. Wilson (ed.), *The Archaeology of Anglo-Saxon England* (Cambridge, Cambridge University Press, 1976), pp. 393–403; P. Stafford, *The East Midlands in the Early Middle Ages* (Leicester, Leicester University Press, 1985), pp. 115–21.

23 G. Fellows-Jensen, *Scandinavian Settlement Names in the East Midlands* (Copenhagen, Akademisk Forlag, 1978).

24 Even in the mid-tenth century, Edgar was created king of the Mercians while his brother was king in the south.

25 Stenton, *Anglo-Saxon England*, pp. 506–12.

26 A. J. Robertson (ed.), *Anglo-Saxon Charters* (Cambridge, Cambridge University Press, 1939), pp. 72–83.

27 Stenton, *Anglo-Saxon England*, p. 505; C. Hart, *The Danelaw* (London, Hambledon Press, 1992), pp. 8–16. Aethelred, the Mercian leader was obviously still in control of southern Buckinghamshire in *c.* 900, as he was involved in the granting of land at Risborough (*S.*, 367 and 219).

28 Buckinghamshire is first recorded as such in 1010 and both Bedfordshire and Northamptonshire in 1011, see Whitelock *et al.* (eds), *Anglo-Saxon Chronicle* under the relevant years; Leicestershire is not actually first recorded as such until 1086.

29 C. S. Taylor, 'The origin of the Mercian shires', in H. P. R. Finberg (ed.), *Gloucestershire Studies* (Leicester, Leicester University Press, 1957), pp. 17–51.

30 Stenton, *Anglo-Saxon England*, p. 502, and for a longer-term and more speculative view of the county's origins see C. Phythian-Adams, 'Rutland reconsidered', in A. Dornier (ed.), *Mercian Studies* (Leicester, Leicester University Press, 1977), pp. 63–84; C. Hart, *The Hidation of Northamptonshire* (Leicester University Department of English Local History Occasional Papers, 2nd Series, 3, 1970), p. 13 and note 3.

31 H. R. Loyn, 'The hundred in England in the tenth and early eleventh centuries', in H. Hearder and H. R. Loyn (eds), *British Government and Administration* (Cardiff, University of Wales Press, 1974), pp. 1–15.

32 Robertson, *Anglo-Saxon Charters*, pp. 72–83, 231–7.

33 C. F. Slade (ed.), *The Leicestershire Survey (c. 1130)* (Leicester University, Department of English Local History Occasional Papers, 1st Series, 7, 1956), pp. 14–29, 68–82.

34 Hart, *Hidation of Northamptonshire*, pp. 39–43; *VCH Buckinghamshire*, 2, p. 245.

35 For instance that recorded in the charter dealing with 'Scelfdune sive Baldinigcotum' (apparently in Buckinghamshire) dated 792, see *BCS*, 264, and that appended to the charter for Wotton (definitely in Buckinghamshire) dated 843x855, see *BCS*, 452, and comments in M. Reed, 'Buckinghamshire Anglo-Saxon charter boundaries', in M. Gelling, *The Early Charters of the Thames Valley* (Leicester, Leicester University Press, 1979), p. 184.

36 *BCS*, 1229.

37 H. R. Loyn, *Anglo-Saxon England and the Norman Conquest* (London, Longmans, 1962), p. 302.

38 For a general exposition on the revolution in organisation associated with the development of states see R. A. Dodgshon, *The European Past* (London, Macmillan, 1987), pp. 130–65.

39 D. P. Kirby, 'The Saxon bishops of Leicester, Lyndsey (Syddensis) and Dorchester', *Transactions of the Leicestershire Archaeological Society*, 41 (1965–6), 1–8.

40 D. Hill, *An Atlas of Anglo-Saxon England* (Oxford, Blackwell, 1981), pp. 147–8.

41 *BCS*, 841.

42 See in particular the second code of Edgar and the eighth of Aethelred II, A. J. Robertson (ed.), *The Laws of the Kings of England from Edmund to Henry I* (Cambridge, Cambridge University Press, 1925), pp. 20–3, 116–29; W. J. Blair, 'Local churches in Domesday Book and before', in J. C. Holt (ed.), *Domesday Studies* (Woodbridge, Boydell, 1987), pp. 265–78.

43 The complete system is only documented for the whole country in the late thirteenth century; see *Taxatio Ecclesiastica Angliae et Walliae Auctoritate P. Nicholai IV c. AD 1291* (London, Record Commission, 1802) though its existence is clearly indicated in episcopal documents from earlier in the century, most clearly for Leicestershire in the 'Matriculus' of Bishop Hugh de Welles, see W. P. W. Phillimore (ed.), *Rotuli Hugonis de Welles, vol. 1* (Canterbury and York Society, 1, 1909), pp. 239–72.

44 R. Fleming, *Kings and Lords in Conquest England* (Cambridge, Cambridge University Press, 1991), pp. 125–6.

45 *VCH Northamptonshire*, 2, pp. 421–4.

46 Whitelock *et al.* (eds), *Anglo-Saxon Chronicle*, p. 65.

47 Rockingham forest, for instance, contained a number of royal manors that covered a considerable proportion of the forest, *DB*, 1, ff. 219–20. Whittlewood contains Whittlebury, where Aethelstan is known to have held an assembly in the early tenth century, see VI Aethelstan 12, 1, F. L. Attenborough (ed.), *The Laws of the Earliest English Kings* (Cambridge, Cambridge University Press, 1922); and Passenham where Edward the Elder stayed in 917, Whitelock *et al.* (eds), *Anglo-Saxon Chronicle*, p. 66. Passenham was also a royal manor in 1086, *DB*, 1, f. 220. Bernwood contained the royal manor of Brill, *DB*, 1, f. 143, where Edward the Confessor is claimed to have built a palace: see F. Barlow (ed.), *Vita Eadwardi Regis* (London, Nelson, 1962), p. 64.

48 W. G. Hoskins and L. Dudley Stamp, *The Common Lands of England and Wales* (London, Collins, 1963), pp. 5–13.

49 *DB*, 1, f. 230.

50 This description comes from a saints' resting-place list: D. Rollason, 'Lists of saints' resting places in Anglo-Saxon England', *Anglo-Saxon England*, 7 (1978), 89.

51 For a general discussion of this and related matters relating to waste districts in Europe see C. Wickham, 'European forests in the early middle ages, landscape and land clearance', in C. J. Wickham, *Land and Power. Studies in Italian and European Social History* (London, British School at Rome, 1994), pp. 155–99.

52 T. D. Hardy and C. T. Martin (eds), *Lestorie des Engles, vol. 1* (London, Rolls Series, 1888), p. 392.

53 For example Newton Bromswold (Northamptonshire) and Leighton Bromswold (Huntingdonshire). There are also a number of examples in the area

of the term 'wold' being used of rough common pastures in the parishes of the area.

54 See for instance the extra-parochial area that survived in the modern period, lying between Old Dalby, Prestwold and Ragdale in north Leicestershire. Examples of intercommoning arrangements are known at many places within the study area. For instance in Buckinghamshire they are known between Dunton and Mursley, F. G. Gurney, 'An agricultural agreement of the year 1345', *Records of Buckinghamshire*, 14 (1941–6), pp. 245–64; Newton Longville and Bletchley, H. E. Salter (ed.), *Newington Longville Charters* (Oxford Record Society, 3, 1921), pp. 18–20; Stewkley and Drayton Parslow, M. W. Hughes (ed.), *A Calendar of the Feet of Fines for the County of Buckinghamshire* (Records of Buckinghamshire, 4, 1940), p. 46; all from medieval sources; between Foscott and Leckhampstead, Preston Bisset and Tingewick, Westbury and Turweston from post-medieval sources, *VCH Buckinghamshire*, 4, pp. 182, 249 and 252. Such arrangements were clearly quite widespread and perhaps even a general phenomenon. For general comments F. Pollock and F. W. Maitland, *The History of English Law*, 2nd edn, vol. 1 (Cambridge, Cambridge University Press, 1898), p. 619.

55 Maps published by John Bryant in 1826 were used for Bedfordshire, Buckinghamshire and Northamptonshire. The early nineteenth-century Ordnance Survey first edition one inch was used for Leicestershire. All were at a scale similar or slightly larger than the modern Ordnance Survey 1:50,000 series. Larger-scale, or earlier, maps, such as those drawn up to accompany acts of enclosure, tithe apportionments, or for purposes of estate management, would have furnished more detail but could not provide a complete or consistent coverage of the study area.

56 See B. K. Roberts, *The Making of the English Village* (London, Longman, 1987) chapters 2 & 9, especially figs 2.3 and 9.6, for details of the categories used by Roberts. Also B. K. Roberts, *Village Plans* (Aylesbury, Shire, 1982).

57 See C. C. Dyer, *Hanbury: Settlement and Society in a Woodland Landscape* (Leicester University Department of English Local History, Occasional Papers, 4th Series, 4, 1991), pp. 32–43 for a discussion of the nature and arrangement of this form of settlement.

58 Larger nucleated clusters are defined for the purposes of this analysis as those settlements which contained more than 25 properties in 1826.

59 See R. F. Hartley, *The Mediaeval Earthworks of Rutland* (Leicester, Leicestershire Museums, Art Galleries and Records Service Archaeological Reports Series, 7, 1983); R. F. Hartley, *The Medieval Earthworks of Central Leicestershire* (Leicester, Leicestershire Museums, Arts and Records Service Archaeological Reports Series, 103, 1989) for plans of settlement remains and existing settlement forms.

60 Hartley, *Mediaeval Earthworks of Rutland*, p. 32.

3

Settlement from prehistory until the Norman Conquest

Prehistoric and Roman settlement

The prehistoric and Roman occupation of the east midlands sets the scene for that of the early medieval period. The suggestion that Saxon incomers in the fifth and sixth centuries found a 'virgin country' of forest and marshes has been refuted by archaeological evidence – from environmental studies, excavation and fieldwork, which has shown that much of England had been largely cleared of woodland, farmed and settled in a process which began as early as 4000 BC. Extensive prehistoric field systems, laid out across these open landscapes and either surviving as earthworks or reflected in modern field boundaries, have now been found in many parts of the country, even on heavy clay soils. Many medieval settlements or field systems have produced evidence, in excavation or fieldwalking, of occupation in the Roman and prehistoric periods. Hoskins's statement that 'The direct prehistoric contribution to the landscape is small'[1] can clearly no longer be accepted, and an awareness of pre-medieval exploitation is an important precondition to our understanding the settlements and landscapes of the middle ages.

However, prehistoric and Romano-British settlement and land use in the east midlands have been less thoroughly studied than in many other parts of the country, such as Wessex. This is at least partly due to extensive medieval occupation and cultivation which has destroyed or obscured much of the evidence for earlier periods. Antiquarian archaeologists had little interest in the region because of the lack of visible remains of pre-medieval sites, and recent archaeological research has been focused on the wealth of medieval sites.[2] Nevertheless, enough work has been done to show that the post-Roman occupants of the east midlands inherited a countryside that had been extensively cultivated and settled for many centuries. There are no parts of the study area that are devoid of evidence for pre-medieval settlement, although there are great variations in the density and character of recorded information. Let us see what is known of the landscape which was handed down to the earliest post-Roman inhabitants.

Environment and land use

Early use of land varied in its intensity across the countryside. Deposits
sealed under a bronze age barrow at Sproxton in Leicestershire show
that woodland clearance was in progress in that area from the early fourth
millennium BC,[3] but elsewhere, as in the Chilterns, woodland survived
until recent times. Excavation has shown the importance of both cattle
rearing and grain production in the economy of the late prehistoric river
valley settlements.[4] Away from the river valleys, in spite of paucity of
evidence, we can suspect a more varied rural economy, with pastoralism
and industrial activity.[5] Generally, by the middle of the first millennium BC
a mostly open landscape supported mixed arable and pastoral agriculture.[6] Farming may have intensified and arable expanded in the final
centuries BC at the time when Belgic-type (late iron age) material appears
in the archaeological record.[7]

   The suggestion has been made that the claylands and high wolds may
have been more easily cultivable in the pre-medieval era than later, either
because of the presence of loess soils or simply because tree cover produces
subsoils which are rich and loamy with good water retaining and draining
capabilities.[8] These characteristics would have remained for a while under
cultivation after the woodland had been cleared. Pressure on the apparently densely inhabited valleys could have encouraged early expansion
onto the claylands, the wolds and even the greensand heathlands.[9] Clearance and cultivation would have led to a deterioration in the soils, and
the creation of colluvial deposits as soil washed down the river valleys.[10] This decline in fertility and manageability of the clayland soils could
have caused settlement to refocus with a greater intensity back onto the
river valleys. This could provide an explanation for the varying distribution and density of archaeological evidence for settlement: simple
distribution maps showing iron age and Roman sites and finds suggest
that the emphasis on the river valleys is more marked in the Roman
period than the iron age.

River valleys

The major river valleys contain most evidence for occupation in the late
prehistoric and Roman periods (Fig. 3.1). This partly results from acci-
dents in the availability of archaeological evidence: crop marks show up
well in alluvial soils, allowing sites to be discovered by aerial photography;
and modern disturbance, such as gravel extraction, provides opportunities
for excavation and casual finds. Even allowing for the relative ease of
discovering sites in the valleys, the sheer density of activity, often of

successive periods superimposed on one another, implies that the river valleys provided a favourable environment for habitation over millennia.[11]

Sites are so densely distributed in the river valleys that neighbouring settlements of iron age date are separated in some places by a kilometre (0.6 mile) or less; in the Roman period settlements can be observed in some places every 500m (550yd).[12] Clearly not all the settlements in either the iron age or the Roman period were in occupation at the same time, but their numbers still impress. Iron age settlements range in type from enclosed complexes to small clusters of two or three huts; in the Roman period isolated farms, villas and villages can be identified. At Lockington (Leics) and Fotheringhay (Northants) are settlements, with regular rows and closes containing buildings lying along tracks and roads, which resemble medieval planned villages (Fig. 3.2).[13] Some settlements in both periods are associated with systems of small rectangular fields enclosed by ditches.

The density of settlement in the river valleys in both the iron age and Roman periods, suggests a general continuity of land use, and numerous iron age sites lie on, or in close proximity to, Roman successors.[14] Research around Medbourne (Leics)[15] has confirmed the impression gained from other parts of the country that the Roman takeover made little impact, particularly in the short term, on rural settlement; villas, although an innovation, were often sited close to iron age sites.[16]

Hill forts, the most visible high status monuments of the late iron age, are (by definition) located out of the river valleys, but other enclosed sites of iron age date on low ground might also have a claim to special status. Villas, the most opulent rural settlements of the Romano-British period, are found most frequently in the river valleys, and indeed in some places, such as the upper Ouse valley in Bedfordshire, almost every parish along the river contains the certain or likely site of one.[17] In both the iron age and the Roman periods the inhabitants of the valleys were probably farming land in territories extending beyond the valleys onto the surrounding slopes, although the evidence for this in the east midlands has been largely destroyed or concealed by later cultivation.

This leads inevitably to speculation as to the survival of these territorial boundaries: later parish and even township boundaries (townships being self-contained subdivisions of parishes, where parishes contained more than one village) have been demonstrated in other parts of the country to have originated before the middle ages,[18] and the repetitive regularity of some of the east midlands parishes, combined with the apparently even distribution of villas, makes it possible that some of these parish or township boundaries may preserve the outline of villa estates or of territories of earlier date.[19]

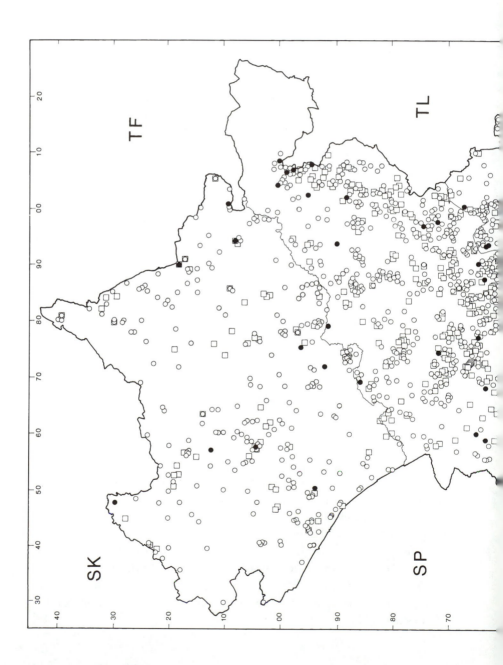

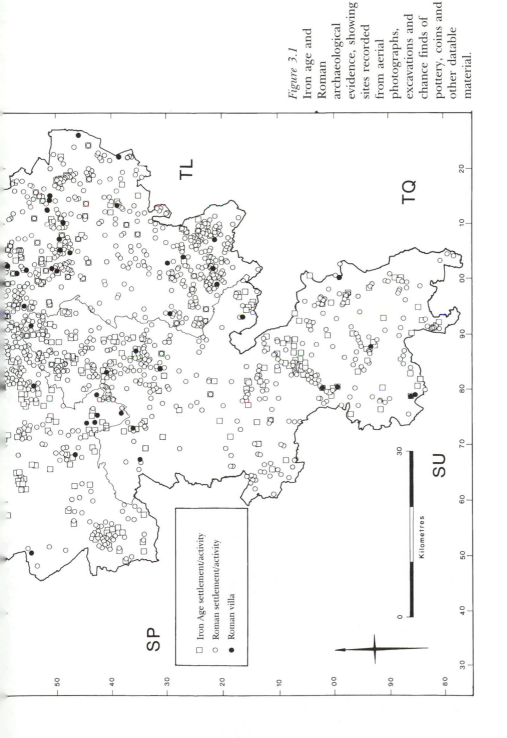

Figure 3.1 Iron age and Roman archaeological evidence, showing sites recorded from aerial photographs, excavations and chance finds of pottery, coins and other datable material.

SP

TL

TQ

SU

Iron Age settlement/activity
Roman settlement/activity
Roman villa

Kilometres

Figure 3.2 Romano-British settlements indicated by crop marks in Fotheringhay and Nassington parishes, Northamptonshire. The ditches which are visible as crop marks define a road running north–south, with rows of boundaries marking enclosures on either side. The rectangular enclosure to the south (12) is the site of a Roman villa. The presence of both villa and 'village' raises questions about the relationship between high-status and low-status rural settlements at this time – was there some anticipation of the medieval manor? The circles mark the sites of prehistoric barrows.

Towns, essentially Roman innovations, also tend to lie in the river valleys. They were linked by the Roman road network, with major routes, of military origin, which in most cases notoriously ignore the terrain. Smaller roads are less easily identified than military ones, but trackways associated with settlements are often visible on aerial photographs, and others may be preserved under medieval and modern lanes. Unlike military roads, they are more likely to follow routes closely related to the local landscape, for example in Buckinghamshire where they link the Chiltern Hills with the low-lying land to the north. These also provided short-distance communications between settlements.

The founding of towns, the improved road network and the demands of the state must have stimulated agricultural production, upon which the economy of villas and farmsteads was based. Other natural resources include the plentiful ironstone deposits in north-east Northamptonshire, already exploited in the iron age and used intensively in the Roman period; coal, mined by the Romans where it was available, for example in north-west Leicestershire; and the limestones of Northamptonshire and Leicestershire, widely used for building.[20] The Nene Valley pottery industry would have obtained its fuel from the woodland resources of the adjacent claylands. The dense occupation of the river valleys, where much of the area's wealth was concentrated, appears to have survived the recession of the third century AD and been sustained up to and beyond the end of the fourth century.

The east midlands claylands

It has often been alleged that the heavy, cold soils of the north Bedfordshire vales and the higher wolds of Northamptonshire and Leicestershire were so inhospitable that they could not be settled or cultivated until the middle ages, when the use of a plough with a mouldboard and a coulter enabled these clays to be worked for the first time. For a while this idea received some tacit support from the absence of archaeological evidence for pre-medieval settlements on these soils. However, the discovery of field systems of probable prehistoric date on similar soils in eastern England shows that intractable clays were no insuperable obstacle to early farmers.[21] Although our area lacks such clear evidence it seems unlikely that parts of it were not also divided up in a similar manner at that date.[22] This supposition is helped by the observation that a number of Romano-British river valley settlements had field systems which extend towards the north Bedfordshire claylands.[23] Traces of pit alignments from aerial photography suggest the former presence of early land divisions across the Northampton Heights.[24]

Evidence for settlements, even in the form of stray finds, is rather
thinly distributed on the claylands, but they are by no means devoid of
indications of human activity. The sparseness of finds is partly a reflection
of the difficulties in conducting archaeological research in these areas.
One piece of detailed fieldwork on boulder clay examined the interior
of the deer park at Brigstock, within the later forest of Rockingham.[25]
Aerial photography and fieldwalking had previously revealed the sites of
several settlements of iron age and Romano-British date.[26] Several of the
iron age cropmark sites are associated with linear ditches lying on a
common orientation (NNE–SSW) which are likely to be the remains of
field boundaries. Fieldwalking produced a few neolithic flints but no
bronze age material.

Several previously unrecorded sites of iron age and Roman date were
discovered at Brigstock, of which a selection were excavated. The earliest
iron age sites date to the fifth to fourth century BC; the majority belonged
to the first century BC; they consisted of small enclosures, both isolated
and clustered together, with sheep dominant among the bones found.
Between the first century BC and the first century AD many of the sites
were abandoned, but occupation continued on new sites, with settlements
of Roman date which were generally larger and more complex, associated
with well-manured infields (detectable as scatters of pottery which had
been deposited with the manure). No occupation could be found after
the end of the second century AD, and Foster has suggested that the area
was then largely abandoned until a medieval hunting lodge was built and
extensive charcoal burning practised, mostly in the thirteenth century.
'Saxon' pottery, however, was found on more than a dozen of the iron
age and Roman sites, and at a handful of other locations within the
park.[27] Only a small area (approximately 100ha or 250 acres), in the west
of the park, lacks any archaeological evidence until the charcoal burning
of the thirteenth century, suggesting that this alone may represent an
area which remained almost continuously wooded from the earliest times
until it was felled in the high middle ages.

Brigstock Park therefore shows shifting but periodically quite intensive
occupation on the boulder clay, within a mostly non-wooded landscape.
Periodic depopulation or deintensification of land-use is suggested by
phases of settlement abandonment, the absence of material from some
periods (such as the bronze age), and the reorganisation of field systems.
The district had a varied economic base in the late prehistoric and Roman,
with much pastoralism.[28] The field boundaries associated with the iron
age and Roman settlements show a regularity of alignment, and could
have influenced the layout of the pale of the medieval deer park. The

picture at Brigstock seems to be echoed in the Milton Keynes vicinity,[29] but we cannot know if it is applicable more widely to other elevated and clayland regions in the study area without much more fieldwork. Other clayland regions may indeed have seen a rather different pattern of settlement and land use: the later forests of Whittlewood and Salcey, for example, contain a large number of Roman villas, which are absent from the higher clays and limestones. Their economies were no doubt stimulated by the proximity of the town of Towcester and the military road of Watling Street.

The Chilterns

A combination of archaeology, place-names and historical evidence has been taken to prove the wooded character of the Chilterns throughout the middle ages. It is assumed also that the woodlands prevailed from the earliest times, and the first incursions were made only in the middle ages. However, the straight lines of sections of prehistoric boundary ditches suggest that the landscape may at an early date have been clear of trees. Permanent settlement in the Chilterns has been supposed to be medieval in origin: Hoskins (for example) asserts that the Chilterns were 'colonised comparatively late', dating the settlement at Fingest from the earliest documentary reference, supported by the twelfth-century date of the church.[30] In fact a number of finds of iron age and Roman date come from within 1km (1090yd) of the church, and the Chilterns generally have produced many prehistoric and Roman sites and finds.

That the Chilterns may have been an area of some importance in pre-medieval times is suggested by the number of high-status or specialised settlements, including enclosures and hillforts, such as Rainsborough Camp. The hills are crossed by the Icknield Way, a major prehistoric route linking Berkshire to the Wash. The hillforts appear to be sited strategically to control access north from the Thames valley, overlooking narrow valleys or the lower land to the north and south. A tradition of high-status settlements continues into the Roman period, with a concentration of wealthy villas often on, or close to, late iron age settlements, including hillforts.[31]

Summary

By the end of the Roman period, most of the study area had been settled or farmed at one time or another. Intensive occupation and exploitation were focused on the river valleys, and in the Roman period these attracted high-status sites such as villas and towns. The higher ground and heavier soils of the wolds and claylands seem to have been settled and farmed more intermittently, depending perhaps on climate and pressure upon resources, and were possibly less densely settled in the fourth century AD than in the last centuries BC or the early Roman period. The Chilterns clearly had a special character, in both the iron age and the Roman period, with concentrations of villas recalling the opulence of the Cotswolds.[32] An important theme in the later history of settlement and landscape is to compare the development of areas such as this with the densely settled river valleys, or the less consistently exploited claylands.

The early middle ages: rural settlement

Archaeological evidence in the east midlands is considerably less plentiful for the early medieval period than for the preceding four centuries (Fig. 3.3). Many districts have no known evidence for settlement between the end of the Roman period and the ninth or tenth century, and for some there is no information before Domesday Book. These places were not necessarily uninhabited during these centuries, but the material culture of the period leaves few visible remains. Much of the pottery was handmade and liable to disintegrate; it tends not to survive in the soil and is difficult to see or date. Many everyday objects were made from wood, fabric or leather which only rarely survives. Finds such as those at Odell in the Ouse valley (Beds), where wickerwork of seventh-century date was preserved in the linings of wells, serve to highlight the absence of such evidence from other sites.[33] As elsewhere in England, the generally small early medieval settlements were provided with wooden buildings which often lack easily discovered features such as stone foundations.

The problems of identifying sites of the early middle ages proved for many years to be self-perpetuating: because little was known about the nature or appearance of Anglo-Saxon settlements, the slight evidence for their presence was overlooked, particularly when earlier or later phases of occupation were the main focus of interest. Consequently research remained focused on material that could be easily recognised, notably metalwork recovered from pagan cemeteries. 'Anglo-Saxon archaeology' for many years involved the typological study of small finds. The richest cemeteries are concentrated in the south-east of England, where inhumation with grave goods was favoured as a means of disposing of the dead. Within the area of our study the rich Kentish-style inhumation of a sixth-century chieftain or prince at Taplow in south Buckinghamshire stands out as an exception.[34] The prevalence of cremation among the pagan population of the east midlands leaves few grave goods, or they are poorly preserved.

Cemeteries of the fifth, sixth and seventh centuries contain vital information about cultural contacts, trade, disease, demography, social status, wealth, religion and attitudes to death. But, however well studied, cemeteries provide limited evidence about rural settlements. Although some were sited near to habitation, as at Harringworth (Northants) or Empingham in Rutland (where burials overlay a sunken-featured building), most seem to have been located at a distance from the living communities, sometimes apparently on the boundaries of territories.[35] Cemeteries may complement the evidence from settlement, but they tell us little about the location and character of the settlements themselves. The number of burials may indicate the size of communities, but only rarely have the cemeteries been completely excavated. Although they do show that people were in residence in a locality, which is valuable as often no other evidence for this exists, our consideration of the period must concentrate on the settlements themselves.

The evidence for continuity and change in the post-Roman landscape

We have seen that by the fourth century most of the east midlands had been settled, sometimes densely, and its resources extensively exploited. The length of occupation of these settlements varies, and settlement foundation, shrinkage, adaptation (including migration and replanning) and abandonment all occurred throughout the Roman period. In the centuries which followed the Roman period, the same processes seem to have continued.

The traditional idea that the end of the Roman period was followed by catastrophic social collapse resulting from invasion and mass migration, with widespread abandonment of towns, villas and farms is reflected in the many Roman settlements which lack evidence for occupation in later centuries. These range from anonymous isolated farmsteads to towns such as *Durocobrivae* (later Dunstable). On some sites which have been excavated, such as Odell (Beds), there is no sign of occupation between the fourth and the sixth centuries.[36] At the villa of Great Casterton in Rutland it has been suggested that the destruction by fire of some buildings can be dated to the early fifth century.[37]

Settlement was clearly not sustainable everywhere in the post-Roman period. Much of the fenland around the Soke of Peterborough, which had been reclaimed from the sea during the first century AD by a complex system of drainage ditches including the Car Dyke, was abandoned soon after the beginning of the fifth century with a combination of adverse climatic conditions, the breakdown in the administrative system needed to maintain efficient drainage, and, doubtless, the reduced pressure on

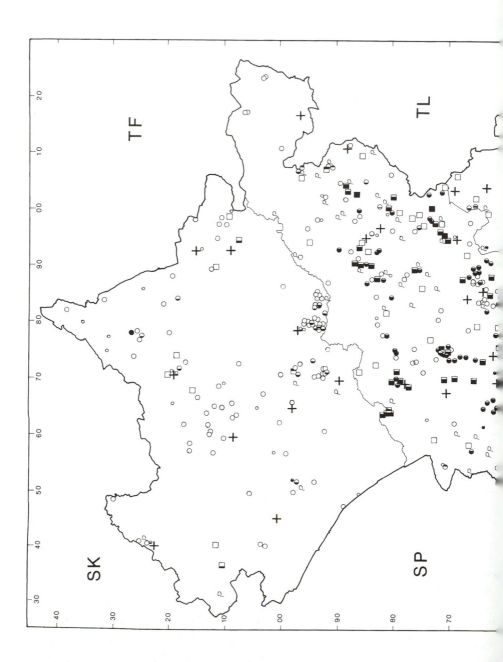

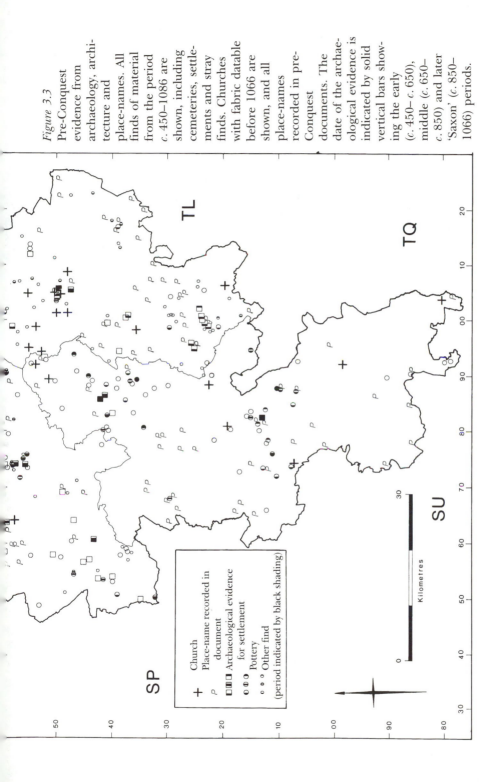

Figure 3.3
Pre-Conquest evidence from archaeology, architecture and place-names. All finds of material from the period *c*. 450–1086 are shown, including cemeteries, settlements and stray finds. Churches with fabric datable before 1066 are shown, and all place-names recorded in pre-Conquest documents. The date of the archaeological evidence is indicated by solid vertical bars showing the early (*c*. 450– *c*. 650), middle (*c*. 650– *c*. 850) and later 'Saxon' (*c*. 850– 1066) periods.

agricultural resources resulting from the collapse of the Roman infra-structure.[38] This area remained largely unoccupied until the twelfth and thirteenth centuries.

Limited evidence for settlement in the fifth to seventh centuries on the claylands leads to the suggestion that this relatively inhospitable environ-ment was abandoned after the end of the Roman period. Most settlements which had been occupied in the Roman period on the heavy soils have produced no early Anglo-Saxon evidence, and many appear never to have been reoccupied following their abandonment in the late Roman period.[39] Researchers working on north Buckinghamshire have com-mented that 'The evidence for continuity of settlement sites from Roman into the pagan Saxon is minimal'.[40]

However, while some of the archaeological evidence may point to the conclusion that many Roman sites were permanently deserted, three reservations should be made in any discussion of continuity and change in the post-Roman landscape. The first concerns local differences: vari-ations in their environment and historical circumstances would have influenced the evolution of settlements in the early post-Roman period. Secondly, it must be remembered that the evidence is very limited, and the way in which it is retrieved and recorded often makes continuity of occupation difficult to observe. Roman material is durable and recognis-able, while evidence for Anglo-Saxon occupation at the same site is more likely to go unnoticed and unrecorded. The third point concerns the proximity of sites to one another. Settlement shift involving the replace-ment of buildings by adjacent structures, or the migration of the population over a short distance, represents a form of continuity. A site with a fifth- or sixth-century farmstead lying adjacent to a late Romano-British settlement and in effect replacing it, could be misinterpreted as representing discontinuity of occupation. We must attempt to establish whether occupation ceased, however briefly, or whether the population moved into a different administrative context, or whether the settlement changed so much that its function was transformed. The archaeological evidence does not allow these processes to be easily recognised.

These considerations lead us to acknowledge the likelihood of a degree of continuity from the Roman to the early medieval period. A strong association between Roman settlements and pagan cremation burials of the fifth and sixth centuries could mean that many Roman sites continued as points of attraction. The large cemetery at Thurmaston in Leicestershire is close to the *civitas* capital of *Ratae* (Leicester), and a number of fifth- to early sixth-century cremation urns have been recovered from a site adjacent to the Roman small town of Sandy in Bedfordshire, and near to the Roman cemetery.[41] In fact, nine of the ten pagan cremation cemeteries recorded in Bedfordshire lie within a few hundred metres (or yards) of Roman settlements. A number of cemeteries, including that at Kempston (Beds) also include both Roman and Anglo-Saxon burials, and suggest some degree of continuity in use.[42]

Notwithstanding the evidence for post-Roman abandonment, many Roman settlements do have evidence for fifth-century occupation. At *Verulamium* (St Albans), in the Chilterns just 10km (6 miles) outside the study area, a Roman lifestyle survived for some time judging from the functioning of the water supply after 450.[43] At nearby Luton, fifth-century handmade pottery of Anglo-Saxon type has been found on a Roman site.[44] Villas such as Latimer (Bucks), Totternhoe (Beds), Brixworth (Northants) and Great Casterton in Rutland, all have evidence of occupation in the fifth century and beyond.[45] Many lower-status settlements, such as four out of the eight known Roman sites in the parish of Toddington (Beds) for example, have also produced material of post-Roman date. Clearly Roman settlements, whether rich or poor, were not all abandoned in the early fifth century.

At other sites there is evidence of post-Roman occupation adjacent or close to Roman settlements. Near Higham Ferrers (Northants), iron age, Romano-British and pre-Conquest (fifth to eleventh centuries) settlements lie within 400m (440yd) of one another.[46] In Brixworth in the same county, many scatters of fifth- to ninth-century pottery, found by fieldwalking, are located within *c*. 200m (220yd) of Roman settlements or villas, and the same is probably true of sites at Medbourne (Leics) and Maxey in the Soke of Peterborough.[47] The implication is that these settlements shifted, but whether this represents unbroken occupation is unclear because of the difficulty in dating the pottery closely. We do not know whether a settlement which yields Roman and handmade post-Roman pottery (which may date from any point between the fifth and the ninth centuries) was abandoned and reoccupied, or continuously occupied.

Change in the function of settlements, which may be inferred from their size and layout, adds a further dimension to the recognition of continuity. On many villa sites post-Roman structures and finds seem no different from the normal early medieval settlement. Sunken-featured buildings (*grubenhäuser*) on the site of the Brixworth villa, for example, are similar to those on small rural settlements such as Maxey. The implication appears to be that these sites continued to be occupied but lost the high status which had previously set them apart from the surrounding farmsteads. Low-status farmsteads which continued to be occupied in the post-Roman period may have functioned as before, like a site at Caldecotte in the parish of Bow Brickhill (Bucks), where Roman field boundaries apparently persisted in use for some centuries after 400.[48] Even when considerable distances separated the Roman and post-Roman occupation sites, the same fields may still have been cultivated.

Exceptions to this levelling of the settlement hierarchy include the villa at Latimer in the Chilterns, where an unusual and very substantial building was constructed in the fifth century.[49] Perhaps in this region factors operated to preserve the social structure, a view which is supported by the large number of sites occupied in both the Roman period and the fifth to seventh centuries in the south of our area. A cluster of such sites around Dunstable in southern Bedfordshire, and others in the major river valleys, contrasts with the scarcity of post-Roman evidence on the heavy claylands and greensand in Bedfordshire; here, the few sites that have been found tend to have no previous occupation. The survival of a Latin word (*funta*, spring) in the Buckinghamshire place name Chalfont is a further clue to the continuation of a native population in the Chilterns. In the other three counties there is a lack of Celtic or Latin elements in place-names.[50]

The end of the Roman period clearly ushered in greater changes in some areas than others. The fenland region provides an extreme example of depopulation, in special environmental circumstances. The situation in the claylands is more uncertain, but finds of the fifth to seventh centuries in north Bedfordshire and Northamptonshire clearly indicate that these regions were not abandoned at the end of the Roman period. Those areas which in the Roman period enjoyed a special importance (such as the Chilterns), or were more densely occupied (the river valleys) appear to have experienced a greater degree of continuity in the following centuries. Towns and villas were most likely to change their functions radically in the fifth to sixth centuries while small rural settlements would have been more likely to persist. Settlement shift occurred before, during and after this transition, and is not in itself evidence of a major dislocation linked to the end of Roman rule.

The nature of settlement in the fifth to ninth centuries.

Work on the settlements of the fifth to ninth centuries, particularly fieldwalking in central and eastern Northamptonshire and in south-east Leicestershire, has indicated a plethora of small hamlets scattered across the landscape. A similar story emerges from finds from observation of a pipeline trench on the chalk ridge north of Dunstable (Beds), where ten sunken featured buildings were found distributed over a distance of 2km (1¼ miles).[51] There is little evidence for differences in function or status.

The large structure on the site of the villa at Latimer appears to have fallen out of use by the late fifth century, and nothing resembling a town existed in our area at this time. Some settlements of the period have no evidence of earlier occupation, and appear to have been newly founded; some may have replaced previous settlements; others appear to continue the occupation of previous Roman sites.

Excavation has confirmed the small size of the settlements, usually containing no more than ten structures at any one time. Excavated examples range from one or two buildings, as at Upton (Northants) or Harrold (Beds), to thirteen or more at Maxey which, however, derived from two separate phases.[52] Most contain sunken-featured buildings and larger timber buildings, built with a variety of techniques: some based on horizontal beams set in slots in the ground, others using vertical timbers in post holes. Unusual evidence for a turf roof was encountered at Puddle Hill (Beds).[53] Ditches appear to have been used to define the limits of the site at Maxey, but the settlement within it shows little sign of planning, apart from regularity of alignment of the post-built structures. These were five to thirty metres (16ft to 100ft) apart and were interspersed with smaller structures and pits.

Small, dispersed settlements may not have been the only type in this period. At Eaglethorpe in Warmington (Northants), for example, field-walking and subsequent excavation around the medieval village and manorial site of Burystead has produced a concentration of fifth- to ninth-century pottery associated with both early and later medieval settlement remains to the south of the manor house.[54] Around the same settlement pottery of the fifth to ninth centuries is distributed over six modern fields. The lack of very clearly defined clusters raises the possibility that the scatter is partly the result of manuring or some other form of rubbish disposal. Evidence of such manuring of both sixth- to seventh- and ninth- to tenth-century date has been tentatively identified near a settlement at Millfield near Blaston (Leics).[55] At Newton-in-the-Willows (Northants), hand-made pottery of middle Anglo-Saxon date (seventh to ninth centuries) and iron slag was spread over 2ha (5 acres) of dark soil indicative of intense occupation.[56] Here the settlement could have been quite large, though shifting, and there is similar evidence from Higham Ferrers in the same county where a very dense scatter of pottery from all phases of the pre-Conquest period covered an area in excess of 1.2ha (3 acres).[57] In the Vale of Belvoir in northern Leicestershire, fieldwalking produced later Saxon pottery in fields around the parish church but no small scatters of earlier pre-Conquest pottery, which led to the suggestion that here settlement of the fifth to ninth centuries had been relatively stable and the sites coincided with those of the medieval nucleated villages.[58]

Dispersed settlements of this period have often been found on lighter soils, particularly those of the river valleys. Other areas of light, easily cultivated soils on the chalk in the south of Bedfordshire and Buckinghamshire have produced much less evidence, though in south Bedfordshire a number of settlements have been found in excavations, indicating occupation, though without much evidence for its scale or distribution. The lack of evidence on the heavy clay soils has been used to deny that the claylands were settled in the fifth to ninth centuries.[59] This is partly because they offer less opportunity for fieldwalking, as fewer of the fields are ploughed; but when research has been possible, they do produce evidence. In Leicestershire, for example, a quarter of settlements of the fifth to ninth centuries are immediately adjacent to boulder clay, and one in ten lies entirely on that heavy soil. Even Brigstock Park, on very inhospitable boulder clay, has produced limited amounts of hand-made pre-Conquest pottery.[60]

Another feature of settlements in the fifth to ninth centuries is their apparent impermanence: they are thought to have been fluid and mobile, in contrast to the more stable sites of the Roman period. Many of the Roman settlements with evidence of continuing occupation appear to have been abandoned by the late fifth or sixth century, so their continuity after *c*. 400 was no guarantee of long-term survival. Others, such as Odell (Beds) or Caldecotte in Bow Brickhill (Bucks), were apparently abandoned in the late Roman period, only to be reoccupied after an interval of a few centuries. Settlement shift continued throughout the period, and various explanations have been offered, from sudden cataclysmic events such as sixth-century famines and plagues, to processes of evolution and adaptation in response to economic, social and environmental factors at various dates. We cannot be certain that settlements in the fifth to ninth centuries were really more unstable than in other periods, and we do not know yet enough in general about the length of occupation of sites.

Dispersal and nucleation in the ninth to eleventh centuries.

In the later pre-Conquest period archaeological evidence is supplemented by documentary sources, such as charters and Domesday Book. But the appearance of a name that corresponds with a later village does not tell us anything about the form of that settlement at the time when a tenth-century charter or the survey of 1086 were written. The small dispersed settlements of *c*. 400–850 which have been found by archaeological research differ profoundly from the nucleated villages which characterise much of the area in the later middle ages. The change from a dispersed to a nucleated settlement pattern must have occurred, according to the archaeological evidence, between the ninth and twelfth centuries. Opinions vary as to the precise timing of the change, and whether it was a rapid transition or a long drawn-out process. Even less is known about any changes in areas where dispersed settlement persisted.

Many small settlements in areas of later nucleated settlement were abandoned or resited before the advent of wheel-turned 'Saxo-Norman' pottery in the mid-ninth century. This is particularly true of those settlements identified by fieldwalking, suggesting that the numerous small scattered hamlets and farmsteads largely ceased to exist after *c*. 850. The apparent abandonment of these dispersed settlements in the ninth century has led to the conclusion that this is the date at which the villages first appeared in their nucleated form.

When settlements of the ninth to eleventh centuries have been found they often coincide with later medieval villages. Typical examples are Tixover in Rutland, where excavation revealed a large amount of Saxo-Norman pottery adjacent to the later medieval village, or Langar (Leics), where similar late pre-Conquest pottery was found by fieldwalking around the edge of the nucleated village.[61] Although the sample of sites that have produced late Saxon pottery is small, in Leicestershire almost nine out of ten findspots of ninth- to eleventh-century material lie in, or very close to, later medieval settlements, and in Northamptonshire and Buckinghamshire the figure is about 80 per cent.[62] There is also no evidence that people at this date were living elsewhere than in the nucleated settlements: deserted tenth- or eleventh-century settlements are almost unknown in the regions of nucleated villages, even in places where intensive fieldwork has taken place.

Whether these nucleated settlements were actually founded anew in the ninth century as a result of a move away from dispersed settlements is a different problem. Excavation has suggested that nucleated villages do not occupy the same sites as pre-ninth-century settlements. However, such negative evidence may be misinterpreted: the seventh-century site at Maxey, for example, apparently deserted by the eighth, lies very close to the edge of the later medieval settlement, suggesting that the village began its life as a hamlet as early as the seventh century, but later shifted its site, perhaps more than once, to its present location.[63] Pre-ninth-century pottery has been retrieved from within the later medieval village of Brixworth as well as from the deserted dispersed sites in its territory, and at Wollaston (Northants)[64] pre-ninth-century occupation has been found at more than one place within the village, suggesting that nucleated

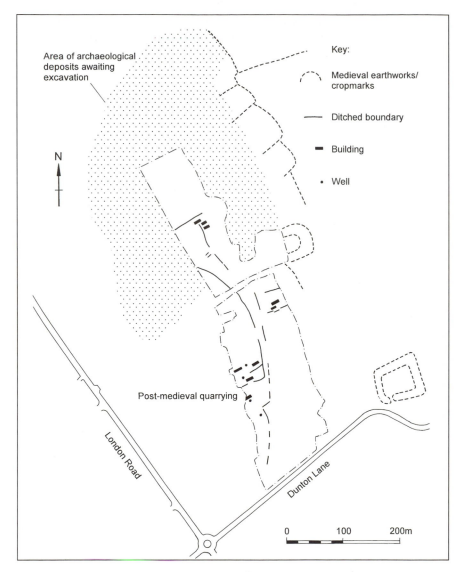

Figure 3.4 Plan of the early medieval settlement at Stratton, near Biggleswade, Bedfordshire. In the phase of Stratton's development in the tenth and eleventh centuries a routeway, defined by boundary ditches, ran northwards from the modern Dunton Lane and curved to the north-west. On either side of the road can be seen at least five houses or groups of houses, some of them accompanied by wells. This phase of the settlement succeeded occupation dated to the fifth to ninth centuries which lay to the west, and was in turn replaced by a twelfth-century village lying along a road a little further to the east (not shown), and also two moated sites. The tenth–eleventh-century phase of Stratton seems to have been developing towards a nucleated settlement with a row plan.

villages may have resulted from the growth or coalescence of earlier small hamlets. So while some dispersed hamlets were abandoned, others could have grown and merged to produce nucleated villages. The absence of earlier occupation from those sections of later medieval villages that have been excavated, may sometimes be explained by the much smaller size of the villages' ninth-century predecessors, which may remain undiscovered under an unexcavated part. Nucleation may have involved a major expansion of an existing place, attracting inhabitants from less favoured sites nearby, rather than a completely new foundation.

These new, large villages of the tenth and eleventh centuries, judging from the few that have been excavated, consisted of rectangular timber buildings of good quality construction, like those destroyed when the castle at Eaton Socon was built over a settlement in the twelfth century.[65] At Stratton in north-east Bedfordshire several post-built rectangular houses dating to the tenth or eleventh centuries lie inside tofts arranged along a road or street, resembling the rectilinear plan of some later medieval villages (Fig. 3.4).[66] The late Anglo-Saxon settlement at Burystead at Raunds (Northants) appears to have been carefully planned with regularly proportioned properties arranged as parallel tofts.[67] The presence of unoccupied tofts within the village plan, also found at West Cotton in the same parish, suggests that the settlement was planned to allow for anticipated growth which did not always occur.[68] This implies considerable organisation and foresight, but perhaps an excess of ambition among those who planned the new villages.

The trend for numerous small dispersed settlements to give way after *c*. 850 to the pull of a single focal settlement did not happen everywhere. While in Leicestershire 69 per cent of sites yielding fifth- to seventh-century material were abandoned in the ninth century or before, in Buckinghamshire 57 per cent of sites of the same period were still occupied in the later middle ages. This reflects partly the different research methods: fieldwalking (the main source of data in Leicestershire) tends to identify abandoned sites, while excavation (the source of most of the Buckinghamshire evidence) takes place more often within existing settlements.

But the main reason for the difference must lie in the fact that in many parts of Buckinghamshire nucleated villages did not develop, and they retained elements of dispersal into modern times. As in Bedfordshire, settlement was often arranged intermittently along winding lanes or on the edges of commons, or consisted of a complex network of small hamlets which were widely scattered. Fieldwork in Norfolk, where green-edge settlement abounds, has shown that the inhabitants migrated to the greens in the tenth to twelfth centuries, at about the same time as nucleation occurred in the midlands.[69]

The early middle ages: higher-status sites and political centres

Political and administrative centres

The absence of a clear settlement hierarchy in the early Anglo-Saxon period reflects a restricted social stratification and the lack of a well defined state structure. In the following centuries archaeologically-visible distinctions in settlement and building forms reappear with aristocratic, religious or commercial functions. The documentary evidence provides more information in this period for specialised and high-status settlement than for the ordinary villages and hamlets (Fig. 3.5).

The earliest political and administrative centres recognisable in the documents are royal vills, places associated with political events and governmental functions from at least the seventh and eighth centuries. Kings stayed at these residences periodically as they moved around their kingdoms. Many of these remained in royal possession over a long period, and some of those of the seventh and eighth centuries are still found in royal hands in 1066 and later. Although no places within our area of study are specifically named in authentic documents as 'royal vills' there are numerous candidates for such centres notably at places where assemblies were held under the auspices of kings: as at Gumley in 749, 772 and about 779, at Croft in 836, Glen in 848 (all Leics); Risborough in 884, Buckingham in 934 (Bucks); Irthlingborough in 787–796 and Whittlebury (Northants).[70] But not all assembly sites need have been permanent settlements, and some meetings were held at traditional open air venues.

Saints' lives also mention royal vills at such places as Weedon Bec (Northants) and Quarrendon (Bucks), while Olney in the same county is identified as such in a post-Conquest chronicle.[71] This evidence, however, may not be reliable. More certain candidates may be found amongst the royal manors of Domesday Book, some of which show clear signs of having been important places well before 1066. Most obvious is Risborough (Bucks), already mentioned as the site of an assembly.[72] The Anglo-Saxon Chronicle records that the king stayed at Passenham (Northants) in 921; and both Luton (Beds) and Aylesbury (Bucks) are associated with events dated to the sixth century in the Anglo-Saxon Chronicle.[73] While we cannot be sure that this records the realities of such an early period, these places were clearly thought to be important at the time of the writing of the Chronicle in the ninth century. Not all of these places

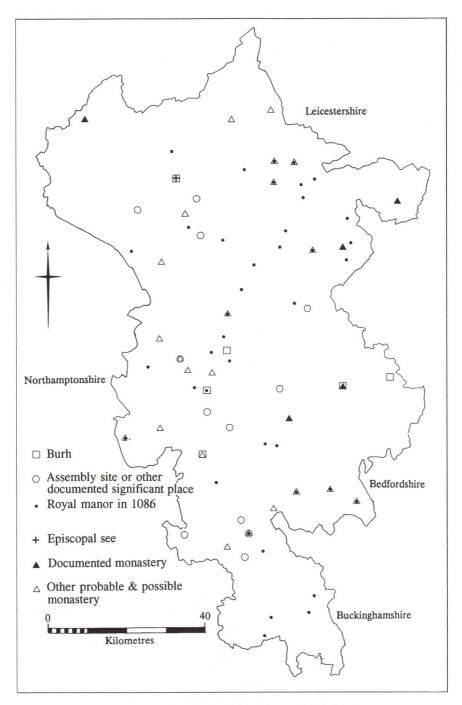

Figure 3.5 Pre-Conquest political, administrative and religious centres.

remained permanently as royal centres, one factor for discontinuity being the Danish invasions, another the vicissitudes of inheritance. Moreover, not all royal possessions were ancient centres: some were only acquired by the king at a late date, like Brill in Buckinghamshire.[74]

The *burh* appeared as a distinct military, political and administrative centre during and after the Danish wars. The *burhs* known in the study area at this time are Buckingham, Bedford, Tempsford, Towcester, Northampton, Leicester and, on the border of our area, Stamford. There is no evidence from within the study area, as there is elsewhere, that *burhs* began before the Danish period.[75] Some of the east midland *burhs*, such as Northampton, had previously functioned as royal vills, and Leicester had been important as a bishop's see, but others may have been founded on greenfield sites.[76]

After the tenth century there is no further reference to *burhs* at Tempsford and Towcester, but the others developed as permanent centres. The distinctive character of the *burh* lay in its combination of royal control and its role as a 'collective' settlement, divided into plots held by different lords, and serving as a refuge and strong-point for the population of its hinterland. The *burh* acted as a 'public' centre, and provided (except in the case of Stamford) the focus around which each of the newly emergent shires developed.

Ecclesiastical and religious centres

Early Anglo-Saxon religious sites can be identified in place names referring to pagan shrines, such as the three Weedons (two in Northamptonshire, one in Buckinghamshire), and the two Harrowdens (one in Northamptonshire, one in Bedfordshire), or to associations with pagan gods, of which Wodneslawe (which was a hundred in Bedfordshire) is the only known case.[77] These names are never habitative ones, indicating that the foci of pagan religion were peripheral to settlement, perhaps located in waste areas, underlining the importance of woods, heaths and moors as public space.[78] They often lay near Roman roads, another feature of the public landscape.[79]

The arrival of the highly structured organisation of the Christian church produced formal and permanent religious centres, notably the see of the bishop of the Middle Angles, established at Leicester. The earliest known monasteries in the study area were at Breedon-on-the-Hill (Leics), Medeshamstede (later Peterborough), and in the vicinity of Oundle (Northants), all of which had been established before the eighth century.[80] Only two other monasteries were explicitly recorded, at Bedford (in existence by 971) and North Crawley (Bucks), but many more can be inferred from a variety of evidence, such as the element 'minster' (Old English for monastery) present in two place-names, Buckminster and Misterton (Leics).[81]

The remarkable church at Brixworth (Northants), a seventh-century aisled basilica, must have been a religious centre of considerable significance. Its status was enhanced by a crypt with an ambulatory, indicative of the housing and veneration of important relics. All the monasteries mentioned housed such relics, and a pre-Conquest church at Wing (Bucks) contains a crypt used in connection with a saint's cult.[82]

A number of other places have associations with particular saints which indicate cult centres. The *Life* of the seventh-century Werburg links her with Weedon Bec in Northamptonshire, while also identifying nearby Stowe as the resting place of the body of Alnoth, a quasi-saint. King's Sutton and Brackley (both Northants) are associated with the activities of St Rumwold.[83] Wistow (Leics) from its very place-name would appear to have been the site of a cult of Wigstan, a Mercian royal martyr of the ninth century. The second element of this name (Stowe), is one that seems often to indicate places of religious significance, perhaps as in Stowe (Northants).

The monasteries at Buckingham and Aylesbury are also identified as the 'resting place' of Anglo-Saxon saints. Domesday Book shows the churches here to be of exceptional status by their possession of more extensive lands than any simple local church. The presence of groups of priests in Domesday, with other signs of 'superiority', also indicates the existence of other early monasteries at Luton, Houghton Regis and Leighton Buzzard (Beds); Haddenham (Bucks); Pattishall (Northants); Oakham, Ridlington and Hambleton (Rutland) and Melton Mowbray (Leics). Groups of clergy, at Daventry and Brigstock (Northants) in the twelfth century, may also represent the vestiges of monastic communities likely to have been established before 1066.[84]

Clearly there were a considerable number of monasteries in the pre-Conquest period, perhaps even enough to represent a network of 'minsters' that could have been the centres of a system of pastoral provision before the emergence of the later medieval parishes. However, monasteries experienced many changes of fortune and some early establishments may not have long survived, particularly those in the area of Danish control: for example, no sign can be found of a monastery in the vicinity of Oundle in the late Anglo-Saxon period. But the Danes may not have been entirely antagonistic towards the church, and some of the monasteries, such as at Breedon, appear to have survived.

Monasteries owed considerable influence to their close association with secular power structures. Frequently they had been founded by ruling families, and were located at important centres such as royal vills and latterly *burhs*. The establishment of monasteries at administrative centres, which might also be the centres of saints' cults, brought an extra significance to those places. In the latter part of the tenth century some monasteries, notably Peterborough, were reformed according to strict Benedictine principles, gaining in prominence and wealth.

Lordly residences and centres

Settlements of the fifth to seventh centuries in the east midlands lack high-status buildings which could be interpreted as aristocratic dwellings. However, early pottery is not infrequently found on or near to later manorial sites, which might mean that lords had lived there for generations. At Eaglethorpe, Warmington, in north-east Northamptonshire, for example a dense concentration of fifth- to ninth-century pottery lay immediately south-west of the manorial site of Burystead.[85] Nearby, the manor site of Furnells in Raunds was occupied from the sixth century onwards.[86]

From the late seventh century, at a time when the earliest laws reveal the presence of a distinct social hierarchy, social stratification becomes more clearly visible in the archaeological record. At Furnells after *c.* 700 a substantial post-in-trench built hall, 19m by 6.8m (62ft by 22ft) was constructed in the second phase of the site. In Northampton a series of late eighth-century buildings, including a hall with stone foundations, has been described as a palace.[87]

Between the ninth and eleventh centuries the nobility experienced a growing territorialisation of their authority, and the king made more numerous formal grants in writing of rights over land to individual laymen.[88] As the lords derived their income from their lands they needed to exercise a good deal of control over the peasant inhabitants, and this is displayed in the well established and widespread manorial lordship found in Domesday Book. The proliferation of local lords, apparently disposing of increased resources, is reflected in substantial buildings or halls. At Furnells in Raunds an aisled hall and associated church were built in the ninth or tenth century.[89] At neighbouring West Cotton a substantial late Anglo-Saxon building adjacent to a mill of ninth- or tenth-century date is likely to be a forerunner of the twelfth-century manor house on the same site.[90] The mill no doubt served as a source of flour for the lord's household, but could also have yielded profits from the nearby peasants.

Some buildings of superior construction stood on sites later occupied by post-Conquest castles, suggesting a continuity in seigneurial occupation. At Higham Ferrers (Northants), for example, part of a late Anglo-Saxon post-in-trench building was found near the centre of the site of the eleventh-century castle, and in the same county the pre-Conquest hall of Sulgrave, measuring 25m (82ft) long with an adjoining stone building, was incorporated as a gatehouse into the earthen rampart of the later ringwork.[91] The motte at Chalgrave (Beds) was constructed in the early twelfth century over an 'earlier' manor, and a moated site at 'Danish Docks' near Bedford produced a considerable quantity of St Neots ware from post holes associated with a stone wall, suggesting a substantial pre-Conquest building.[92] However, the majority of moated and manorial sites show no sign of occupation before the twelfth or thirteenth century.[93]

Local lordship in the ninth, tenth and eleventh centuries demonstrated its growing influence in the proliferation of local churches, the precursors of parish churches. Domesday Book records 112 priests and nineteen churches in our four counties, mostly as the possessions of rural manors. This was not a complete record, particularly for the two southern counties. Twenty-five existing parish churches have surviving pre-Conquest fabric, mostly of tenth and eleventh centuries.[94] But again these must represent only a fraction of the total, as the original timber buildings have not survived, or early stone fabric has been replaced or concealed in later rebuilding. By 1086 there would have been hundreds of churches in the area, indicating the scale both of the resources to build them, and the size of the congregations that they served. The late Anglo-Saxon laws relate possession of a church to thegnly status, and churches represent one aspect of the growing capacity of lords to command and organise local societies.[95] The seigneurial character of many of these churches may sometimes also be seen in their close physical relationship to lordly centres, as at Earls Barton (Northants) and Clapham (Beds).[96]

All of these high-status sites – royal vills, aristocratic residences, religious buildings of varying size and importance – represent a growing network of centres and structures in the landscape with a degree of permanence, all of which served as centres for gathering peasants to pay rents and dues, and attend courts and ceremonies. They were clearly potential nodal points around which larger settlements could form.

Markets, trade and urbanism

In contrast with signs of continuity in the countryside in the post-Roman period, the Roman market economy, with its towns acting as production and trading centres, failed to survive the transition to the early medieval world. The towns rapidly lost their urban characteristics, and there is no evidence for any trading settlements in the east midlands in the sixth and seventh centuries. Towns or specialised market centres could not play a role in an economy in which, for example, pottery was hand made, fired in bonfires and used in the immediate locality. The implication is of household production for personal use, although the discovery of vessels in the Nene Valley whose fabric appears to derive from the Charnwood area, some 60km (40miles) away, may suggest a rudimentary exchange system.[97] This is in marked contrast to the mass production, and interregional and international distribution, of ceramics in the Roman period. Evidence for trade or exchange comes from cemeteries. Pottery vessels containing cremations at several sites around Kettering (Northants) had been decorated using the same stamp, implying centralised production followed by local distribution.[98] Vessels associated with disposal of the dead seem to have been 'traded' more than other goods, and this distribution may have been restricted to the upper ranks of society. Wider cultural contacts indicated by stylistic influences on metalwork are also apparent from cemetery finds. Otherwise the evidence in the east midlands of the fifth to seventh centuries points to a subsistence economy of local manufacture for local consumption.

In the seventh to ninth centuries, urban trading centres reappear in other parts of the country, such as the 'emporia' of *Hamwic* in Hampshire or Ipswich in Suffolk, but none are known within our area. A limited number of coins of this period, such as silver sceattas of the seventh and eighth centuries, are known from the east midlands, with a concentration in and around Dunstable (Beds). Pottery made at Ipswich (of the period 650–850) has been found at Castor, Thrapston and Brixworth (Northants).[99] Hurst has suggested that as these were probably monastic sites, perhaps the use of Ipswich ware was confined to an elite; sherds of the same ware from near Higham Ferrers may also be associated with a site of high status.[100] Exchange may have occurred at royal vills or occasionally at gatherings of people attending courts or religious ceremonies.

Burhs of the late ninth and tenth centuries seem to represent the earliest fixed regular trading centres in the east midlands. A number of these became towns no doubt because their administrative function, and royal protection, stimulated the development of an increasingly market-orientated economy. Northampton and Leicester had been political and religious centres before the burghal fortification, and may have already begun to develop as trading places as a by-product of those functions. The economic significance of the *burhs* was also enhanced by the siting of mints within them. Royal policy regulated the production of coinage, and ensured that money was both widely available and reliable. Leicester had a mint during the Danish period, and mints appeared at Bedford and Northampton in the 940s or 950s. By the time of the Norman Conquest a number of the east midlands *burhs* (and in particular the shire centres) were involved in the production and trade of everyday goods as well as luxuries, and had become fully fledged urban centres with large populations involved in a variety of non-agricultural occupations. Calculations based on Domesday indicate that the populations of Leicester and Northampton each exceeded 1,500.[101]

The existence of smaller centres of exchange before the Conquest is suggested by place-names containing the element *port* ('market'), such as Newport Pagnell (Bucks), a borough by 1066.[102] Lamport (Bucks) and Langport (Northants) may have been early markets.[103] Domesday Book also records markets at Arlesey, Leighton Buzzard and Luton (Beds); Aylesbury (Bucks); Melton Mowbray (Leics), Higham Ferrers, King's Sutton and Oundle (Northants), a number of which have already been mentioned as royal vills or the sites of minster churches.[104] Five of the eight had gained borough status by the twelfth or thirteenth centuries.

The growth of towns and permanent market centres was accompanied by increasing craft specialisation, most strikingly demonstrated by the change in pottery across the region. Late pre-Conquest pottery, unlike that of preceding centuries, was thrown on a fast wheel and fired at a higher temperature in specialised kilns, to produce a much harder and finer fabric. Stamford ware and St Neots-type ware are the wares which are most common in the east midlands in the ninth to eleventh centuries, and examples are found widely distributed across the region, at a considerable distance from their places of manufacture. This clearly marks a change from household production for local use to industries, often sited in towns such as Stamford and Leicester. Some wares were still produced in the countryside, and St Neots ware may have been made at a number of rural sites, including places just outside Northampton and Bedford, poised to exploit the markets in these towns.

The growth of crafts, trade and towns had implications for life in the countryside. For example, the similarity of plan of many nucleated villages with those of towns may imply some degree of imitation. Regular town plans with long thin plots extending at right angles to streets seem to have been conceived in Wessex by *c.* 900, but are not so apparent in the midlands. In St Peter's Street in Northampton, buildings of early tenth century date which were arranged in an irregular, random fashion with no regard for the later street line, were not replaced until the eleventh century or later by dwelling houses laid out on a regular plan.[105]

Urbanisation had an indirect effect on rural settlement by increasing the number of people engaged in a variety of non-agricultural activities, and this created a demand for food, raw materials and fuel from the countryside. Both lords and peasants would have been encouraged to produce a surplus for exchange in the market, which would have changed the social and economic character of settlements previously geared to subsistence farming.

The early middle ages: village territories and estates

Vills

Our understanding of social developments in the ninth to eleventh centuries would be greatly aided by documents describing the peasants and their communities, like the detailed surveys found in continental Europe. Such material is available in abbreviated form in Domesday Book, but we cannot be sure how far we can apply the picture given in that great panoramic view of English rural society to the centuries before 1086. If we cannot study directly the places and people at the heart of the rural territories, we can find out something about their outer limits, and thereby hope to glean some information about peasant life. Although the documents cannot tell us whether nucleated villages had formed by the tenth century, they provide some data about the lands within which the settlements were sited.

The relatively small village territories, often as small as 400ha (1,000 acres), that are known to have existed in the eleventh to thirteenth centuries, were probably already in existence 200 years before the Norman Conquest. Some boundaries were very old indeed. Reference has already been made to the view that some medieval parishes were based on the land attached to Roman villas. A study of Claybrooke on the Leicestershire/Warwickshire border has suggested that the *territorium* associated with the Roman roadside settlement at High Cross (*Venonae*) survived into the early middle ages,[106] and at Brixworth (Northants) the discovery of a Roman villa near to the seventh-century church, has lent support to the idea of continuity between Roman and medieval estate units. Inevitably there are many uncertainties about these theories. For example, we do not know if a relatively small roadside settlement like High Cross would have had a *territorium*,[107] and in the case of villas and their medieval successors there can be no proof of continuous occupation in the fifth and sixth centuries. The coincidence may derive simply from the tendency of Anglo-Saxon elites to associate themselves with sites of past importance as a means of legitimising their authority.

Another approach to the problem is to look at stretches of boundary to see whether or not they coincide with datable linear features.[108] This seldom provides straightforward evidence. When parish boundaries ignore the Roman roads or linear earthworks such as Grim's Ditch in the Chilterns we are left with the possibility either that these boundaries are even older than these pre-medieval features, or that those who defined the boundaries did not regard these landmarks as sufficiently significant features to incorporate them into their lines of demarcation. We are on safer ground with those parish boundaries which follow Roman roads of the first century AD, such as Watling Street. The boundary must have been laid out, or significantly altered, after the first century AD; they may be Roman in origin, or many centuries later.

We can be sure that many units of land later used as parishes existed by the tenth century. The Aspley Guise (Beds) charter of 969 describes a boundary very similar to that of the later parish, which defines the edges of Aspley with reference to the apparently clearly defined territories of surrounding villages, Woburn, Marston Moretaine and so on. The pre-Conquest charters of the Badby (Northants) area are similarly useful in indicating the existence of the full network of local territories coinciding with those of the later medieval villages.[109] A rational basis for boundaries can be seen in their tendency to follow 'natural' divisions in the landscape, such as rivers and watersheds, so that each place was provided with meadow, arable and pasture in strips of land which stretched up the side of a valley from the river to the higher ground. It is a particular feature of the valleys, such as that of the Great Ouse in north Bedfordshire, that the parishes are laid out in a regular and repetitive fashion, with similarly sized units all having access to a balance of local resources.

In wastes and dense woodland, territories may not have become clearly defined until later. Villages would have the right to share wood and pasture along with their neighbours, a situation prone to disputes. In the extreme cases of Charnwood and Leicester Forest, firm boundaries were apparently not drawn until modern enclosure.[110]

Before the Conquest larger units are said to have broken up as land was exploited more intensively. In eastern Bedfordshire, for example, an oval area defined by the River Ivel and its watershed with the Ouse may actually have been known as the territory of 'Ivel'. By the time of Domesday it had been split into three units, later parishes, called Northill ('North Ivel'), Warden and Southill ('South Ivel'). New settlements may have been created as a result of this process. At Badby, where all of the village territories had been formed before the Conquest, we still find one of them called Newnham ('the new homestead'), which evidently had a shorter history than the others.

The agriculture of the valleys and claylands, where the nucleated villages were to form, is likely to have involved the cultivation of extensive arable fields. Some of the tenth-century charter boundaries – Aspley Guise and Badby have already been mentioned, but others are documented for Linslade, Olney and Chetwode and Hillesden in Buckinghamshire – also mention in their descriptions of landmarks along the edge of the territory such features as headlands, acres and furrows, which are clearly referring to cultivated land.[111] Later in the middle ages such features were elements of open field systems with intermixed strips and a degree of communal control of cropping. We cannot be sure that fully developed open fields had emerged by the tenth century, but we can suppose that already the ploughs were working at the very edge of the land units within which the settlements lay. The argument has been made on topographical grounds that a form of open field system existed in Northamptonshire by the tenth century, but it differed from the later version in that the strips were longer and not subdivided in the complex pattern found in the later medieval and early modern periods.[112]

Multiple estates in the east midlands

One concept which has influenced our thinking about early medieval local territories, and thereby the study of settlement, is that of the 'multiple estate'. This argues that before the tenth century the countryside lay in large estates which served as both administrative and agrarian units, and these included a number of later independent manors, vills or parishes. It is sometimes implied that they date back to pre-medieval or even pre-Roman origins. Some writers treat the large estate as a unity, and refer to it as a 'land unit', partly because it is not possible to examine the interior of the estates in any detail. Others emphasise the federal character of the estate, with its structure of component elements which performed different functions, as sheep pasture, arable land, and so on; hence the term 'multiple'. These federations broke up in the course of the late Anglo-Saxon period giving rise to the pattern of smaller vills and parishes familiar in the post-Conquest period, though these units could have already had a distinct existence in the heyday of the estate. This process has been seen as representing a fundamental shift in the structure of society, and is thought to be associated with the changes in the pattern of settlement which occurred around the same time. These ideas have been applied to the study of many areas in the east midlands, notably in work on Fawsley hundred, King's Sutton and Raunds (Northants),

Claybrooke (Leics), and Brill (Bucks), and more generally over North-amptonshire.[113]

A good example of the reconstruction of such an estate is Brown's work on Daventry and its surrounding parishes in western Northamptonshire.[114] Drayton lay in the same parish as Daventry, and the adjacent Welton had once been a chapelry of Daventry too. As the ecclesiastical links often reflected secular matters, this implies that all these places had once formed a single large estate, assessed at thirty hides. To the south-east lay another group of villages, Badby, Newnham, Dodford and Everdon, that appear together in a charter of 944 as a single block of thirty hides. Perhaps together they had originally belonged to the Roman villa that lay on Borough Hill near Daventry. But payments of churchscot by Badby and other churches to Fawsley, a centre of royal administration, and the attachment of a number of places in the vicinity to the soke of Fawsley, make it possible to envisage an even larger combination of places centred on Fawsley.

However, the assumptions behind such arguments contain many un-certainties. The evidence on which many reconstructions are based (with the exception of the pre-Conquest Badby charter and a few others like it), is invariably late. In particular the geography of dues and connections, like churchscot payments, is not recorded until the twelfth century or after, and there is a distinct possibility that some of these links were created only at a relatively late date. For example sokes, the organisations through which sokemen owed payments to a central manor, have some-times been thought to pre-date the formation of the hundred in the tenth century because they cut across hundred boundaries. But we know that sokes could be altered, and even created anew (as happened at Ged-dington, Northants) in the post-Conquest period, so that they are not necessarily a guide to ancient administrative arrangements.[115] The large estates that have been identified seem to vary greatly in size; the analysis of the Daventry/Fawsley area has led to the identification of thirty-hide, sixty-hide and even larger units. Some 'multiple estates' are much smaller than these. The concept seems suspiciously variable, if the same pheno-menon can operate on such different scales.

The assumption that the sequence of events must always have taken the form of a fission of large estates into smaller manors, vills and parishes is qualified by some evidence of fusion, in which relatively small parcels of land were merged into larger units. In the case of Badby, for example, Brown has shown that Everdon was added to the Badby estate in the early tenth century. One circumstance that could lead to the forging of new links would be the desire of a minor lord to seek the protection of a more powerful neighbour; or some additions may have been newly established areas of settlement and cultivation, taken in from wastes which had previously belonged to no particular estate.

Place-names sometimes indicate the former connections between places (such as Great and Little Addington, Northants), which were clearly created by the splitting of a single place called Addington.[116] Other names may suggest subsidiary places with specific agricultural functions, like Barton ('barley farm') and Hardwick ('dairy farm'), or those inhabited by subordinates, such as Carlton ('ceorls' settlement') or Walton ('welsh, or slaves', settlement'). These constituent parts of estates look like creations in the course of management, and specifically by the imposition of manorial organisation during the later part of the pre-Conquest period, and are unlikely to be primeval. It suggests that the estates were subject to dynamic change before fragmentation, and that their conservative character should not be overemphasised. In this context the distribution of such 'manorial' place-names, which are found in Leicestershire and Northamptonshire but not in southern Bedfordshire and Buckinghamshire, must point to social differences across our study area, with perhaps a more assertive imposition of lordship in the two northern counties, a likely by-product of the upheavals of the Danish conquest and the English reconquest.

The connection between 'multiple estates' or 'land-units' and the history of settlement is thus a complicated one. A simple assertion that the fragmentation of the great estates provided the context for the nucleation of villages is not convincing: firstly because, as the 'multiple estate' hypothesis itself proposes, many of the constituent parts of the estates had a separate existence long before fragmentation; secondly, because we cannot be sure that multiple estates, or large local units, were universal – some places lay outside the system altogether and we tend to know most about former royal estates – so some land from a very early date could have been held by other lords in small units; thirdly, because we cannot assume a once simple world in which large blocks of land belonged to single lords, and where multiple and complex lordship developed only at a late date – 'land units' may have been divided between lords as early as the seventh and eighth centuries, when we know of ranks of secular aristocrats; and fourthly, because fission of large units was not the only change of which we are aware – land units merged and expanded, as well as falling apart.

Conclusion

By the mid-eleventh century many elements of the later medieval and modern countryside had begun to take shape – territories and their boundaries, the towns, the institutions of lordship and the church; and at least some of the nucleated villages were already in existence. This was partly a development based on a legacy from the Roman and prehistoric past: there were varying degrees of continuity in the use of land, and such continuity was most marked in the river valleys. The Chilterns changed their character from a centre of prosperity and high-status settlements to remote and thinly populated margins. Even in the high claylands, the story is not a simple retreat from inhospitable conditions. But there were important discontinuities either at the end of the Roman period or in the subsequent three centuries in terms of the abandonment or migration of settlements, and in changes in the economy and in political structures.

The archaeological evidence of the fifth to eleventh centuries suggests a simple story of the nucleated village supplanting small and unstable farms and hamlets after *c*. 850, but there may have been local tendencies towards nucleation before 850, and of course dispersed settlement patterns persisted in many districts. The reality of nucleation remains an important development deserving explanation, and the documentary evidence suggests some contexts – firstly, the rise of a growing number of administrative and religious centres which could serve as nuclei for settlement. But we are mainly aware of simultaneous developments – or, at least, changes – for which no very precise chronology can be given: as the lords and their residences became more prominent from the ninth century or earlier, and towns and commerce were growing up in the tenth and eleventh centuries. Extensive cultivation was present by the tenth century, and many parish churches were being built in the century and a half before 1050. The village territories, though not properly documented until the later part of our period, could have had a former existence as parts of larger estates, and indeed owe at least part of their boundaries to much earlier land divisions.

Notes

1   W. G. Hoskins, *The Making of the English Landscape* (Harmondsworth, Penguin, 1955), p. 20.
2   See, for example, Royal Commission on Historical Monuments England, *An Inventory of the Historical Monuments in the County of Northampton* (London, Her Majesty's Stationery Office, 1975–82); B. Croft and D. Mynard, *The*

Changing Landscape of Milton Keynes (Aylesbury, Buckinghamshire Archaeological Society, Monograph Series no. 5, 1993), Leicestershire Museums Archaeological Reports series, Bedfordshire parish surveys.

3   P. Clay, *Two Multi-Phase Barrow Sites at Sproxton and Eaton, Leicestershire* (Leicester, Leicestershire Museums, Art Galleries and Records Service Archaeological Reports Series, 2, 1981), pp. 21–4.

4   See Croft and Mynard, *Milton Keynes*, pp. 8–10, for a summary of the findings from excavations at the iron age settlements of Furzton and Pennylands.

5   The evidence from Brigstock suggests the dominance of sheep: P. Foster, 'The Brigstock Survey: an intensive field survey on upland boulder clay in Northamptonshire', in M. Parker Pearson and R. T. Schadla-Hall (eds), *Looking at the Land – Archaeological Landscapes in Eastern England* (Leicester, Leicestershire Museums, Arts and Records Service Archaeological Reports, 1994), pp. 46–50.

6   The Milton Keynes area in Buckinghamshire was characterised in the bronze age by an 'open grassland environment which supported a pastoral economy', Croft and Mynard, *Milton Keynes*, p. 7; Sproxton in Leicestershire indicated an open pastoral environment with some arable: Clay, *Sproxton and Eaton*, pp. 10–14.

7   A similar intensification, accompanied by some reorganisation of field systems, has been identified in Yorkshire, mid-first millennium BC (information from A. Fleming).

8   J. A. Catt, 'The contribution of loess to soils in lowland Britain', in S. Limbrey and J. G. Evans (eds), *The Effect of Man on the Landscape: the Lowland Zone* (C. B. A. Research Report, no. 21, 1978), pp. 12–20.

9   Foster, *Brigstock Survey*, p. 47.

10 See S. Limbrey, 'Changes in the quality and distribution of the soil of lowland Britain', in Limbrey & Evans (eds), *Effect of Man*, pp. 21–7.

11 See A. Simco, *The Roman Period* (Bedford, Bedfordshire County Council Survey of Bedfordshire, 1984), pp. 24–5 for an example of the density and complexity of settlement in the Ouse valley.

12 See S. Parry, 'Raunds area survey', in Parker Pearson and Schadla-Hall (eds), *Looking at the Land*, pp. 36–42, fig. 10.2 for a plan of the evidence from the Raunds area survey which illustrates this point.

13 Some resemble medieval village plans, for example Cople and Willington (Beds), Simco, *Roman Period*, p. 32; Lockington (Leics), P. Liddle, *Leicestershire Archaeology: The Present State of Knowledge. vol. 1 – to the end of the Roman Period* (Leicester, Leicestershire Museums, Art Galleries and Records Service Archaeological Reports Series, no. 4, 1982), p. 24; Fotheringhay in Northamptonshire, Royal Commission on Historical Monuments England, *County of Northampton, vol. 1, Archaeological Sites in North-East Northamptonshire* (London, Her Majesty's Stationery Office, 1975), pp. 40–1.

14 Examples include Odell and Wyboston (Beds) and Medbourne (Leics), Raunds (Northants), Westbourne, Caldecotte and Wavendon Gate (north Bucks) (information from county SMRs).

15 P. Liddle, 'The Medbourne area survey', in Parker Pearson and Schadla-Hall (eds), *Looking at the Land*, pp. 34–6.

16 For example, Lockington (Leics), Brixworth (Northants), Totternhoe (Beds), Latimer and Bancroft (Bucks) (information from county SMRs).

17 Simco, *Roman Period*, p. 29.

18 D. Bonney, 'Early boundaries in Wessex', in P. Fowler (ed.), *Archaeology and the Landscape* (London, A. and C. Black, 1972), pp. 168–86; A. Goodier, 'The formation of boundaries in Anglo-Saxon England: a statistical study', *Medieval Archaeology*, 28 (1984), 1–21.

19 The settlement remains between Cople and Willington lie in parishes which are regular in layout, extending over the valley so as to include all types of land.

20 S. S. Frere, *Britannia*, 3rd edn (London, Guild Publishing, 1987), pp. 287–9.

21 See T. Williamson, 'Early co-axial field systems on the East Anglian boulder clays', *Proceedings of the Prehistoric Society*, 53 (1987), 419–31 for examples around Scole and Dickleburgh in Norfolk; O. Rackham, *The History of the Countryside* (London, Dent, 1986), p. 158, around the Elmhams and Ilket-shalls in Suffolk; W. Rodwell, 'Relict landscapes in Essex', in H. C. Bowen and P. Fowler (eds), *Early Land Allotment* (British Archaeological Reports, 48, 1978), pp. 89–98, for examples around Thurrock, Orsett, Little Waltham and Braintree in Essex.

22 In ridge and furrow landscapes the earlier boundaries are not preserved in modern field boundaries, but underlying linear features are often visible on aerial photographs or during fieldwork. The destruction by ploughing of ridge and furrow in eastern Yorkshire, Cambridgeshire and eastern Bedfordshire is revealing features preserved underneath: personal comment by Roger Palmer.

23 Foster, 'Brigstock Survey', fig. 12.4.

24 Personal comment by Glenn Foard and records in county SMR; and see D. Wilson, 'Pit alignments: distribution and function', in Bowen and Fowler (eds), *Early Land Allotment*, pp. 3–5 for a distribution map of pit alignments in the study area, and a discussion of their function 'separating blocks of land, bounding individual fields or defining lanes which pass between fields'.

25 Foster, 'Brigstock Survey', pp. 46–50.

26 See RCHME, *North-East Northamptonshire*, pp. xxxiv–xxxv and 20–4.

27 Some of these appear to be quite significant concentrations of 10–50 sherds, which may reflect the close interval of fieldwalking (2m or 6ft 6in). No precise date for this pottery can be given.

28 Frere, *Britannia*, p. 287.

29 Croft and Mynard, *Milton Keynes*, p. 8.

30 Hoskins, *English Landscape*, pp. 86–94.

31 Latimer in particular is an opulent courtyard villa, located close to the Buckinghamshire boundary with Hertfordshire. It overlies an iron age building, and has an unusual second-century mosaic floor. After a period of apparent decay in the third century, at least two large sub-Roman buildings were constructed on the site. See Frere, *Britannia*, p. 287; P. A. Rahtz, 'Buildings and rural settlement', in D. M. Wilson (ed.), *The Archaeology of Anglo-Saxon England* (Cambridge, Cambridge University Press, 1976), p. 56.

32 Frere, *Britannia*, p. 271; J. Percival, *The Roman Villa: an Historical Introduction* (London, Batsford, 1976), pp. 97–8, 100.

33 B. N. Eagles and V. I. Evison, 'Excavations at Harrold, Bedfordshire, 1951–53', *Bedfordshire Archaeological Journal*, 5 (1970), 17–55; B. Dix, 'Odell: a

river valley farm', *Current Archaeology*, 66 (1979), 215–18; but a well lining is recorded at Aldwinkle (Northants), see L. Webster and J. Cherry, 'Medieval Britain in 1971', *Medieval Archaeology*, 16 (1972), 158.

34 J. Campbell (ed.), *The Anglo-Saxons* (Oxford, Phaidon, 1982), p. 39.

35 S. Young and J. Clark, 'Medieval Britain in 1980', *Medieval Archaeology*, 25 (1981), 175; D. Wilson and D. G. Hurst, 'Medieval Britain in 1967', *Medieval Archaeology*, 12 (1968), 160; L. E. Webster and J. Cherry, 'Medieval Britain in 1975', *Medieval Archaeology*, 20 (1976), 165.

36 Dix, 'Odell', 215–18.

37 P. Corder, *The Roman Town and Villa at Great Casterton, Rutland* (Nottingham, University of Notingham, 1951–61), 1st report, pp. 18–19; 2nd report, pp. 32–3.

38 H. C. Darby, *The Changing Fenland* (Cambridge, Cambridge University Press, 1983), pp. 1–40; Frere, *Britannia*, pp. 268–9.

39 For example, D. Hall, 'The late Saxon countryside: villages and their fields', in D. Hooke (ed.), *Anglo-Saxon Settlements* (Oxford, Blackwell, 1988), pp. 99–122.

40 Croft and Mynard, *Milton Keynes*, p. 15.

41 D. Kennett, 'Pottery from the Anglo-Saxon cemetery at Sandy', *Medieval Archaeology*, 14 (1970), 17–33.

42 County SMR.

43 Frere, *Britannia*, pp. 368–9.

44 County SMR.

45 At Great Casterton destruction in *c*. 400 has been identified by the excavator, yet there is still fifth-century occupation: see note 37 above.

46 M. Shaw, 'Saxon and earlier settlement at Higham Ferrers, Northamptonshire', *Medieval Settlement Research Group Annual Report*, 6 (1991), 15–19.

47 D. N. Hall and P. Martin, 'Brixworth, Northamptonshire: an intensive field survey', *Journal of the British Archaeological Association*, 132 (1979), 1–6; Liddle, 'Medbourne area survey', 34–6; P. V. Addyman, 'A dark age settlement at Maxey, Northamptonshire', *Medieval Archaeology*, 8 (1964), 23.

48 Pottery of the fifth to ninth centuries was found in the upper layer of fill of ditches defining Romano-British fields: L. E. Webster and J. Cherry, 'Medieval Britain in 1979', *Medieval Archaeology*, 24 (1980), 218.

49 K. Branigan, *Latimer. Belgic, Roman, Dark Age and Early Modern Farm* (Chess Valley Archaeological and Historical Society, 1971), pp. 89–99, 187–9.

50 M. Gelling, *Signposts to the Past* (London, Dent, 1978), pp. 63–86. On the possible inclusion of the southern part of our area in an enclave of British rule into the fifth and sixth centuries, see K. R. Dark, *Civitas to Kingdom* (Leicester, Leicester University Press, 1994), pp. 86–9.

51 L. E. Webster and J. Cherry, 'Medieval Britain in 1971'. *Medieval Archaeology*, 16 (1972), 147; C. L. Matthews and J. Schneider, *Ancient Dunstable* (Dunstable, Manshead Archaeological Society, 1989), p. 101.

52 D. A. Jackson, D. W. Harding and J. N. L. Myres, 'The iron age and Anglo-Saxon site at Upton, Northamptonshire', *Antiquaries Journal*, 49 (1969), 202–21; D. M. Wilson and D. G. Hurst, 'Medieval Britain in 1965', *Medieval Archaeology*, 10 (1966), 172; Eagles and Evison, 'Excavations at Harrold', 17–56; Addyman, 'Maxey', 20–73.

53   C. L. Matthews, 'Saxon remains on Puddlehill, Dunstable', *Bedfordshire Archaeological Journal*, 1 (1962), 48–57.

54   *Medieval Settlement Research Group Annual Report*, 6 (1991), 40; *ibid.*, 7 (1992), 40.

55   S. M. Youngs, J. Clark, D. R. M. Gaimster and T. Barry, 'Medieval Britain and Ireland in 1987', *Medieval Archaeology*, 32 (1988), 259–60.

56   L. E. Webster and J. Cherry, 'Medieval Britain in 1972', *Medieval Archaeology*, 17 (1973), 147.

57   Shaw, 'Higham Ferrers'.

58   M. Hills and A. Liddon, 'The Vale of Belvoir survey', *Transactions of the Thoroton Society*, 85 (1981), 13–25; S. Losco-Bradley and H. M. Wheeler, 'Anglo-Saxon settlement in the Trent Valley: some aspects', in M. Faull (ed.), *Studies in Late Anglo-Saxon Settlement* (Oxford, Oxford University Department for External Studies, 1984), pp. 101–14.

59   Hoskins, *English Landscape*, pp. 33–44.

60   For example, handmade 'Saxon' pottery of indeterminate date has been found at Brigstock: Foster, 'Brigstock Survey'; at some sites in Northamptonshire: Hall, 'Late Saxon countryside'; and possibly in Chellington in North Bedfordshire: A. Brown and C. Taylor, 'The origins of dispersed settlement; some results from fieldwork in Bedfordshire', *Landscape History*, 11 (1989), 61–81. The information about Leicestershire sites comes from the county SMR.

61   S. M. Young and J. Clark, 'Medieval Britain in 1981', *Medieval Archaeology*, 26 (1982), 190; Hills and Liddon, 'Vale of Belvoir'.

62   For example, 85 per cent of recorded medieval settlements in Northamptonshire have no evidence of any pre-Conquest occupation, only 6 per cent are documented in the late pre-Conquest period and only 7 per cent have produced archaeological evidence for the ninth to eleventh centuries. The data for Bedfordshire are too few to make such a calculation.

63   Addyman, 'Maxey'.

64   Hall and Martin, 'Brixworth'; C. C. Taylor 'Polyfocal settlement and the English village', *Medieval Archaeology*, 21 (1977), 189–93.

65   P. V. Addyman, 'Late Saxon settlement in the St. Neots area: I, the Saxon settlement and Norman castle at Eaton Socon, Bedfordshire', *Proceedings of the Cambridgeshire Antiquarian Society*, 58 (1965), 38–73.

66   B. S. Nenk, S. Margeson and M. Hurley, 'Medieval Britain and Ireland in 1991', *Medieval Archaeology*, 36 (1992), 193–4.

67   S. M. Youngs, D. R. M. Gaimster and T. Barry, 'Medieval Britain and Ireland in 1987', *Medieval Archaeology*, 32 (1988), 265.

68   Personal comment by Glenn Foard.

69   A. Davison, *The Evolution of Settlement in Three Parishes in South East Norfolk* (Norwich, East Anglian Archaeology, no. 49, 1990).

70   W. de G. Birch (ed.), *Cartularium Saxonicum* (London, Whiting, 1885–93) (henceforth *BCS*), 178, 210, 230, 416, 455, 552, 704; F. L. Attenborough (ed.), *The Laws of the Earliest English Kings* (Cambridge, Cambridge University Press, 1922), 6 Aethelstan, 12,1.

71   C. Horstman (ed.), *The Life of St. Werburg of Chester by Henry Bradshaw* (Early English Text Society, 88, 1887), pp. xxii–xxiii; K. Bailey, 'Osyth, Frithuwold and Aylesbury', *Records of Buckinghamshire*, 31 (1984), 41; W. T. Mellows

(ed.), *The Chronicle of Hugh Candidus* (London, Oxford University Press, 1949), p. 65.

72 *DB*, 1, f. 143.

73 Whitelock *et al.* (eds), *Anglo-Saxon Chronicle*, pp. 66, 13.

74 F. Barlow (ed.), *Vita Eadwardi Regis* (London, Nelson, 1962), p. 64.

75 J. Haslam, 'Market and fortress in England in the reign of Offa', *World Archaeology*, 19 (1987), 76–93.

76 See Asser's comments: S. Keynes and M. Lapidge (eds), *Alfred the Great* (Harmondsworth, Penguin, 1983), p. 101.

77 J. E. B. Gover, A. Mawer and F. M. Stenton, *The Place-Names of Northampton-shire* (English Place-Name Society, 10, 1933), pp. 30, 45, 125; A. Mawer and F. M. Stenton, *The Place-Names of Buckinghamshire* (English Place-Name Society, 2, 1925), p. 85; A. Mawer and F. M. Stenton, *The Place-Names of Bedfordshire and Huntingdonshire* (English Place-Name Society, 3, 1926), pp. 91, 100.

78 Pagan cemeteries were also often sited away from settlements.

79 D. Wilson, 'A note on OE *heorg* and *wēoh* as place-name elements repre-senting different types of pagan Saxon worship sites', *Anglo-Saxon Studies in Archaeology and History*, 4 (1985), 179–83.

80 *BCS*, 454 and 841 (dated 848 and 675 × 692 respectively; F. M. Stenton, 'Medeshamstede and its colonies', in D. M. Stenton (ed.), *Preparatory to Anglo-Saxon England* (Oxford, Oxford University Press, 1970), pp. 179–92; C. Plummer, *Venerabilis Baedae Opera Historica* (Oxford, Oxford University Press, 1896), vol. 1, p. 330.

81 Whitelock *et al.* (eds), *Anglo-Saxon Chronicle*, p. 76; J. Blair, 'Secular minster churches in Domesday Book', in P. H. Sawyer (ed.), *Domesday Book: a Reassess-ment* (London, Arnold, 1985), pp. 108–9; E. Ekwall, *The Concise Oxford Dictionary of English Place-Names* (Oxford, Oxford University Press, 1936), pp. 69, 313.

82 H. M. Taylor and J. Taylor, *Anglo-Saxon Architecture* (Cambridge, Cambridge University Press, 1965), 1, pp. 108–14; 2, pp. 665–72.

83 Horstmann, *St. Werburg*, pp. xxii–xxiii; D. W. Rollason, 'Lists of saints' rest-ing places in Anglo-Saxon England', *Anglo-Saxon England*, 7 (1978), pp. 89–90; Breedon, North Crawley and Aylesbury were listed as sites of relics in post-Conquest sources: Mellows (ed.), *Hugh Candidus*, pp. 59–64.

84 M. Franklin (ed.), *The Cartulary of Daventry Priory* (Northamptonshire Record Society, 35, 1988), pp. 215, 328; another possible example may be found in thirteenth-century evidence of possible vestiges of collegiate organisation at Brigstock (Northants), see C. D. Ross (ed.), *The Cartulary of Cirencester Abbey, Gloucestershire* (London, Oxford University Press, 1964), nos. 720 and 728.

85 *Medieval Settlement Research Group Annual Report*, 6 (1991), 40.

86 G. Cadman, 'Raunds 1977–1983: an excavation summary', *Medieval Archae-ology*, 27 (1983), 107–22.

87 Cadman, 'Raunds 1977–1983', 110; J. Williams, M. Shaw and V. Denham, *Middle Saxon Palaces at Northampton* (Northampton, Northampton Develop-ment Corporation, 1985).

88 Loyn, *Anglo-Saxon England and the Norman Conquest*, p. 199; H. R. Loyn, 'Gesiths and thegns in Anglo-Saxon England from the seventh to the tenth

centuries', *English Historical Review*, 70 (1955), 529–49; H. R. Loyn, 'The king and the structure of society in late Anglo-Saxon England', *History*, 42 (1957), 96–100.

89 Cadman, 'Raunds, 1977–1983', 116–18.

90 D. R. M. Gaimster, S. Margeson and T. Barry, 'Medieval Britain and Ireland in 1988', *Medieval Archaeology*, 33 (1989), 204.

91 B. Nenk, S. Margeson and M. Hurley, 'Medieval Britain and Ireland in 1991', *Medieval Archaeology*, 36 (1992), 255–6; D. M. Wilson and D. G. Hurst, 'Medieval Britain in 1961', *Medieval Archaeology*, 6–7 (1962–3), 333–4; L. Webster and J. Cherry, 'Medieval Britain in 1972', *Medieval Archaeology*, 17 (1973), 147.

92 D. M. Wilson and S. Moorhouse, 'Medieval Britain in 1970', *Medieval Archaeology*, 15 (1971), 145; L. E. Webster and J. Cherry, 'Medieval Britain in 1974', *Medieval Archaeology*, 19 (1975), 249.

93 For example, Hardmead and Stoke Goldington (Bucks), Stagsden (Beds), and Badby (Northants): D. M. Wilson and D. G. Hurst, 'Medieval Britain in 1969', *Medieval Archaeology*, 14 (1970), 188, 189, 191–3.

94 See the sixteen churches belonging to Taylor's period C, Taylor and Taylor, *Anglo-Saxon Architecture* 1, pp. 43–7, 71, 158–9, 222–6, 261–2, 285, 335–7, 376–7, 411–12, 455–6; and 2, pp. 483–4, 488–9, 571–2, 594–6, 626–7, 678–80. There is a tantalising glimpse of a wooden church in a mid-eleventh-century charter referring to Studham (Beds): M. Gelling, *Early Charters of the Thames Valley* (Leicester, Leicester University Press, 1979), p. 22.

95 D. Whitelock (ed.), *English Historical Documents*, 1, 2nd edn (London, Eyre and Spottiswoode, 1979), p. 468, note 7.

96 For Clapham see L. E. Webster and J. Cherry, 'Medieval Britain in 1974', *Medieval Archaeology*, 19 (1975), 249; J. Blair, 'Introduction: From minster to parish church', in J. Blair (ed.), *Minsters and Parish Churches: The Local Church in Transition* (Oxford University Committee for Archaeology, monograph 17, 1988), p. 11.

97 M. McCarthy and C. Brooks, *Medieval Pottery in Britain AD 900–1600* (Leicester, Leicester University Press, 1988), p. 61.

98 See J. N. L. Myres, *Anglo-Saxon Pottery and the Settlement of England* (Oxford, Oxford University Press, 1969), p. 128.

99 L. E. Webster and J. Cherry, 'Medieval Britain in 1971', *Medieval Archaeology*, 16 (1972), 158; J. Hurst, 'The pottery', in Wilson (ed.), *Archaeology of Anglo-Saxon England*, pp. 283–348.

100 *Medieval Settlement Research Group Annual Report*, 6 (1991), 18.

101 H. C. Darby, *Domesday England* (Cambridge, Cambridge University Press, 1977), p. 366.

102 Mawer and Stenton, *Place-Names of Buckinghamshire*, p. 21; *DB*, 1, f. 148.

103 Mawer and Stenton, *Place-Names of Buckinghamshire*, pp. 48–9; Gover *et al.*, *Place-Names of Northamptonshire*, p. 127.

104 *DB*, 1, ff. 143, 209, 212, 219, 221, 225, 235.

105 J. H. Williams, *St. Peter's Street Northampton: Excavations 1973–1976* (Northampton, Northampton Development Corporation, 1979), pp. 140–3.

106 C. Phythian-Adams, *Continuity, Fields and Fission, The Making of a Midlands Parish* (Leicester University Department of English Local History, Occasional Papers, 3rd Series, 4, 1978), p. 30.

107 A. S. Esmonde Cleary, *The Ending of Roman Britain* (London, Batsford, 1989), p. 198.

108 See D. Bonney, 'Early boundaries and estates in southern England', in P. H. Sawyer (ed.), *English Medieval Settlement* (London, Arnold, 1979), pp. 41–51; and D. Hooke 'Early medieval estate and settlement patterns: the documentary evidence', in M. Aston, D. Austin and C. Dyer (eds), *The Rural Settlements of Medieval England* (Oxford, Blackwell, 1989), pp. 9–30.

109 Boundary clauses are discussed in A. E. Brown, T. R. Key and C. Orr, 'Some Anglo-Saxon estates and their boundaries in south-west Northamptonshire', *Northamptonshire Archaeology*, 12 (1977), 155–76; A. E. Brown, T. R. Key, C. Orr and P. Woodfield, 'The Stowe charter: a revision and some implications', *Northamptonshire Archaeology*, 16 (1981), 136–47.

110 L. Fox and P. Russell, *Leicester Forest* (Leicester, Leicestershire Historical Series, 1948), p. 78.

111 *BCS*, 792, 883, 1189 and 1229.

112 D. Hall, *Medieval Fields* (Aylesbury, Shire, 1982), pp. 45–55.

113 Brown *et al.*, 'Anglo-Saxon estates'; F. Brown and C. Taylor, 'Settlement and land-use in Northamptonshire: a comparison between the iron age and the middle ages', in B. Cunliffe and T. Rowley (eds), *Lowland Iron Age Communities in Europe* (British Archaeological Reports, International Series, 48, 1978), pp. 77–89; G. Cadman and G. Foard, 'Raunds, manorial and village origins', in M. Faull (ed.), *Studies in Late Anglo-Saxon Settlement* (Oxford, 1984), pp. 83–99; Phythian-Adams, *Continuity, Fields and Fission*; M. Reed, *The Buckinghamshire Landscape* (London, Hodder and Stoughton, 1979), pp. 74–6; G. Foard, 'The administrative organisation of Northamptonshire in the Saxon period', *Anglo-Saxon Studies in Archaeology and History*, 4 (1985), pp. 185–222; M. Franklin, *Minsters and Parishes: Northamptonshire Studies* (unpublished Ph.D. thesis, Cambridge, 1982).

114 A. E. Brown, *Early Daventry* (Leicester, University of Leicester, Department of Adult Education, 1991).

115 The soke of Geddington appears in the early twelfth-century Northamptonshire Survey, *VCH Northants*, 1, pp. 383–5, while Geddington had been nothing but a member of Brigstock in 1086, *DB*, 1, f. 219.

116 Gover *et al.*, *Place-Names of Northamptonshire*, p. 177, discusses Addington, 'Eadda's farm'.

4

Rural settlement *c.* 1066–1500

This chapter examines the settlement pattern of the four east midland counties in the 450 years following the Norman Conquest. Recorded post-Conquest settlements are much more densely distributed than known settlements of pre-Conquest date. This is due to a number of historical and archaeological circumstances. The increasing sophistication of the bureaucracy of the state and lords in the later middle ages resulted in the writing and preservation of large numbers of administrative documents. We consequently know of the existence of many settlements in the eleventh, twelfth or thirteenth centuries because their names are recorded in Domesday Book, deeds, tax lists and manorial surveys, although in the majority of cases, there is no recorded archaeological evidence for their occupation at this date. Archaeological evidence from excavation or fieldwalking alone would, in some districts, produce a picture almost as incomplete and biased as that for the period 400–1066. But the evidence is generally more plentiful, because pottery of the later middle ages is abundant and easily recognised, and abandoned settlement sites are often visible as earthworks.

This chapter is concerned with the physical aspects of rural settlement – settlement form, nucleation and dispersal, shrinkage and desertion – but uses, as any study of the medieval period must do, evidence of excavations, earthworks and chance finds, in combination with information from maps and documents.

Settlement form

The distribution of finds and sites of the tenth and eleventh century suggests that many settlements then in existence continued to be occupied well into the later middle ages, and in many cases up to the present day (see pp. 92–4). The evolution of settlements in the middle ages did not cease once villages had been founded; settlements continued to grow (often undergoing reorganisation and replanning), to spawn extensions, to shift, to migrate and to contract. Settlement intensified both in already densely settled regions, and in those with a sparser distribution of people, such as the Chilterns, parts of the claylands, and the Fens (see chapter 5 for documentary evidence for population densities). This expansive trend in most areas probably reached its apogee some time during the thirteenth century, presumably reflecting the growth of population up to *c*.1300. In the next two centuries settlements tended to shrink, and many were totally abandoned as population levels declined.

Direct evidence for the form of settlements in the eleventh to fifteenth centuries comes from excavation and field survey of earthworks, and much can be inferred from modern maps. While there have, inevitably, been many changes in the nature of individual settlements in the centuries between the late middle ages and the earliest maps, evidence from archaeology can be used to show that in general the maps reflect an earlier situation. As we have seen, the contrast between areas of nucleated villages, and those where dispersed settlement forms (interrupted or irregular rows, common-edge settlements, single farmsteads) predominate, can be identified from the early nineteenth-century maps, and we can now examine the distinction in the light of earlier evidence.

Nucleated villages

These were even more common in many parts of the study area in the middle ages than in the early nineteenth century. Many settlements which in the nineteenth century survived only as hamlets or isolated farmsteads, or in many cases had completely vanished, have extensive earthwork remains which show them to have been nucleated villages in the middle ages. Many are surrounded by ridge and furrow reflecting large-scale cultivation. Such sites are common in eastern Leicestershire, across most of Northamptonshire, and in the clay vales and river valleys of Bedford-shire and Buckinghamshire. They provide the best evidence for the variations in layout and size of medieval nucleated villages. Without universal excavation, it is impossible to be certain how many settlements had taken on a nucleated form before *c*.1100. Some, such as Burystead (Raunds) in Northamptonshire, had been organised into villages by that date. A little detailed documentary evidence can be interpreted to suggest that nucleation had occurred by the twelfth century. For example a charter for Dodford (Northants) of *c*.1160 describes a messuage (house) lying 'at the end of the vill of Dodford towards Flore', which must imply that the village consisted of houses grouped together.[1]

Villages in the study area generally adopt one of two basic forms. The regular linear row has rectangular tofts and crofts arranged in an orderly line at right angles to the street, on one or both sides. This seems to have been the most common form of medieval village, and in many cases tofts are regular in size. On the Northampton Heights, Winwick, Silsworth

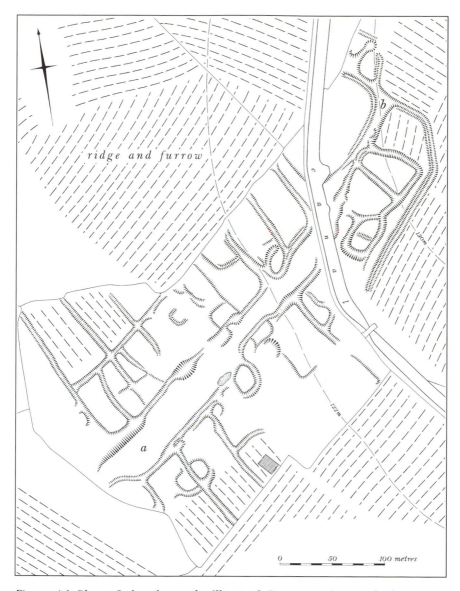

Figure 4.1 Plan of the deserted village of Downtown in Stanford-on-Avon, Northamptonshire, a regular linear row settlement. The site consisted of a wide holloway marking the village street, with about twenty tofts on both sides, some of them containing house platforms. The site is surrounded by ridge and furrow. Pottery of the twelfth to fourteenth centuries suggests the period of occupation. The site is cut by the canal. It has now been destroyed by ploughing.

(in Watford parish), Stanford-on-Avon, Downtown (in the same parish) (Fig. 4.1), Little Oxendon, Marston Trussell, Hothorpe in the same parish), Little Creaton (in Creaton parish) and Nobold (in Clipston parish) are just a few examples of deserted or shrunken settlements which have this regular linear plan (Fig. 4.2).[2]

Regular row settlements may extend to a length of less than 100m (110yd) or more than 2km (1¼ miles), although the very big nineteenth-century examples such as Arlesey and Langford in Bedfordshire may be largely the result of post-medieval growth. The layout of many of these regular rows resembles that of planned towns, and some are in fact market villages. Rockingham (Northants) is one example of a settlement where the granting of a market charter in 1271 may have led directly to the deliberate replanning of the settlement as a regular row with a wide central street on an accessible, level site away from the castle.[3] The form

Figure 4.2 Aerial photograph of a linear row settlement at Carlton Curlieu, Leicestershire. A series of rectangular tofts containing house platforms runs at right angles from the holloway just below the centre of the photograph. The southern section of the village is of the linear row type; the remainder of the settlement has a more irregular plan. The village seems to have shrunk severely in the seventeenth century.

Figure 4.3 Aerial photograph of a gridded cluster settlement at Ingarsby, Leicestershire. At least twenty rectangular tofts are linked by holloways intersecting at right angles. The modern farm, which has a large moated and banked enclosure at one side and the earthworks of a pond on the other, stands on the site of a grange of Leicester Abbey. The village had a dozen households in 1381, but was deserted by 1469.

of these linear settlements was also influenced by topography and pre-existing landscape features. These included the presence of a road or a river which would encourage linearity in the settlement plan. Such regular rows appear to have a long currency in the east midlands. The beginnings of such a settlement at Stratton can be dated to the tenth century; in others, such as Mallows Cotton on the boundary between Raunds and Ringstead (Northants), occupation appears to be entirely post-Conquest.

On some sites occupation, at least on a small scale, predates the creation of the large, regularly planned row village. An example is Isham, in the Ise valley in Northamptonshire, where pottery as early as the ninth century lay near the parish church, in the centre of the nucleated village.[4] The present village layout, and earthwork remains of an abandoned part of the medieval settlement, indicate a regular double row plan, the result of a phase of replanning, probably entirely or in part of late pre-Conquest date.

The second type of plan among nucleated villages, the gridded cluster, forms a block rather than a row (Figs 4.3, 4.4). These are less common

Figure 4.4 Aerial photograph of a gridded cluster settlement at Crafton, Buckinghamshire from the north. The settlement remains consist of a rectilinear pattern of holloways and ditches defining at least twenty tofts. The site is surrounded by ridge and furrow, and on the west side tofts seem to have expanded over former arable land.

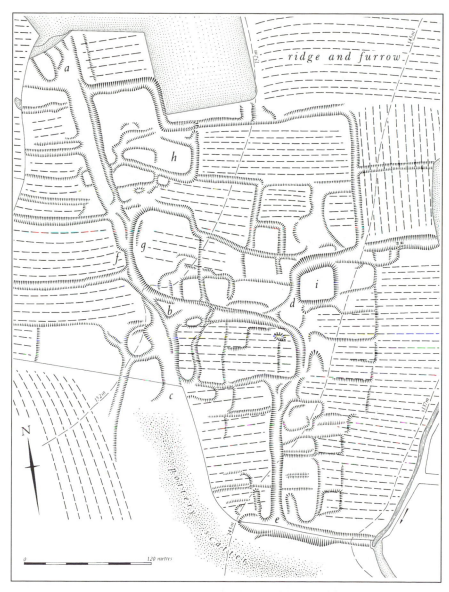

Figure 4.5 Plan of the deserted village of Sulby, Northamptonshire. For a description of this complex site, see text. After desertion the site was entirely ploughed over, as is shown by the ridge and furrow. The main holloway is *a–b–c*, and *i* marks the probable site of the parish church. The village had eighty-nine tax payers in 1377 (suggesting at least thirty households), but was reduced to less than ten households by 1428, and the site had become a pasture by the early sixteenth century.

Figure 4.6 Aerial photograph of the deserted village of Sulby, Northamptonshire. This photograph, taken from the north-east, can be compared with the plan in Figure 4.5.

than row settlements, but occur in numbers across the limestone country of the Northampton Heights and in eastern Leicestershire and Rutland. In existing settlements of this kind, the initial impression is often of a disorganised huddle, but this is probably the result of a series of changes in layout in post-medieval times. Surveys of shrunken or abandoned examples of such settlements reveal evidence of a regular layout. Kelmarsh, Braunston and Muscott (Northants) are made up of a number of sub-square tofts and crofts grouped together to form a compact block.[5] A similar plan is identifiable in many sites in Leicestershire, such as Eye Kettleby, Hamilton and Sysonby.[6] Parallels can be found among a number of sites such as Sysonby Grange or Thrussington Grange, which are monastic granges rather than villages, and is similar to other seigniorial grange sites such as Cottesbrook.[7]

Many nucleated settlements form large agglomerated clusters in which elements of both row and grid plans are visible, and other, less regular elements besides. In these settlements several different phases of development have taken place, often focusing around a central point such as a road junction, church or manor house. Sulby in north-west Northamptonshire is a classic example which is now completely deserted; hence the complexities of its medieval layout can be seen free of later development (Figs 4.5, 4.6).[8] The earthworks extend over an area 500m by 400m (550yd by 440yd) and consist of clear remains of holloways, toft boundaries and house sites. The plan was very complex. To the west a number of tofts are arranged in a regular row along a major broad holloway. A narrower holloway which branches off from this runs initially east for about 100m (110yd) and then bifurcates. Closes along this holloway may belong to another phase of the village development. From the fork one holloway turns north and runs around a substantial platform which may be the site of the church, while the other runs south for 200m (220yd). The closes along this lane are small but very regular and appear to belong to yet another phase. Finally the lane turns eastward out of the settlement. A further development appears to be represented by a block of closes occupying the north-east of the site, and there are other areas of more confused remains. Pottery of twelfth- to fourteenth-century date has been found on the edge of the site. Most of the tofts are covered with ridge and furrow, showing that the site was cultivated after desertion.

Many other examples of these complex agglomerated settlements were not abandoned, but are still inhabited and evolving today. Evidence of their plans and development are often found in areas of earthworks within or around shrunken settlements. For example at Harringworth in Northamptonshire a still surviving nucleus of settlement around the church was probably the site of the earliest medieval occupation. To the south-east a grassy field contains the earthwork remains of a number of tofts arranged along a road which is still in use. The quite irregular tofts are associated with short or non-existent crofts, set within a narrow strip of land between the road and ridge and furrow. This appears to be a medieval extension to the settlement, which may overlie earlier arable fields, but it was later abandoned as the settlement contracted.[9]

Dispersed settlements (Fig. 4.7)

The absence of large medieval villages, whether deserted, shrunken or still inhabited, in such districts as the Chilterns must mean that nucleated settlement never existed there. Settlement in the greensand, much of the low claylands and the chalk of the Chilterns was largely dispersed in the middle ages. Some nucleated settlements, or at least 'proto-nucleations' once existed in south Bedfordshire, judging from earthwork remains of small clustered sites, for example at Battlesden, Lower Stondon or Faldo.[10]

Figure 4.7 Aerial photograph of the deserted hamlet of Moreton in Dinton, Buckinghamshire. A number of ditches and holloways define a series of enclosures (tofts), some rectangular, some irregular in shape. The site appears to have gone through a number of phases of development, as shown for example by an irregular enclosure overlying a narrow rectangular toft. The site lies in a stream valley, near a moated site, and surrounded by ridge and furrow.

Only exceptionally did such sites attain any size. Even the largest deserted and shrunken sites, such as Gravenhurst and Cainhoe, cannot rival the earthworks of large deserted villages further north in Northamptonshire and Leicestershire, in either area or in complexity.

Dispersed settlements inevitably embrace a variety of forms, divided here into four main categories: isolated single farmstead units, small hamlets, attenuated or interrupted rows and common-edge settlements. Although a focal point within each parish or manor can usually be identified, consisting of a church and perhaps a manor house, settlement often did not concentrate around this, and many townships or parishes containing dispersed settlements lacked a distinctive centre.

Few dispersed settlements in our area have produced archaeological evidence for medieval occupation, but this is largely due to a lack of research. Often the only evidence for the medieval period comes from the names in written records such as the numerous hamlets called 'end' and 'green' found in some parishes. But of course the first reference in a document does not date the origin of a settlement. High rates of population growth between the eleventh and fourteenth centuries in these regions, accompanied by historical evidence for assarting, has suggested that many dispersed settlements were late foundations. But in view of the many small settlements of the period 400–900, it seems likely that at least some of the hamlets recorded in the thirteenth century had a much earlier beginning. Shifts and migrations continued to take place so that a place-name may have moved, and a farmstead named in the fourteenth century may have stood on a site different from that of the building which carries the same name on a nineteenth-century map.

Single farmsteads are found in all periods. Many small sites of the fifth to ninth centuries may have functioned as individual farmsteads, but from the ninth century onwards these were mostly abandoned, or they may have expanded into larger settlements. A large number of modern farms which have produced evidence for medieval occupation are in fact on the sites of abandoned medieval villages, not farmsteads. Grange sites such as Sysonby Grange (Leics) may have been founded as farms, but represent a rather specialised type of dispersed settlement as they were the centres of demesne farms cultivated directly by lords, not peasants.[11] Fieldwalking, combined with documentary evidence, has led to the suggestion that the later village of Grafton Regis (Northants) may have been a single farmstead before *c.* 1200: the low density of pottery of ninth- to twelfth-century date accords well with the record in Domesday Book of a single bordar and plough for Grafton.[12] It lies in the Tove valley, a tributary of the Nene, in an area of mainly nucleated settlement in the medieval period,

but less than 3km (2 miles) from the mixed settlement region of Whittlewood forest. This example points to the variable and changing nature of
settlement in the ninth to twelfth centuries, when the pattern was evidently
evolving faster in some areas than others.

A large number of farms inhabited in recent times are recorded by
name in the twelfth to fourteenth centuries in the Chilterns, but none of
them have produced archaeological evidence for occupation in the medieval period, and there is apparently no sign of earthwork or soil
mark remains around them which could indicate former large settlements. So it would appear that many isolated farms in existence by the
thirteenth century continued to be occupied in much the same form until
the present day.

Farmsteads can also be found in areas of dispersed settlement interspersed with hamlets, often in areas of historic woodland. The parish of
Cranfield in central Bedfordshire has six named settlements, three with
'end' names.[13] Hartwell, in southern Northamptonshire, lies within Whittlewood Forest. At least seven separate small medieval settlements have
been recorded in the parish.[14] Five of these have earthwork remains of
abandoned sites. Some, such as Elms Farm and Hartwell End Farm were
little more than farmsteads; other more extensive sites, such as Chapel
Farm and an earthwork site south of Hartwell Green, may have included
ten or more small tofts. The earliest medieval pottery from any of the
hamlets dates from the twelfth or thirteenth century, but earlier evidence
may remain undiscovered. This need not be regarded as entirely new
settlement of the middle ages, because the deserted hamlet of Bozenham
coincides with a Roman site.

Many peasant holdings were located, not in isolation as farmsteads,
but along lanes or tracks near to neighbours. The resulting settlements
have been termed interrupted or attenuated rows and are commonly
found in some areas of dispersed settlement on modern maps. At Scald
End (Thurleigh parish), on the boulder clay in north Bedfordshire,
fieldwalking and survey have revealed that the settlement which now
consists of houses spaced along a road was occupied more densely in the
middle ages, but that it still retained its distinctive pattern of closes
containing houses set at intervals and separated from neighbours by plots
used for agriculture (Fig. 4.8).[15] A similar pattern was noted at Hobb's
End in the nearby parish of Odell, in the Ouse valley.

As one result of this fieldwork, Brown and Taylor have remarked that
the origins of these superficially similar settlements may be very different.
Some are probably of pre-Conquest origin, while others are later, either
associated with the clearance of woodland, or laid out over arable land.

Figure 4.8 Aerial photograph of the interrupted row settlement at Scald End in Thurleigh, Bedfordshire. Fieldwork has shown that, although more houses were occupied along the road in the high middle ages than now, the layout of houses had a similar character to that which still exists.

They suggest that the peak of the post-Conquest expansion in that area may date to the middle or end of the twelfth century, and was rather short-lived. In north Buckinghamshire, loosely nucleated rows of houses have been excavated at Westbury, also known as Shenley Brook End. The settlement appears to have developed in the thirteenth century, when houses were sited on the ends of a field system, and the whole site shows a degree of dynamism, with much replanning.[16]

Similar patterns of attenuated rows of cottages and holdings around the edges of common land are found in the Chilterns and south Bedfordshire. Judging from the evidence of nineteenth-century maps they vary in the way in which they are organised. In central Bedfordshire, settlements such as Ickwell, Thorncote Green and Beeston on the green-sand heathlands are arranged intermittently but quite neatly around the fringes of relatively small areas of common, sometimes called 'greens' (meaning extensive pastures, not the open space found at the centre of some nucleated villages). The regularity of these examples could be the result of deliberate planning. In the Vale of Bedford, greens or commons are sometimes much larger and less regularly shaped, like Kempston West End, Cranfield and Wootton where the common land forms a long thin strip along a road. The associated settlement has an irregular appearance perhaps resulting from modern roadside squatting.

Further south in Bedfordshire the commons or greens are generally wider and of very variable shape, which is likely to be the result of piecemeal enclosure of parts of commons which were formerly even larger. Tofts at Stanbridge and Tilsworth arranged on the periphery of the common land are the major settlements within their parish and contain the parish church. This arrangement could well be of twelfth- or thirteenth-century date. However, a similar settlement at Eggington has produced archaeological evidence of occupation dating between the sixth and ninth century. In south Buckinghamshire, much of the Chilterns contains even larger green- or common-edge settlements. These, however, are frequently located on the edge of parishes and often lie across several parish boundaries. They have names which tend to appear in the documentary record no earlier than the thirteenth century and which frequently change. Although the settlements have an apparent unity through being arranged around the same area of common land they divide up into numerous small units, each with a different name. Little archaeological work has been carried out around any of these settlements, so it is difficult to establish any date for them. The diversity of their form and siting may reflect varied origins, and indeed many will have originated or at least been extended with modern population expansion.

Moated sites

Defined as sites surrounded by a broad and shallow ditch, often water filled, moated sites have long been associated with dispersed settlement because, although they are found in many nucleated villages, usually set apart from the tofts, the majority are sited in relative isolation in land-scapes containing farmsteads and hamlets. They are especially useful sites for the purposes of our survey because their construction, unlike that of other dispersed sites, is fairly closely datable. The great majority of moated sites that have been excavated belong to the period 1180–1320, so that we can presume that they reflect the foundation or at least consolidation of settlement around the thirteenth century. They are also, unlike the rather elusive earthworks of deserted peasant farmsteads, relatively easily discovered because of the distinctive character of the moat itself.

Nearly 800 moated sites are known in our four counties, of which more than 300 lie in the small county of Bedfordshire, one of the densest distributions in England.[17] They are most common on heavy soils (Fig. 4.9). The mapping of moated sites here uses three categories:

1 occupied moated sites, containing a farm or house in the early nineteenth century,

2 abandoned moated sites lying more than 250m (275yd) from an existing settlement, and

3 moated sites lying in or near (i.e. at a distance less than 250m (275yd) from) an existing village or hamlet.

Details were also recorded of the distance of the site from:

i the church of the parish in which it lay (a line on the map being used to indicate the position of the church in relation to each moated site), and

ii the nearest river or stream.

Buckinghamshire

The distribution of moated sites in Buckinghamshire shows a marked preference for the gault clay of the northern edge of the Chilterns, and the low-lying Oxford clay between the Thame and the Ouse. Moated sites are scarce in the Chilterns, although a few appear around Missenden and Beaconsfield, and others towards the Thames valley. Most of these are abandoned or incorporated into a settlement, and all but two lie more than 1km (1090yd) from their parish churches. Some may have originated as distant granges within the large Chiltern manors. A number of parishes on the edge of the Chilterns (e.g., Ellesborough, Stoke Mandeville, Great

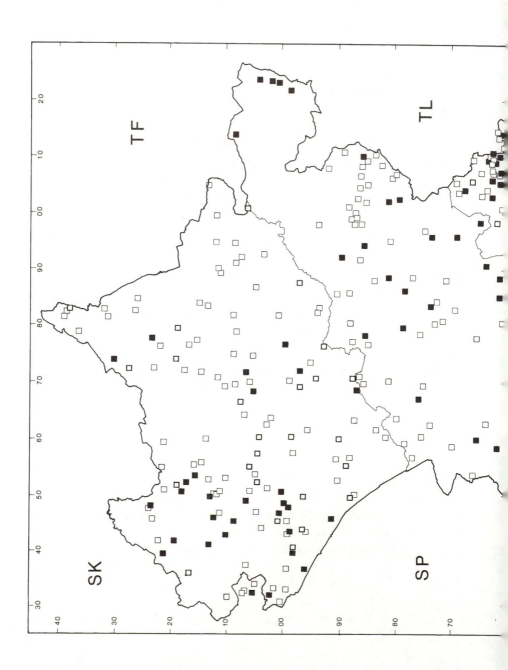

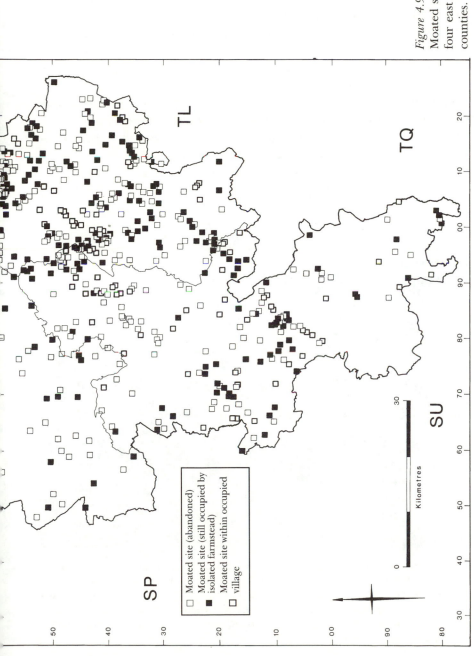

Figure 4.9
Moated sites in the
four east midland
counties.

and Little Kimble, Dinton with Ford and Upton) each contain from four to six moated sites, most of which are still occupied by farms.

In the clay vales to the north the density of moats thins out a little, with two to five sites per parish. Quite a high proportion of the moated sites in this area are abandoned. In all 46 per cent of moated sites in existing villages north of the Chilterns lie immediately adjacent to the church. These settlements have a distinct core consisting of a church and a moat, presumably the site of a manor house. A number of moated sites in the centre of the county are located at some distance from a church, but very close to streams or rivers (Fig. 4.10). In these cases water appears to have been a major consideration in determining their sites. Sites with no houses now standing within them most often occur in such locations, and some of these sites may never have been inhabited, but were instead connected with water control and supply, being used for example as fish ponds.[18]

Figure 4.10 Aerial photograph of the Vaches isolated moated site at Aston Clinton, Buckinghamshire, from the east. The area enclosed by the moat was rectangular, *c.* 120m by 120m (130yd square). To the east are traces of buildings, perhaps agricultural in purpose, or a gatehouse, and the earthworks of a large fishpond. To the west a curved boundary ditch can be seen. The site lay 1.5 km (1 mile) from the village of Aston Clinton.

Moated sites occur in a distinct concentration in north-east Buckinghamshire, coinciding with the underlying Oxford clay and continuing in an even more dense distribution further east in Bedfordshire. Many of these sites lie in the small townships of the Ouzel valley, very close to the river. There are one or two in each township; at Woolstone, Willen or Moulsoe they are in pairs, with an abandoned moat sited near to another which is still occupied as if one were replacing the other. These moats are likely to have surrounded manor houses.

Bedfordshire

Among Bedfordshire's numerous moated sites, the densest distribution occurs on the Oxford and boulder clay in the parishes north and south-west of Bedford. Here they form a major component of the settlement pattern, and in some cases almost every messuage within an interrupted irregular row settlement is surrounded by a moat. This association of moated sites with dispersed woodland settlement has been noted throughout the country, and is commonly explained by the need to provide a secure site for occupation on newly cleared land, in which the clays, often associated with woodland, gave an ideal water-retaining soil for the moat. They can reflect the creation of new holdings by enterprising, free peasants and gentry who prospered from reclamation and the land market, and were keen to show off their achievement and to assert their higher status, real or imagined; but some of the holdings may date back to Domesday and before.[19]

The largest numbers of moats occur in the parishes of Thurleigh, Bolnhurst, Cranfield and Marston Moretaine, in each of which from eleven to thirteen are known: neighbouring parishes commonly also contain from seven to ten. Few such moats are abandoned, particularly in Cranfield, where all but three are still occupied by farms. While the majority of the moats in these areas lie in interrupted row settlements, there are a number of others situated away from larger settlements, close to the parish boundaries. No simple rule allows us to predict that moats should be numerous in particular terrains or settlement zones. Not all regions with dispersed settlement patterns contain plentiful moated sites. As in Buckinghamshire, they are virtually absent from the Chiltern fringes in Bedfordshire. Nor are they found on all clay soils, as can be judged from their scarcity among the nucleated townships of the north-west of the county, despite the extensive boulder clay.

Moated sites are more sparsely distributed in the Ouse and Ivel valleys. They fall into two groups in terms of location: the first are found in the river valleys, mostly in or close to existing settlements; the second are sited away from the watercourses, towards the parish or township boundaries.

Very few moated sites are found on the greensand. In the Flitt valley, those that do exist lie on patches of boulder clay, and are probably manorial sites. Further south a number of moats cluster on the mixed boulder and gault clay immediately north of the Chilterns.

Northamptonshire

Although there is a smaller number of moated sites in Northamptonshire, a few concentrations can be noted, most notably in the Lyveden valley. These lie on the edges of several Nene valley townships around Oundle including Oundle itself, Benefield, Stoke Doyle and Wadenhoe, near the point where boundaries meet. In two cases, namely Stoke Doyle and Pilton, a second moat, presumed to be the site of the manor house, lies within the nucleated village in the Nene valley bottom. The Nene valley, a zone of nucleated settlement, is generally poorly endowed with moated sites, and the cluster near Oundle coincides with a group of incompletely nucleated villages.

The moated sites which are thinly scattered across the Northampton Heights tend to be associated with villages; many which are no longer inhabited lie in the earthwork remains of deserted settlements. They are probably the sites of former manor houses like that excavated at Badby.[20] A number of moated sites in the forest regions of Whittlewood and Salcey are, in contrast, mostly still occupied. Moats which lie within 50m (55yd) of churches have been noted in considerable number in the county, and confirm the strong ties between church and manor.

Leicestershire and Rutland

Of the 130 moats known in Leicestershire slightly more than half are now abandoned. The densest distribution is to be found in the west, on the watershed between the Soar and Sence, in the area around the forest of Charnwood. This coincides with an area of dispersed settlement. In this area the majority of moated sites are still occupied, nearly all by isolated single farms. As they often lie more than 1km (1090yd) from the church, the moats were not obviously created to fortify or enhance the importance of the main manor house, but resemble in their peripheral siting other isolated farmsteads. In the immediately adjacent valleys of the Soar and the Sence, moated sites are fewer in number and are more commonly deserted. Most of those which are still occupied lie in villages, and they are generally close to churches. In some parishes, such as Kirby Muxloe and Ratby, moated sites are paired, with one occupying a low-lying site near the church, while another is found on high ground or some distance from the village.

Figure 4.11 Aerial photograph of a moated site in a deserted settlement at Owston, Leicestershire. The existing village of Owston is accompanied by large areas of earthworks, some of them marking the site of Owston Abbey, and this clearly visible moated site.

East of the River Soar, a thin scatter of moated sites extends across most of the county, with fewer on the wolds and more on the higher land between the Soar and Rutland (Fig. 4.11). With the exception of a handful in or around the valleys of the Welland and the Wreake, more than 95 per cent are abandoned. There is no obvious explanation for this unusual degree of desertion: abandoned moats are recorded both close to churches and at some distance, both within deserted villages and in isolation. As this part of the county is notable for its high proportion of deserted and shrunken settlements, the moated sites appear to have been part of the general late-medieval retreat of settlement.

Summary

Moated sites in the study area tend to be most common in some, but not all, areas of dispersed settlement, and their distribution seems usually to correlate with that of heavy soils. There appear to be three different uses for moated sites implied by their siting within their territorial unit. Firstly, moats which lie within villages are generally presumed to have surrounded manor houses and functioned partly as assertions of superior status, although they must also have had a minor defensive role, and are related to water control systems, for example for fish-ponds. Secondly, moats which lie towards the periphery of parishes or townships are likely to have served as houses of sub-manors, or secondary manors created in the course of land clearance. Some 'moats' may not have been intended as habitations, but served as elaborate ponds. Thirdly, those moats which occur with such frequency in dispersed settlements in the Bedfordshire claylands, cannot all have been constructed as manor houses, and some could have belonged to the wealthier and more pretentious free peasants who aped the lifestyle of the gentry.

There were also functional and economic influences on the creation of moats. The lack of moated sites in the Chilterns, which was an area of dispersed woodland settlement and contained its share of prosperous and aspirant freeholders, must be explained in terms both of the free-draining qualities of the chalk, and social factors at present unknown.

Problems of classification and definition

While it is possible to identify several regions of distinctly 'nucleated' and 'dispersed' settlement patterns, the present research has shown the variability within, as well as between, those areas. 'Nucleated' and 'dispersed' patterns were subject to much local variation: the settlement patterns of the Chilterns and the Vale of Bedford, though both dispersed, are very different, just as the nucleated villages of Rutland and Rockingham Forest have little in common.

Elsewhere, the linear villages of many of the river valleys, with their history of continuous and intensive occupation, probably followed a distinct path of development, as did the nucleated agglomerations of eastern Leicestershire; the linear settlements of Rockingham Forest may have emerged at quite a late date, as did the market settlements of dispersed south Bedfordshire – yet they fall within the umbrella term 'nucleated'. The pattern was not fixed, as areas originally with dispersed settlement became nucleated, and then later fragmented back into isolated farms when the villages were deserted. Some villages formed after the middle ages.

Many settlements cannot easily be classified because they have both nucleated and dispersed elements. Many polyfocal settlements fall into this category (Fig. 4.12). Settlements which contain more than one main plan element or focus are defined as polyfocal, and most large clustered settlements in the study area exhibit this characteristic in some degree. They occur in all regions and though most often nucleated they can, if the foci are widely separated, be regarded as dispersed. They could have developed from the fission of large villages, as seems to have occurred in the major river valleys, or from the coalescence or fusion of hamlets as happened in areas of dispersed or mixed settlement, particularly the Chilterns, the high ground in north Buckinghamshire, and southern and central Bedfordshire. In the Flitt valley in south Bedfordshire, a number of the coalesced, clustered settlements in an area of general dispersal were granted market charters in the thirteenth century, and this may have stimulated the growth and merger of initially small dispersed hamlets into larger polyfocal groupings. The documents for Harlestone (Northamptonshire) record the names of these hamlet settlements, such as *Walbek* and *Hoddele*, at the end of the thirteenth century.[21] The type is uncommon in the main river valleys.

The processes lying behind the observed modern settlement plan are sometimes difficult to identify, and in some cases both fusion and fission may have been at work. Warmington in Northamptonshire, with its hamlets of Southorpe and Eaglethorpe is a good example of this problem.[22] The name 'Southorpe' implies a secondary foundation, and has been described as a 'daughter' hamlet. Eaglethorpe, however, to which the same term is applied, has produced evidence from fieldwalking for occupation throughout the pre-Conquest period, implying that at least part of the polyfocal plan of Warmington emerged as a result of infilling and coalescence of the previously separate hamlets. Excavations at Tattenhoe (Bucks) have shown that one part of this polyfocal settlement was occupied from the eleventh century, and was then abandoned in the late thirteenth century at the same time that a tightly-nucleated group of eight houses developed nearby.[23]

Smaller settlements can also pose problems of classification such as Kirby (Deene parish) north-east of Corby in Northamptonshire.[24] This small Domesday manor contains a single settlement set within open fields,

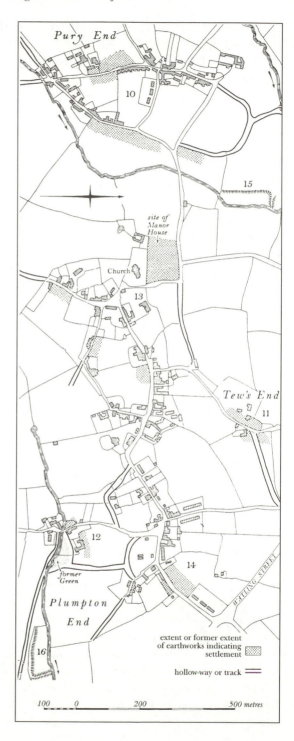

Figure 4.12 Plan of a polyfocal village at Paulerspury, Northamptonshire. Paulerspury stretches over 2km (1¼ miles), and consists of five or six distinct elements. It was a single manor at the time of Domesday, but the village seems to have developed from the partial fusion of once separate hamlets. All of the foci still have inhabitants, but also show signs of shrinkage.

superficially suggestive of a classic nucleated village, yet its plan, surveyed in detail as a deserted settlement, reveals a straggle of tofts extending intermittently over 400m (440yd), an arrangement more characteristic of dispersal. At Fawsley in Northamptonshire, two small deserted settlements, separated by little more than 100m (110yd), lay within the same manor and appear always to have been regarded as one unit for administrative purposes.[25] Lying within the ridge and furrow remains of open fields they have been defined as a 'double village', but they are so small and separate they resemble many dispersed settlements.

In general, characteristics such as a single settlement in its parish or township, large size, a high degree of compactness, a common field system and evidence of regular planning are all features of the classic nucleated east midlands village at its peak of development. However, many nucleated villages lack one or more of these criteria: acquiring such features could have been a gradual process and one which continued long after nucleation at the focal point of a territory. The variations in the form of nucleated villages suggest their origin in diverse routes of development: one of these was migratory nucleation by which smaller, dispersed settlements gave up their inhabitants; another was the merging of adjacent hamlets; but perhaps both could take place in the history of a single village.

Desertion and shrinkage

Deserted and shrunken settlements are known from all periods and indeed, as we have seen, most known pre-ninth-century settlements are deserted. The most visible phase of decline came, however, in the later middle ages, and this process has left us with a mass of archaeological evidence in the form of earthworks of abandoned streets and houses, or pottery scatters in modern ploughed fields. Many villages recorded in documents of the thirteenth and fourteenth centuries were left as an empty pasture or a single farm in the fifteenth and sixteenth centuries.

Deserted and shrunken settlements in the area have been mapped in conjunction with all recorded medieval settlements known from archaeological or historical sources (Fig. 4.13). Each settlement was placed in one of six categories as follows:

1 existing villages or hamlets with no recorded evidence of shrinkage,

2 existing villages or hamlets with a very limited extent of shrinkage not exceeding *c.* 30 per cent of the area still occupied,

3 existing villages or hamlets with shrinkage not exceeding *c.* 60 per cent of the area still occupied,

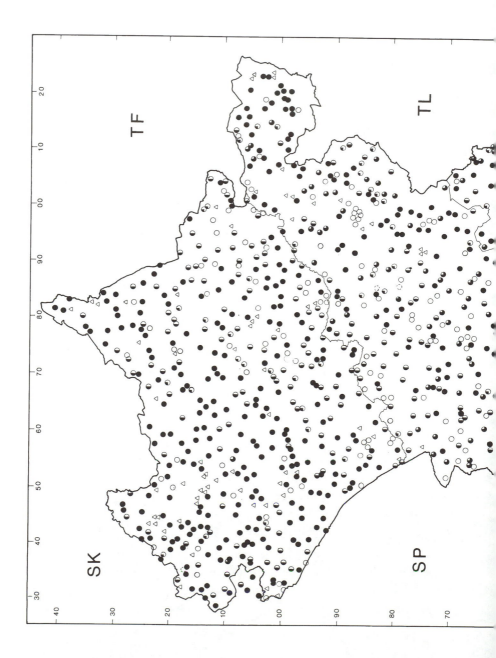

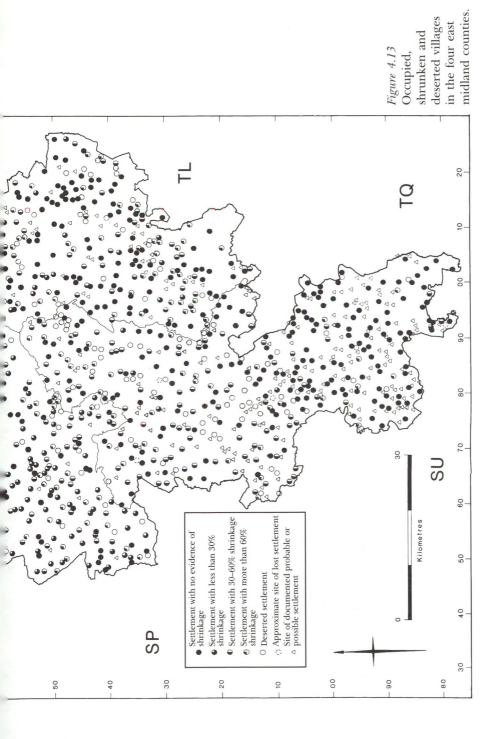

Figure 4.13
Occupied,
shrunken and
deserted villages
in the four east
midland counties.

SP

TL

TQ

SU

Settlement with no evidence of
shrinkage

Settlement with less than 30%
shrinkage

Settlement with 30–60% shrinkage

Settlement with more than 60%
shrinkage

Deserted settlement

Approximate site of lost settlement

Site of documented probable or
possible settlement

Kilometres

0   30

30   40   50   60   70   80   90   00   10   20

50

40

30

20

10

00

90

80

4 extensively shrunken settlements with only vestigial hamlet or farmstead occupation remaining,

5 totally deserted settlements, and

6 farmsteads for which there is documentary evidence of medieval
occupation, but no corroborative archaeological or architectural evidence.

The analysis of deserted and shrunken settlements in the study area is
inevitably biased by a number of factors. The archaeological evidence is
itself incomplete, as the remains of former houses, boundaries and roads
may have been ploughed away or built over at a later date. Nor can we
be sure of the dating of the abandonment of settlements marked by
earthworks or cropmarks, still less of the causes, whether sudden depopulation, gradual desertion, or migration to another site.

Table 4.1: Settlement desertion and shrinkage in the east midland counties

	deserted	extensively shrunken	shrunken	slightly shrunken	total of recorded villages & hamlets
Beds	27	43	40	18	460
Bucks	83	39	80	6	625
Leics & Rutland	72	14	134	1	539
Northants	82	53	96	125	557
All five counties	264	149	350	150	2,181

Buckinghamshire

The striking contrast in Buckinghamshire is between the Chilterns and
the rest of the county. Only a handful of settlements in the Chilterns has
as yet produced any archaeological evidence for contraction, and these
are mostly clustered around Great Missenden and Princes Risborough.
The region is known from documents to have experienced a loss of
population, and it went through the same social and economic changes
as other parts of the study area. Perhaps its wood–pasture resources, its
flexible field systems and proximity to London gave its inhabitants some
economic advantages, but we cannot rule out the possibility that later
land use has removed earthwork evidence of isolated house sites, or that
there has been a lack of systematic research.

The rest of the county displays a considerable number of deserted and
shrunken settlements (see Table 4.1). Some of these, such as Eythrope
and Putlow, Upton in Dinton, Simpson, or Walton and Caldecotte in Bow
Brickhill, lie in river valleys (the Thame and Ouzel) often quite close to

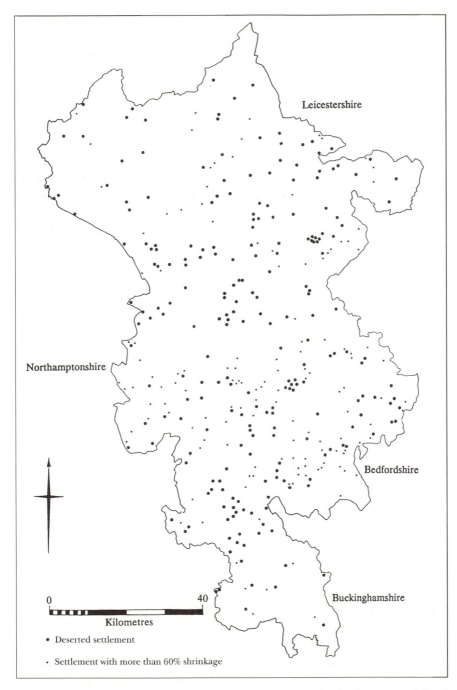

Figure 4.14 Deserted and severely shrunken settlements in the four east midland counties.

other settlements both occupied and deserted, suggesting that the proximity of other villages made some of them vulnerable to decline. Many, even when they had their own field systems, were often subordinate to other villages.[26] The major settlements, such as those mentioned in Domesday Book, were rarely completely deserted, although many of these do contain large areas of shrinkage. In the river valleys, however, most settlements show little or no physical evidence for contraction.

Apart from the main river valleys, many small deserted settlements lie close to the periphery of parishes (e.g., Westbury in Shenley, Stearthill in Little Horwood, Biggin in Grandborough, Littleton in Waddesdon, and others whose medieval names are unknown). Most of these parishes also contain settlements which are only slightly shrunken, if at all, and these are usually those carrying the names of Domesday manors, which may indicate their superiority as administrative centres. Some parishes, however, contain no existing settlements (e.g., Hogshaw, Fleet Marston, Quarrendon and Woodham) while others contain only very small hamlets of just a few cottages (e.g., Creslow and Dunton); all these have archaeological evidence that occupation was formerly much more extensive.

Bedfordshire

The vast majority of the very shrunken or deserted settlements in Bedfordshire lie in the major river valleys or on the chalk or clay soils, and are much less common among the dispersed settlements on the greensand heathlands (Fig. 4.14). Indeed the only dispersed parish which contains a number of known deserted settlements is Old Warden, where the major landowner was the Cistercian monastery of Warden Abbey.

In contrast, other areas of dispersed settlement, those of the heavy claylands of north Bedfordshire, contain evidence for deserted and shrunken settlements. The pattern here is quite distinct: the subsidiary settlements, lying towards the parish boundaries, are nearly all either very shrunken or totally deserted, but the central settlements are in no instance deserted, and show a much lesser tendency to shrinkage. The subsidiary settlements appear to have been especially vulnerable to abandonment. Over the whole of England, judging from tax assessments of the early fourteenth century, smaller and poorer settlements were more likely to be deserted, presumably because they were more sensitive to the impact of economic and agrarian recession.

Deserted and shrunken settlements are recorded in relatively small numbers in the river valleys in Bedfordshire. Few of the more important and well established settlements in the Ouse valley (using a reference in Domesday to identify such places), have any evidence for contraction, and only around Bedford itself are there any such settlements with extensive shrinkage, such as Elstow and Eastcotts. The densest distribution of shrunken sites occurs on the gault clay in the south of the county, particularly the parishes of Harlington, Pulloxhill, Westoning, Barton in the Clay, Streatley and, slightly to the south-west, Eggington, Battlesden and Chalgrave. This is an area of very irregular settlement pattern, with large numbers of small clusters, many with 'end' place-names. Many other deserted settlements are not named in documents, and lie close to parish boundaries, suggesting their peripheral status.

Northamptonshire

The distribution of deserted medieval settlements in Northamptonshire does not fall into a definite pattern. Deserted and shrunken settlements are nearly as common along the Nene valley as in the Northampton Heights, and are only slightly more densely distributed in the south-west. They are least common on the edge of the Fens. Few townships in the Northampton Heights contained settlements which were not subject to some shift or contraction. In this area, unlike the Nene valley, many of the places named in Domesday are extensively shrunken or even deserted. As we have seen, the shrinkage of settlements in the Heights reveals them to have been very regular and notably uniform in plan at the time of their contraction, with elements such as a distinctive gridded layout repeated from village to village.

The two main forest regions of Northamptonshire, Rockingham, and Salcey with Whittlewood, present very different pictures of desertion and shrinkage. The area south-east of Rockingham village itself, in the core of the forest, has few shrunken or deserted settlements among its nucleated villages. In contrast in Salcey and Whittlewood, a much more dispersed settlement pattern, characterised by frequent interrupted rows and 'end' place-names, contains a high proportion of shrunken places and several deserted ones. Many of these are very small and appear to be the remains of farmsteads and green-edge settlements.[27] A distinct pattern of very small, shrunken settlements, including Foscote, Wood Burcote, Caldecote, Duncote and Heathencote, occurs in the area around Towcester and appears also to form part of the dispersed settlement pattern. The 'cote' place-name element present in most of these settlements suggests their secondary or subsidiary status.

Leicestershire and Rutland

Settlement shrinkage and desertion in Leicestershire is especially widespread in the east and south, and least common around Charnwood and in the valleys of the Soar and its tributaries (Fig. 4.15). The greatest number of deserted and shrunken settlements occurs in eastern High Leicestershire, incorporating the old county of Rutland. Across much of this region, there is scarcely a single village which does not contain physical evidence of considerable contraction. Parishes such as Leighfield and Noseley are now 'empty' in that they contain no occupied settlements beyond one or two farms. In contrast with north Bedfordshire, most deserted settlements in this region lie centrally within their townships, surrounded by the remains of their own field systems, and most of these settlements had names which appear in Domesday Book, including Bescaby, Sysonby, Baggrave and Keythorpe (all Leics). Some deserted settlements lie on parish or township boundaries such as those at the point where Pickworth (Leics), Horne and Great Casterton (Rutland) meet, or at the junction of the boundaries of Whissendine, Ashwell and Langham (all Rutland), suggesting that peripheral settlements were, as elsewhere, vulnerable to decay.

Deserted and shrunken settlements appear less commonly in the river valleys. In the Soar valley, very few settlements are completely deserted, although Prestwold is one exception. Sites of abandoned settlement occur less often in the Wreake valley than in High Leicestershire and the Wolds, although there is one cluster of such sites around Melton Mowbray, and one of deserted and shrunken sites in Rutland around Stamford. Abandoned sites are much less common in the west of the county, and are almost entirely absent from Charnwood. The settlement pattern is much more confused here than in the nucleated east, and there is a larger number of small settlements. Indeed some only appear in the documents as late as the fifteenth or sixteenth century.

Patterns of desertion in the east midlands

Deserted and extensively shrunken settlements are concentrated in areas of nucleation, particularly the major river valleys, and on the limestone plateaux of Northamptonshire and Leicestershire. In Northamptonshire, archaeological evidence for contraction has been noted in 64 per cent of all recorded medieval settlements. In Bedfordshire, Buckinghamshire and Leicestershire, all of which contain larger areas of dispersed settlement, the figures are 33, 33, and 41 per cent respectively. Northamptonshire also has the highest percentage of deserted and very shrunken settlements, at 24 per cent of the total. In the other counties the proportion ranges from 15 per cent to 19 per cent. In particular regions of dispersed settlement, like the Chilterns and Charnwood, few deserted and shrunken

Figure 4.15 Aerial photograph of the shrunken village at Burton Overy, Leicester-shire. Although a village still exists at Burton Overy, it is surrounded on all sides by rectangular enclosures and holloways indicating that it has lost a high proportion of its inhabited houses since the peak of its development in the middle ages. It was a large place, with thirty-four households in 1086 and more than forty in the late fourteenth century. Some shrinkage occurred between 1381 and the mid-sixteenth century, by which time the number of households had fallen to thirty-two.

settlement sites are recorded. How do we explain the vulnerability of nucleated settlements to desertion or very extensive contraction?

Desertion and nucleation

In eastern Leicestershire and Rutland, and north-west Northamptonshire, all of the settlements in many townships were almost wholly abandoned, and most surviving villages show evidence of contraction. Here population decline or displacement must have been much more severe than in the southern counties, even to the point of catastrophe, and much of eastern Leicestershire even today is very thinly populated. To some extent this is easily explained in terms of the economic and social stress of the fourteenth and fifteenth centuries: the drop in population following plague epidemics in 1348–9 and subsequent outbreaks; agrarian crises caused by a switch from cereal growing to pasture; internal strains within communities short of labour and threatened by the ambitions of a few better-off yeoman farmers; and depopulation by lords wishing to turn arable land into sheep pasture (see chapter 5 below). But only a minority of villages was deserted totally, while others suffered varying degrees of contraction. Evidently some factors rendered some settlements more vulnerable to depopulation than others.

Extensively shrunken or deserted settlements are generally less common in the main river valleys than in the other areas where nucleation predominates. While many villages in river valleys have some evidence for shrinkage, it is rarely extensive, and very few were totally deserted. Although regular row settlements are more common in river valleys, and clustered agglomerations occur more frequently in other districts with nucleated villages, there is no statistical correlation between clustered nucleations and settlement contraction. Geographical location counted for more than settlement form in this: river valleys are inherently less likely to experience sustained shrinkage, having been favoured for sustained settlement at all periods, at least from late prehistory. A combination of advantages, such as in soils and communications, has attracted settlers and discouraged emigration. The enduring pull of the riverside environment helped to insulate these villages from adverse trends in the later middle ages.

Four other patterns in the distribution of deserted settlements can be observed. The first concerns the incidence of deserted or shrunken settlements around market towns, even in the river valleys, where deserted settlements are otherwise generally scarce. The Ouse valley has very few very shrunken or deserted settlements, except around Bedford, where the shrunken settlements of Elstow, Medbury and Harrowden all lie less than 3km (2 miles) from the town. A similar pattern is notable around Buckingham and Newport Pagnell in Buckinghamshire, Oundle and Towcester in Northamptonshire, Loughborough and Melton Mowbray in Leicestershire. Perhaps outward migration from the villages was intensified by the 'pull' of the nearby towns or, as some of these towns were in decline at this time, the town and its surrounding villages and hamlets could have shrunk together. Whichever factor was at work, the pattern emphasises the interdependence of towns and rural settlements and the likely role of migration in settlement history.

A second pattern is the tendency for the more important and larger settlements to escape desertion. In most areas settlements recorded in Domesday Book are less likely to be shrunken than others. This is not to imply that the earliest settlements were the most enduring, because many places that were in existence in the eleventh century do not appear in the survey. Rather, it suggests that a place carrying the name of the manor is likely to have been an administrative centre and to have had some importance within the settlement hierarchy which protected it from decline.

A third tendency, which follows from the second, was for the less favoured villages to be vulnerable to desertion. The 1334 tax assessments show that villages that were eventually deserted each paid on average about half the level of tax of all villages. For example, in Leicestershire the average tax quota was 47s. per village, but the assessment for the villages that would later be deserted was only 26s.[28] The villages that were later to be deserted even appear smaller than those that survived at the time of Domesday. The subsidiary settlements, the smaller villages, the poorer villages, were all more vulnerable to desertion or severe shrinkage.

A fourth tendency to be noted is the correlation between deserted or very shrunken nucleated villages and geology. It is immediately striking that 42 per cent (123 out of 291) of all recorded deserted and very shrunken villages lie on or adjacent to boulder clay: 22 per cent lie *exclusively* on boulder clay. Superficial comparison of these figures with those for other geological formations suggests that the presence of boulder clay, with the heavy, unmanageable soils which it tends to produce, must have been the major factor in the failure of these settlements. However, closer examination suggests that this conclusion is unduly simplistic because very few deserted medieval villages occur on either Oxford or Gault clay, both of which tend to produce soils which are even less tractable than boulder clay. In addition, if recorded settlements of all types (nucleated, dispersed, deserted, populated) are taken into the equation, a very different pattern becomes apparent. Of all recorded settlements which lie solely on boulder clay, 21 per cent are deserted, as are 23 per cent on upper oolitic limestone. Only 7 per cent of recorded settlements lying solely on Oxford clay are deserted or very shrunken. These figures suggest that it is not heavy soils, or even the environment of the cold limestone wolds, which precipitated a village towards terminal contraction.

Desertion and dispersed landscapes

Very few deserted and shrunken settlements are recorded in areas of dispersed settlement. This partly reflects the problems of identifying and interpreting the evidence. Deserted hamlets and farmsteads are hard to find, using either archaeological or historical evidence. The earthworks of a single toft which can be as small as 60m by 60m (200ft by 200ft), rarely stand out well either from aerial photographs or on the ground. Large villages tend to produce very pronounced earthworks, with deep holloways incised by the passage of many people, carts and animals, which are less likely to form around a place inhabited by only one or two families. If the land is now cultivated, the dispersed settlements ought to be discoverable from pottery scatters, but these tend to cover only a small patch of ground, and they are not easily distinguished from the effects of manuring. Documents tend not to mention each individual farmstead, and so sites cannot be noticed as easily as deserted villages which will appear in, and disappear from, tax lists or manorial surveys. These problems of discovery are by no means insuperable, if researchers are prepared to examine individual parishes very closely, literally field by field, and to use good series of documents with a high level of topographical detail such as deeds and manorial court rolls.

Despite the deficiencies in the evidence, we can tentatively conclude that dispersed settlements seem to have suffered less desertion than nucleated villages. Desertion in the nucleated regions like eastern Leicestershire could leave a township or parish completely empty, apart from a single farm or two; in dispersed areas the individual units were more self-sufficient, not being closely tied into large communal field systems, and whereas villages shrank to a critically small size at which they no longer formed a viable community, the people of small settlements were less interdependent. Therefore dispersed communities might be greatly thinned, but the whole township rarely went into a terminal collapse. They were also more likely to be reoccupied. Once a village's fields had been converted into an enclosed sheep pasture, there could be no question of the village's revival. The vested interest of the farmer, or grazier, lay in specialised pastoral agriculture. In an area of dispersed settlements, the abandoned holdings could more easily be reoccupied or new houses created on wastes or roadsides as the fortunes of agriculture or levels of population revived in the late fifteenth and sixteenth century. At an earlier date, some of the people settling in the regions of dispersed settlement may have been refugees from depopulated villages.

Conclusion

The archaeological evidence, above all the earthwork remains, confirms that the early nineteenth-century maps of then surviving villages and hamlets are a useful guide to the form of medieval settlement. The frontiers between nucleated villages and dispersed settlements did not change greatly between the later middle ages and the nineteenth century. The study of the medieval evidence, combined with that from more recent maps, confirms the view that while a broad distinction between nucleated and dispersed settlements provides a useful aid to analysis, there were many intermediate and complex forms which do not fall readily into one category or another. These exceptions are found everywhere, like the isolated moated sites found in districts otherwise dominated by large nucleated villages.

Despite these qualifications, the impression may be given from the comparison between medieval and modern settlements that we are studying stable and conservative phenomena. In fact the analysis of the archaeology of deserted sites and the topography of surviving villages demonstrates the complexity of their history, with many additions and reorganisations during their period of development, and above all the widespread shrinkage and total abandonment of the later medieval centuries. This tells us not just about the tendency for settlements to change, but also about their vulnerability, or capacity for survival. The higher-status settlements were least likely to succumb, and the small and poor places were apparently the first to go. However those located on the supposedly inhospitable clays were not deserted in especially large numbers, which seems to tell us that settlement of the clays may not have been the last resort of a land hungry peasantry. Most important of all, the survival of many small settlements must tell us something of the resilience and adaptability of the dispersed settlements, when they were tested by the crises of the later middle ages.

Notes

1 For these early nucleations see notes 66 and 67 in chapter 3 above. A lack of regularity has been noted at Tattenhoe in Buckinghamshire, R. A. Croft and D. C. Mynard, *The Changing Landscape of Milton Keynes* (Aylesbury,

Buckinghamshire Archaeological Society, 5, 1993), pp. 159–64; for Dodford, G. R. Elvey (ed.), *Luffield Priory Charters, vol. 2* (Northamptonshire Record Society, 26, 1975), p. 2.

2   Royal Commission on Historical Monuments, England, *Archaeological Sites in North-West Northamptonshire* (London, Her Majesty's Stationery Office, 1981), pp. 49–50, 59–60, 138–42, 159–61, 175–7, 189–91 and 199–201.

3   C. C. Taylor, 'Medieval market grants and village morphology', *Landscape History*, 4 (1982), 21–8; RCHME, *Archaeological Sites in Central Northamptonshire* (London, Her Majesty's Stationery Office, 1979), pp. 126–30.

4   RCHME, *Central Northants*, pp. 99–101.

5   RCHME, *North-West Northants*, pp. 22–3, 111–13 and 182–7.

6   R. F. Hartley, *The Medieval Earthworks of North-East Leicestershire* (Leicester, Leicestershire Museums, Art Galleries and Records Service Archaeological Report Series, 88, 1987), pp. 9, 14–15, 30 and 44; R. F. Hartley, *The Medieval Earthworks of Central Leicestershire* (Leicester, Leicestershire Museums, Arts and Records Service Archaeological Reports Series, 103, 1989), pp. 8, 16.

7   RCHME, *North-West Northants*, pp. 54–7.

8   *Ibid.*, pp. 184–6.

9   Royal Commission on Historical Monuments, England, *An Inventory of Archaeological Sites in North-East Northamptonshire* (London, Her Majesty's Stationery Office, 1995), p. 50.

10 Information on these and other sites derived from the county SMR.

11 Hartley, *North-East Leics*, pp. 15 and 37.

12 A. E. Brown, 'Field survey at Grafton Regis: a village plan explained', *Landscape History*, 13 (1991), 73–7.

13 A. Mawer and F. M. Stenton, *The Place-names of Bedfordshire* (Cambridge, English Place Name Society, 1926), pp. 60–1.

14 RCHME, *An Inventory of Archaeological Sites in South-West Northamptonshire* (London, Her Majesty's Stationery Office, 1982), pp. 74–80.

15 A. E. Brown and C. C. Taylor, 'The origins of dispersed settlement: some results from fieldwork in Bedfordshire', *Landscape History*, 11 (1989), 60–81.

16 R. Ivens, P. Busby and N. Shepherd, *Tattenhoe and Westbury* (Buckinghamshire Archeological Society Monograph Series, no.8, 1995), pp. 213–15.

17 A. Aberg (ed.), *Medieval Moated Sites* (CBA Research Report, no. 17, 1978), pp. 1–4.

18 Of the abandoned moats, 33 per cent lie within 50m (55yd) of streams or rivers, compared with 17 per cent of moats in existing villages. H. E. J. Le Patourel, 'The excavation of moated sites', in Aberg (ed.), *Moated Sites*, pp. 40–1, discusses empty moats. C. C. Taylor, 'Moated sites: their definition, form and classification', in Aberg (ed.), *Moated Sites*, pp. 5–14, discusses sites such as rabbit warrens and gardens which have been in the past wrongly identified as moats.

19 B. K. Roberts, 'The historical geography of moated homesteads: the forest of Arden, Warwickshire', *Transactions of the Birmingham and Warwickshire Archaeological Society*, 88 (1976–7), 61–70 on new holdings, but for older origins, A. E. Brown and C. C. Taylor, *Moated Sites in Northern Bedfordshire* (Leicester, University of Leicester Department of Adult Education, Vaughan Paper no. 35, 1991).

20 RCHME, *North-West Northants*, p. 8; D. M. Wilson and D. G. Hurst, 'Medieval

Britain in 1968', *Medieval Archaeology*, 13 (1969), 270–3; D. M. Wilson and D. G. Hurst, 'Medieval Britain in 1969', *Medieval Archaeology*, 14 (1970), 191–3.

21 D. Willis (ed.), *The Estate Book of Henry de Bray* (Camden Society, 3rd Series, 27, 1916), pp. 23 and 108.

22 RCHME, *An Inventory of Archaeological Sites in North-East Northamptonshire* (London, Her Majesty's Stationery Office, 1975), pp. 106–11.

23 Ivens, Busby and Shepherd, *Tattenhoe and Westbury*, pp. 7–47.

24 RCHME, *North-East Northants*, pp. 33–4.

25 RCHME, *North-West Northants*, pp. 88–91.

26 Caldecotte (in Bow Brickhill parish) apparently did not have its own field system, although there is evidence for earlier occupation, iron age, Roman, and late Saxon: Croft & Mynard, *Milton Keynes*, pp. 61–70.

27 For example, Hartwell, RCHME, *South-West Northants*, pp. 74–80.

28 M. W. Beresford and J. G. Hurst (eds), *Deserted Medieval Villages* (London, Lutterworth Press, 1971), p. 23.

5

Historical evidence for settlement, society and landscape, *c.* 1066–1500

Population and wealth

Domesday Book shows that the four east midland counties in 1086 formed one of the more heavily populated parts of the country, but with lower densities of people than in parts of East Anglia and Kent.[1] Our counties had an average of 7.8 recorded people per square mile (3.1 per sq km), which can be taken to represent an actual population in excess of 35 per square mile (13.5 per sq km), assuming that each person listed was head of a household containing at least 4.5 members. We know that Domesday tends to omit certain categories of people: rent-paying tenants, for example, or specialists such as millers, so all figures must be taken to represent a minimum. There were significant variations within the area at local level ranging from 1 to about 16 recorded people per square mile (0.4–6.2 per sq km), perhaps from 5 people to over 70 (1.9–27 per sq km). Viewed county by county, Leicestershire and Rutland had the greatest density of population of the four with 8.1 recorded people per square mile, equivalent to 36 (3.2–13.9 per sq km) followed by Bedfordshire, Northamptonshire and Buckinghamshire (Fig. 5.1).

Within the counties, the area west of the Fosse Way in Leicestershire had an average of little more than 4 recorded people per square mile (1.5 per sq km), while the remaining two-thirds of the county to the east registered an average of 10 per square mile (3.9 per sq km). Throughout the study area populations tended to be higher in the east, largely due to the concentration of people in the major river valleys and in the other lower-lying areas, such as the Vales of Aylesbury and Belvoir. People were more thinly distributed on the higher ground, which is in the western part of the area, but also in north Bedfordshire, central Buckinghamshire and the Northampton Heights. The wooded upland regions supported the most sparse populations, notably Charnwood in western Leicestershire and the Chiltern Hills in southern Buckinghamshire, and in some parts of Whittlewood and Rockingham forests in Northamptonshire.

What were the effects of population growth in the two centuries after 1086? The next source after Domesday Book for the population of the whole area, the Poll Tax of 1377, was levied after both the substantial increase up to *c.* 1300 and the reduction following the harvest failures in the early fourteenth century, the Black Death of 1348–9 and successive plagues in the 1360s. The best sources from the time of the demographic peak around 1300 are surveys such as those of the Hundred Rolls, which contain lists of tenants from the royal inquest of 1279–80 for parts of Bedfordshire, Buckinghamshire and Leicestershire, and extents compiled for individual manors by landlords and the crown after the death of a tenant-in-chief. The lay subsidies of the late thirteenth and early fourteenth centuries give figures for single counties or at least substantial parts of counties.[2]

The surveys found in manorial records and the Hundred Rolls provide lists of tenants which can be compared with the numbers in Domesday Book. However just as Domesday omits categories of people, so the later surveys tell us little about sub-tenants, who might be mentioned but are not usually enumerated, and we do not know if all of the tenants were actually resident at the places where they held land.[3] Nor can we always be sure, with the changes in property such as the letting of sub-manors and the losses and gains in the land-market, that the manors of 1086 and *c.* 1300 covered the same amount of territory.

The Hundred Rolls for north-west Bedfordshire and north Buckinghamshire show that the numbers of tenants increased respectively by 130 per cent and 110 per cent, so the population of the villages more than doubled. In south-west Leicestershire the increase averaged 55 per cent, though with much variation; while Markfield, for example, had an increase in its tenants of more than tenfold, at some other places the number of tenants actually decreased between 1086 and 1279.

The most detailed population evidence around 1300 derives from manorial court rolls, based on a painstaking count of every person mentioned in the records. The courts met so frequently and regulated people's lives so comprehensively, that we can expect that most adult residents would be named over a five-year period. Bennett, from the court rolls of Brigstock in Rockingham Forest (Northants), has calculated the male population for several decades either side of 1300. The numbers were growing steadily until a peak of 495 adult males in the 1310s, which could represent a total of 1,300 men, women and children, after which it declined to 394 adult males on the eve of the Black Death. Brigstock's population could have been six times the figure for 1086.[4] Figures have also been calculated from the court rolls of Iver (Bucks) on the edge of

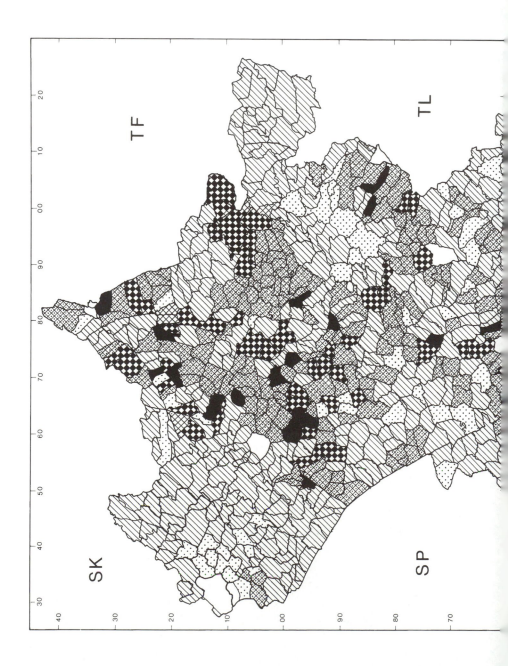

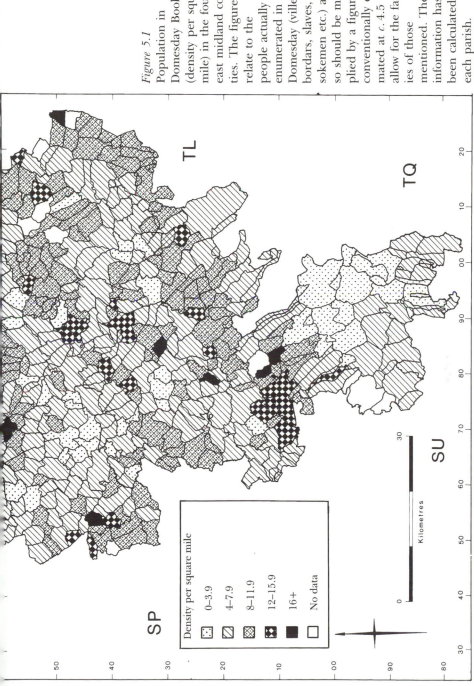

Figure 5.1
Population in Domesday Book (density per square mile) in the four east midland counties. The figures relate to the people actually enumerated in Domesday (villeins, bordars, slaves, sokemen etc.) and so should be multiplied by a figure conventionally estimated at *c.* 4.5 to allow for the families of those mentioned. The information has been calculated for each parish.

Density per square mile

- 0–3.9
- 4–7.9
- 8–11.9
- 12–15.9
- 16+
- No data

Kilometres

0   30

SP   TL

SU   TQ

the Chilterns, where in the 1330s the population has been estimated at 454 adult males, giving a total of 1,200 people, at least five times the Domesday figure.[5] However, the rate of increase between 1086 and 1300 over the four counties as a whole must have been rather less than in these manors, particularly in view of the great quantity of woodland clearance at Brigstock, and it may be that the method of calculation in *c.* 1300 exaggerates the population somewhat by including some non-residents who appear in the manorial court rolls.

The 1377 poll tax allows us to count the numbers of tax-payers, as it was levied at a standard rate of 4*d.* on everyone over the age of fourteen. It provides perhaps the most reliable indication of the rural population, as relatively small numbers of people were excluded, though the amount of evasion is inevitably uncertain. The tax reveals an average density of 39.7 tax-payers per square mile (15.3 per sq km) across the four counties as a whole, an actual population density of about 80 per square mile (30.9 per sq km); this is double the figure for 1086.[6] Of the individual counties, Bedfordshire had the highest density of population with 43.6 tax payers per square mile (16.8 per sq km), followed by Northampton-shire, Leicestershire and Rutland, and Buckinghamshire, the latter having a density of 33.1(12.8 per sq km).[7] By 1377, Bedfordshire had become the second most densely populated county in the whole of England after Norfolk, but in fact the greatest increase is found in Northamptonshire where the population had more than doubled. The differences presum-ably arose mainly from the growth before the Black Death, and we can assume that between 1086 and *c.* 1300 population expansion was greater in Bedfordshire and Northamptonshire than in the other two counties, and that the overall increase lay in the region of three or four times.

If we turn from population to general economic development, a useful source is the 1334 subsidy which was based on assessments of the value of moveable goods.[8] These had been calculated for each household in the thirteenth and early fourteenth centuries, but in 1334 it was decided to negotiate a lump sum with each village, taking note of earlier detailed assessments, and to leave the community to divide up the payment among themselves. The resulting tax quotas are generally regarded as a useful indication of relative prosperity, and the tax has the great virtue of covering the whole country in a comprehensive and standardised fashion (Fig. 5.2). In 1334 the major river valleys had consistently high densities of wealth, among them the Nene valley which stands out as having a higher tax assessment than the surrounding countryside. In Bedfordshire the river valleys are less distinct, as if during the expansion of the twelfth and thirteenth centuries regions such as the Vale of Bedford had caught up with the well-favoured fertile river valley. The Soke of Peterborough, which had benefited from the reclamation of the Fens, provides another example of a strong increase in fortunes since 1086.

In spite of the expansion on to new land and general growth in intensity of land use, the districts with low densities of wealth in 1334 are the same areas which showed up as underdeveloped in 1086, notably the woodlands, particularly Charnwood and the Chilterns, and on a smaller scale Bernwood and Leighfield forests. The taxable wealth of Rockingham and Whittlewood forests was not exceptionally low, suggesting an impressive amount of development since 1086. As a further indication of the expansion which had favoured the previously underdeveloped districts, the differences between the areas of highest and lowest population were narrower in the fourteenth century than in 1086. The percentage increases between 1086 and 1377 were by far the greatest in those areas where population had been least dense, ranging above 200 per cent, while districts of relatively high population had increased by about 60 per cent, so the growth of the twelfth and thirteenth centuries had helped to close a gap.

Agriculture and land use

In the east midlands, as in the rest of England, Domesday reveals a fairly consistent correlation between the density of population and the intensity of arable exploitation, as indicated by the numbers of plough teams. A density of 3–4 ploughs per square mile (1–1.5 per sq km) would imply that about half of the land was under cultivation, if each plough is reckoned to have been able to cope with about 100 acres (40ha) each year. Such densities are found in eastern Leicestershire and Rutland, the Nene valley in Northamptonshire, central Buckinghamshire and most of Bedfordshire (Fig. 5.3). The coincidence between the distribution of population and ploughs indicates the primary importance of grain production in the region.

As might be expected, the woodland recorded in Domesday Book shows an inverse correlation with both population and plough teams.[9] The districts with greater density of woodland, most notably south Buckinghamshire (including the Chilterns), south and eastern Bedfordshire, south-western and north-eastern Northamptonshire (the areas of the later royal forests of Whittlewood and Rockingham) and eastern Leicestershire and Rutland (the location of Leighfield/Rutland Forest) all had both fewer people and fewer ploughs.

However the Domesday woodland does not provide a full indication

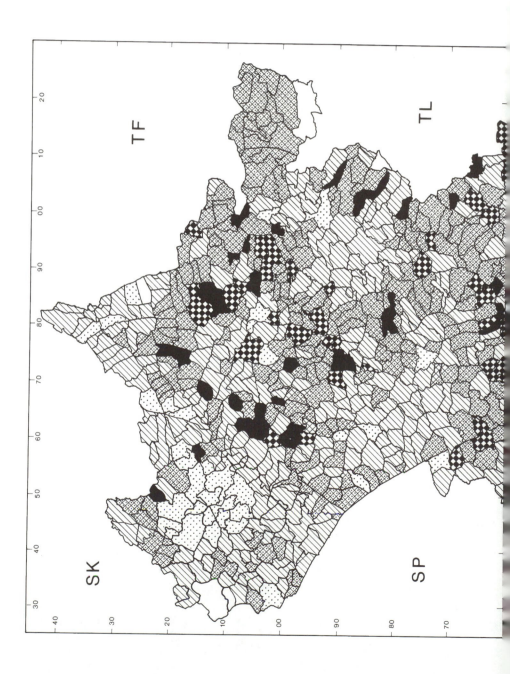

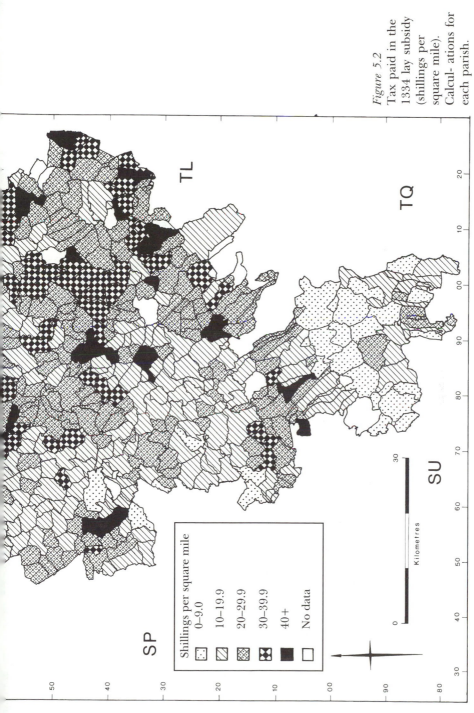

Shillings per square mile

⠿	0–9.0
▨	10–19.9
▩	20–29.9
▦	30–39.9
■	40+
☐	No data

SP

TL

TQ

SU

0   30
Kilometres

Figure 5.2
Tax paid in the
1334 lay subsidy
(shillings per
square mile).
Calcul- ations for
each parish.

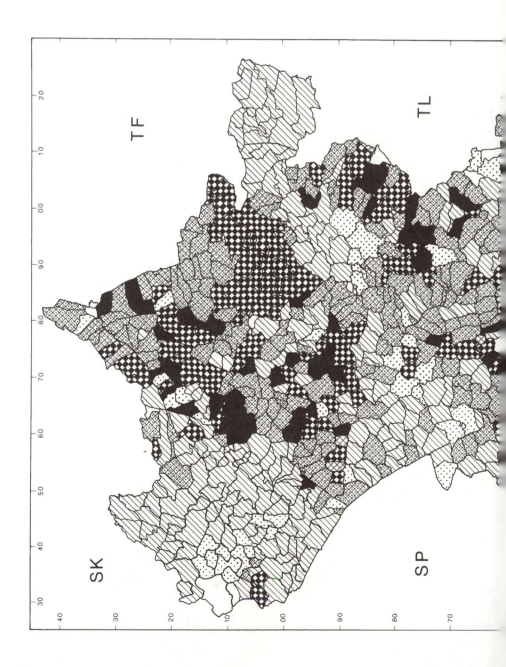

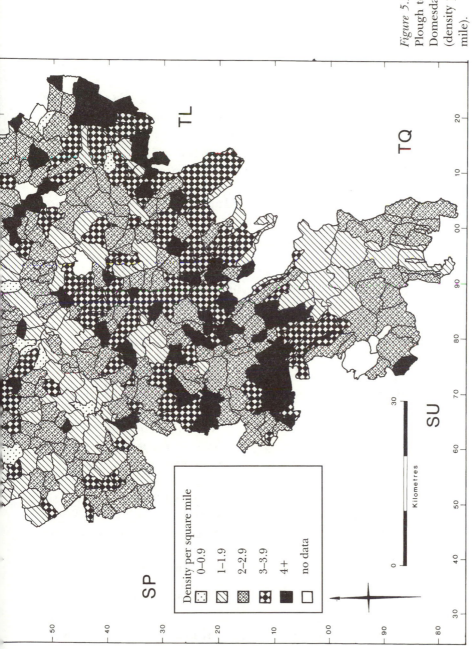

Figure 5.3
Plough teams in
Domesday Book
(density per square
mile).

of uncultivated land in 1086. The thinly populated Charnwood and Northampton Heights, which are known to have retained extensive areas of grazing land in the later middle ages, have little or no woodland reported in the Domesday survey. This is partly because they lacked tree cover, and were occupied by heaths or moors. Another reason for under-recording of these territories is that Domesday was focused on the manorial assets which generated income for their lords. Thus wastes and woodland in common use, and which were not under direct control, lay outside the survey's vision.

Woods and wastes provided valuable resources, especially for pasture, and the potential of woodland to support animals is made especially clear in the Domesday convention (used in Bedfordshire and Buckinghamshire) of measuring woods by the number of pigs that they could feed. The hundreds, sometimes thousands, of pigs mentioned show that some communities had a significant involvement in this branch of animal husbandry. These places had similar ratios of population to ploughs as in districts with little woodland, suggesting that pastoralism was not so much an alternative to arable, but complementary to it.

The two centuries after 1086 saw extensive clearances of wood and cultivation of waste; a process that was no doubt linked to the rapid growth in population at that time, creating a need (and providing a pool of labour) to expand cultivation. Assarting is documented throughout the four counties, but much valuable evidence comes from the records of the royal forests, especially the judicial enquiries into the breaches of forest law: offences against the 'vert' – removing vegetation for agriculture – were regulated, as they eroded the cover for the beasts of the chase.

In the early thirteenth century, clearances which offended against forest law are recorded at more than sixty places in Whittlewood and Salcey forests, at a similar number of places in Rockingham Forest, and in a further twenty or so in Leighfield/Rutland Forest.[10] The acreages of assarts in Rockingham, Salcey and Whittlewood forests between *c.* 1200 and *c.* 1350 total more than 6,000 acres (2,400ha).[11] These account for a relatively small proportion of the many square miles covered by these forests, but these figures do not account for all the assarting, which sometimes took place by permission. While most of the individual assarts consisted of just a few acres (though cumulatively such parcels amounted to a considerable area), much larger areas of clearance are occasionally recorded. For example, at Rushton in the forest of Rockingham 500 acres (200ha) of assarts are mentioned, an area of about one quarter of the entire parish.[12]

The figures from the records of the forest courts begin in the thirteenth century, but substantial clearance had already taken place before this. In

1189 Peterborough Abbey was granted permission to clear 400 acres (160ha) in one place in the forest at Oundle. In the Soke of Peterborough, then part of the same forest, royal charters indicate the clearance of at least 2,000 acres (800ha) under the same abbey between the mid-twelfth century and 1216, most of it confined to the west of that district.[13]

Outside the royal forests the process of reclamation appears more patchily in grants of assarts in charters, lists of assarts in manorial surveys, and records of field or furlong names, such as 'brech', 'stubbing' and 'redding'. At Cranfield in Bedfordshire 450 acres (180ha) of assarts were recorded in the second half of the thirteenth century.[14] At Kensworth on the edge of the Chilterns, a survey of 1222 lists more than 290 acres (120ha) of assarts as well as others of unspecified size.[15] A similar scale of clearance seems to be indicated at Groby (western Leicestershire) where, in an Inquisition Post Mortem survey of 1288, assized rents of recent assarts in Charnwood totalled £7 5s. 2d.[16] Numerous incidental references to assarts or clearance demonstrate the large scale of reclamation in Charnwood and the Chilterns, and also on the lower greensand ridge of central Bedfordshire and Leicester Forest.[17]

Villages with the largest clearances in the twelfth to fourteenth centuries have above average population growth in the same period, as at Cranfield. Population expansion also occurred in districts which lacked the room for growth, with large numbers of people and little or no woodland recorded in 1086. Without the ability to expand the area of cultivation by clearing woods, increasing pressure on existing resources led to the more intensive use of land. Elsewhere this can be seen in the reduction of the extent and frequency of fallow, the introduction of new crops such as legumes, as an alternative means of feeding livestock and restoring soil fertility, and a more systematic use of manure and marling. The replacement of the ox by the horse for pulling carts and ploughs also contributed to easier contacts with the market, and faster cultivation.[18]

Technical innovations were not confined to areas of high densities of population. Some of the best indications of 'improving' agricultural methods come from the Chilterns,[19] where population was always more thinly spread, and where even in the thirteenth century a good proportion of the countryside lay in rough pastures. Here the managers of demesnes took special measures to marl and manure the soil, used horses rather than oxen, and practised forms of convertible husbandry by which arable was turned over to pasture periodically to recover heart. This could be explained by pressure on good arable land, which was intense in a district of generally poor soils. Surveys of the late thirteenth and fourteenth centuries consistently give a lower value to arable in Chiltern manors than

comparable documents in the major river valleys.[20] Evidently the uncultivated areas were of such poor quality or so inaccessible that they were
useless as arable. An alternative explanation of the innovative methods
of the Chilterns could be that the lack of population pressure gave the
cultivators the breathing space to experiment and try out alternative
techniques; and also that the region was stimulated to produce more, not
by the burden of excess people, but by the demands of the nearby London
market.

'Improving' practices in the thirteenth and fourteenth century may not
always have achieved the desired effect in the long term. On the greensands of central Bedfordshire, an area of poor soil, in spite of considerable
cultivation of legumes, land was frequently valued at a low level comparable to that of the Chilterns, and according to the complaints to the tax
assessors in 1341 the soil was often only good for growing poorer grains
like rye, and was very quick to lose its fertility in adverse conditions.[21] As
this inquiry makes clear, this was an area where land was quickly abandoned even before the Black Death.

Field systems and agrarian organisation

Much medieval agriculture in the four counties was organised in the
common field system, known as the 'midland system', which is distinguished by the regularity of its layout and rotations.[22] Detailed evidence
of both its operation, and in particular detailed maps of fields, furlongs
and strips, come from the sixteenth, seventeenth and eighteenth century.
However, key features of the system were in place by the twelfth and
thirteenth centuries.

In the midland system a community of cultivators held their arable
land in intermixed narrow strips. Adjacent strips were grouped into
furlongs, which themselves were brought together into two or three large
fields of approximately equal size. In many instances the arable lay in
almost continuous tracts over most of a parish or township, with other
resources such as meadow, woodland and permanent pasture being located on its fringes (Fig. 5.4). The operation of the system was based on
the community's disciplined cultivation and regular fallowing of fields
according to a cycle. Each cultivator's holding consisted of strips of land
divided approximately equally between the fields, to ensure that the same
proportion of land could be cropped in each year. Thus at Wolverton
(Bucks) in the early thirteenth century a half-yardland holding of 16 acres
(6.4ha) was described as consisting of 8 acres in the west field and 8 acres
in the east field.[23] Each cultivator only ploughed and planted the strips

Figure 5.4 Aerial photograph showing extensive ridge and furrow at Frisby, Leicestershire, enclosed in the seventeenth century. The large cultivated area is dramatically displayed by this view of a part of a field system. Notice the windmill mounds in the bottom right-hand corner. The modern farm has been built over the abandoned field system. The enclosure hedges have been planted on boundaries between furlongs in the original field system, helping to preserve its original subdivisions.

of his or her holding, but had common rights of pasture over entire fields after they had been harvested and when they lay fallow. The cultivators also had common rights of grazing on the permanent pasture, haymaking in the meadow, and were able to take fuel from the woodland.

The operation of the whole system was regulated by the community, either through a manorial court or by a separate meeting, which issued by-laws. Recorded examples of these show particular concern over the regulation of pasturing rights, laying down the precise times of year when animals could be placed on the various parts of common land, and the number of animals that each tenant could graze there. The midland system involved a complex package of rights and obligations, and depended on a delicate balance of individual and communal interests, maintained by self-discipline, neighbourly pressure and the ultimate sanction of the court.

Frequently in the midland field systems, arable accounted for as much as nine-tenths of the village territory, and represented a productive asset of overwhelming importance for the villagers. No doubt the shared interests in the fields provided the community with its sense of identity and cohesion; and running the fields, electing officers, and disciplining wrong-doers gave the village the experience of administration that could be applied to tax collecting and other functions of government.

Post-medieval field systems

It is only between 1500 and 1800 that we have a large sample of evidence for types of field system. The largest proportion of places had three common fields organised in a regular fashion. Two fields were sometimes in use, but there was also a significant minority of places where there were more than three, mostly ranging from four to ten, but occasionally as high as forty-nine. Bedfordshire had by far the largest proportion of cases of such multiple fields, where in the eighteenth century only 8 per cent of vills for which there is evidence had three fields, all others having more. In Northamptonshire, however, in the sixteenth to nineteenth centuries, 53 per cent of our examples had three fields, 42 per cent having more, and comparable figures are found in Buckinghamshire, and Leicestershire and Rutland.

How was agriculture organised in a village with multiple fields? One answer is that fields were grouped for cultivation and fallowing into 'seasons', sometimes three in number, so they closely resembled regular three-field villages in their agricultural methods. This is recorded in Bedfordshire and southern Buckinghamshire. However this still differed from the regular systems in that the fields were often not adjacent, and the groupings were impermanent and might be changed from year to year.[24] This allowed greater flexibility in cropping, and could exist in conjunction with extensive areas of land lying in closes. Enclosed land could be subject to rights of common pasture when fallow, but was usually in the hands of an individual or a small group of cultivators. Again, such land could be cropped with considerable flexibility. The agrarian organisation of the irregular field systems had a collective aspect, in that grazing was still regulated by the community, but common rights were not as restricted as under the midland system, and the number of closes gave greater scope for individualism.

Medieval field systems

Some villages with a multiplicity of common fields in the sixteenth and seventeenth centuries may have changed from a more regular 'midland' system which had two or three fields before 1500. Indeed 90 per cent of villages for which we have evidence in the twelfth and thirteenth centuries had two-field systems (Fig. 5.5). Most of these lay in southern and eastern Bedfordshire, central and northern Buckinghamshire and western Northamptonshire. Three-field systems are recorded less frequently before 1300, but have been found widely scattered across the four counties, most frequently in northern Bedfordshire and northern Buckinghamshire. These three-field arrangements are often recorded in or around woodland environ- ments, although two-field systems are also found in the same landscape. It was once believed that all three-field systems evolved out of the two-field systems as communities felt pressurised by growing population to reduce the amount of land under fallow from a half to a third. Well-documented examples of such changes are, however, rare and it is now argued that the two- and three-field systems developed together, and that the preference of villages for two rather than three fields depended on complex calculations of the number of animals to be kept on the fallow, and the yields of grain. In our area, however, the high proportion of three-field systems recorded after 1500 compared with earlier evidence of their relative rarity, suggests some change from two to three fields, though in unknown circumstances.

In many vills numerous common fields or other elements of irregular organisation are recorded in the twelfth to fourteenth centuries. These are found in the Chilterns and in central and northern Bedfordshire, on the clay plateau north of the Ouse, in the vale to its south, and on the ridge of lower greensand that bisects the county.[25] In Bedfordshire the irregular systems of the middle ages coincide approximately in their distribution with the post-medieval occurrence of multi-field systems.

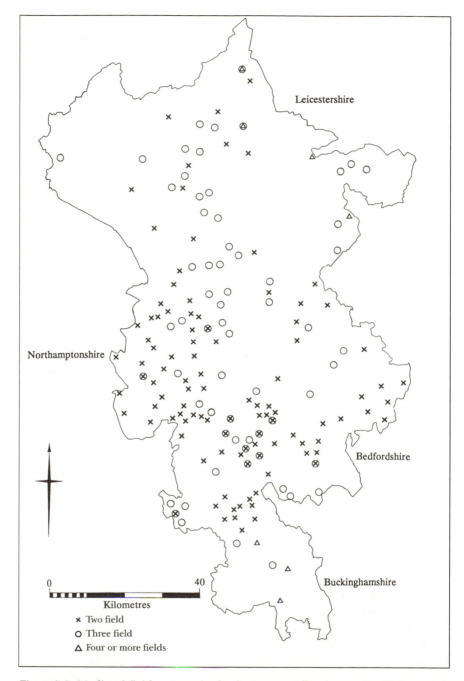

Figure 5.5 Medieval field systems in the four east midland counties. This records all known documentary references which allow the type of field system to be identified, dating from the period before 1500.

Often the irregular fields were associated with the districts with many dispersed settlements.

Origins of field systems

Irregular field systems are often found in districts with substantial amounts of uncleared land, whereas the two- and three-field townships were often those where cultivation had extended by the thirteenth century (or earlier) over most of their territories. The absence of sufficient resources of permanent pasture has been assumed to have forced communities to take maximum advantage of the temporary pasture of the fallow field.[26] Regular fallowing was necessary to restore soil fertility when ample supplies of manure were not available – the land was rested, and received manure directly as the animals grazed. A large fallow area required everyone in the village to agree to leave their adjacent lands uncultivated at the same time, thereby introducing the discipline of cultivation in rotation. However a regular arrangement of fields is sometimes found associated with ample areas of permanent pasture, like Harrold in north-west Bedfordshire, a two-field village where the demesne in the early fourteenth century had 100 acres (40ha) of pasture, and presumably the peasants also had access to ample grazing. Regular field systems in association with extensive pasture resources are also found in Bernwood and Rockingham, the Northampton Heights and Charnwood and Leicester forests.[27]

One of the few early medieval descriptions of changes to a field system relates to Segenhoe (Beds), in the twelfth century, in which a major concern in the rearrangement was that the land of the vill should be divided according to equal shares,[28] indicating the importance of the notion of fairness within the community. Everyone in a village with a midland system and with a standard holding – a yardland (*c.* 30 acres or 12ha) or half yardland – was given equal access to arable and pasture. The scattering of parcels resulted from a wish to allocate equal quantities of both good and bad land to each cultivator. It is therefore likely that the basis of the regular field systems lay only partly in practical consideration for dealing with a pasture shortage, but also in an idea of the best form of social organisation, which might be borrowed and imitated from one village to another.

The midland field system and the reorganisation of landscapes

Whether the impulse behind the adoption of midland field systems lay in economic necessity or the wish to engineer a more even distribution of resources (and the two are not mutually exclusive), everyone agrees that they involved a degree of conscious planning. However, the character and chronology of planning and reorganisation are still debated. On one hand it has been suggested that in Northamptonshire the midland systems were created around the ninth century.[29] Alternatively, it is argued that the origins of the system can be traced as far back as the seventh century and lay in a slower, evolutionary process, perhaps involving several stages of reorganisation, which may not have been completed in some villages until after 1200.[30]

All can agree that regular field systems are described in the twelfth century with strips of individual holdings distributed equally across two or three fields.[31] The debate really revolves around the analysis of later evidence, and interpretation of the likely route by which the fields developed to this point. In western and central Northamptonshire, detailed reconstructions of many field systems, through a combination of medieval and modern documents and maps, show a high degree of regularity. The strips of each holding are found to have been evenly distributed across all the furlongs of the field system, and to have followed a cycle, each tenant holding lands in strict order, with each of an individual's plots always adjoining those of the same neighbours. It is also possible to relate the number of standard yardland holdings to the fiscal assessment of the villages in hides, implying that the peasant tenements and their particular strips were allocated by some authority ruling over many villages. Great Billing (Northants), for example, was assessed for tax purposes at four hides, and would be expected to contribute to the geld, if it was levied at 2s. to the hide, a sum of 8s. The peasants of Great Billing are recorded in later documents as holding 48 yardlands, at a rate therefore of 12 yardlands to the hide. Conventionally the hide contained four yardlands, but the hides here are fiscal assessments, and the yardland relates to tenurial arrangements, and in Northamptonshire the fiscal hide seems to have been equated to ten or twelve tenurial yardlands.[32]

An alternative explanation of the regularity of the arrangements would lie in the reorganisation of field systems over the medieval centuries, so that the very systematic allocation of land recorded for the first time in the twelfth century (but, in more cases, at some time between the thirteenth and the eighteenth centuries) reflected the orderly minds of the administrators of a much later period than the pre-Conquest originators of the system.

There is evidence that a once regular system soon began to break down under pressures such as the land market and divided inheritance. Some strips of a holding may have the same neighbour, but never is this the case for all of them. Strips in most holdings have only a limited number of different neighbours, which may be evidence of former greater regularity which has been reduced by tenurial changes subsequent to the allocations of land. For example, at Irthlingborough (Northants) in the early four-teenth century a yardland of 25 acres (10ha) is described in 26 parcels: in six cases the adjoining land was held by John Godwyne, in another five by Richard Joye, in four others by Geoffrey Aunore and in the rest by other neighbours.[33] This suggests a cycle of deterioration in the order of the system, followed by a reimposition of regularity at intervals. There are instances elsewhere of such reorganisation having taken place in the late middle ages or in the modern period.[34]

Social structures and social organisation

Domesday Book classifies the population of our four counties into four main groups: villeins, bordars, sokemen and slaves, all in some way dependent on manors. The villeins are by far the most numerous, making up about 50 per cent of the recorded population, while the bordars account for about 30 per cent. Our current understanding of these two groups is that the villeins held a relatively large holding of a yardland (*c.* 30 acres or 12ha) or half yardland, while the bordars were smallholders typically with 5 acres (2ha) or so. They were subordinated to lords, and often owed labour services, but were not regarded as legally unfree. The other two social groups, the sokemen and the slaves, were defined in terms of legal status rather than the quantity of land that they held. The slaves were unfree, owned and controlled by their lords and working almost entirely for them. However, opinion is divided whether by 1086 the slaves were housed and fed by the lord, or had the use of at least a cottage.[35] Sokemen, on the other hand, were free, owing only light obligations to their lords.

Table 5.1: Analysis of Domesday population for the four east midland counties

county	villeins	bordars	slaves	sokemen	others	total
Beds	1,888	1,156	480	90	11	3,625
Bucks	2,901	1,314	842	20	18	5,095
Leics & Rutland	2,643	1,362	403	1,904	116	6,428
Northants	3,452	1,808	680	849	93	6,882
Total	10,884	5,640	2,405	2,863	238	22,030
	(49%)	(26%)	(11%)	(13%)	(1%)	(100%)

The proportions of villeins and bordars did not vary greatly across the whole area, though there might be some local concentrations of one type.

Distinct regional patterns can be discerned in the incidence of the other two groups. Sokemen are very rare in the two southerly counties: only 90 are recorded in Bedfordshire and 20 in Buckinghamshire, but more than 800 appear in Northamptonshire, representing about 12 per cent of the total recorded population, and in Leicestershire nearly 2,000, accounted for 30 per cent. In both of these counties sokemen were more numerous towards the east.

Slaves, conversely, occur in greater numbers in the two southern counties. In Buckinghamshire and Bedfordshire they account for 17 per cent and 13 per cent respectively of the recorded population, but considerably less in the northern counties. There are no places with populations entirely of slaves, but there are a few settlements, such as at Tingewick and Newport Pagnell (Bucks), where they account for more than 60 per cent of the total. The uncertainty about slaves' domestic arrangements means that we do not know whether to count them individually or as heads of households.

Slaves are conventionally assumed to have been workers on the demesne; male slaves seem to have served as ploughmen, as suggested by the consistent ratio between their numbers and those of demesne ploughs that has been found in many parts of the country.[36] This relationship is visible throughout our area, although there were plenty of places with demesne ploughs but no slaves. In Leicestershire in particular, nearly half of the manors provided with demesne ploughs lack slaves, while in Buckinghamshire that figure is only a tenth. In Leicestershire there must have been greater emphasis on other sources of demesne labour, either from the services of tenants, or from some form of hired work. Female slaves (57 are recorded in Northamptonshire, for example) may have worked as dairymaids.

Slavery seems to have been in decline in the eleventh century, and indeed had by then begun to disappear in the eastern part of the country, including the eastern districts of our area. Many of the bordars, and perhaps some of the sokemen, recorded in 1086 were former slaves, or the descendants of former slaves who, judging from their relatively small holdings, had been granted land by lords. This process by which slaves, who were dependants of the manor, were converted into peasants with houses and land which became their hereditary possessions, has a direct relevance to the problem of village origins. Lords allocating demesne land to ex-slaves must have made decisions as to whether to assign them a compact group of plots next to the manor house, or cottages scattered about the fields, thus propelling the settlement in a nucleated or dispersed direction. As we have seen, these decisions would not usually have determined the plan of the whole settlement, since slaves, at the time they are recorded in detail, represented a small minority of the population of most manors.

At the opposite end of the range of status among the peasantry are the sokemen. They are sometimes found living in groups on 'sokeland', without any demesne arable at all. In Northamptonshire forty-eight places, and in Leicestershire as many as eighty-four, had no demesne ploughs in 1086; these may in some cases be identified as 'sokeland', attached to a central manor, but often scattered over a considerable distance.[37] Although free, the bulk of sokemen were nevertheless clearly subject to lords but, as they were separated from the manorial demesne, they were not subject to heavy labour services. At Tilbrook in north Bedfordshire, the population in 1086 was almost entirely made up of a group of twenty sokemen and, although subject at that time to a Norman lord, before 1066 this manor had apparently been held by those same sokemen themselves.[38] Here, apparently, sokemen had been the lords of their own lands at least until the Conquest, and therefore presumably lay outside the conventional manorial regime. Some continental scholars would argue that the sokemen enjoyed a special relationship with the crown, and that their origins lie in the settlement of peasants by the state, in return for military services and the payment of taxes.[39] But this hypothesis is not supported by English evidence, and it would be best to regard the sokemen as privileged peasants, better able than others to exercise choice in the location and form of their villages or hamlets.

The villeins and the bordars cumulatively represented the main productive forces in eleventh-century society. Tenant ploughs accounted for around three-quarters of the total in the four counties, and this could rise locally, in the Chilterns, to as much as 80 per cent. Most of the beasts who pulled these implements were owned by the more substantial peasants, the villeins. We have seen that the archaeological evidence suggests that in districts of nucleated settlements, villages were forming or had formed in the eleventh century, and the villeins and bordars would have been the majority of the inhabitants of such places. A brave attempt to reconstruct the appearance of a village in 1086 has been made for Kibworth Harcourt (Leics).[40] Working backwards from an estate map and a good series of manorial records, the village plan of the fourteenth and fifteenth centuries can be drawn with a fair amount of certainty. More conjecturally, the various yardland and cottage tenements can be reconstructed for 1086, giving a two-row village with 10 holdings of villeins, 7 free tenants (being 6 sokemen and a 'frenchman') and 5 cottars, assumed to have been granted plots of demesne land. The problem with this method of reconstruction is that, rather like the use of later field evidence to reconstruct pre-Conquest strips and furlongs, it could have been upset by a complete replanning in, say, the twelfth century. The original Domesday settlement may have been an uncoordinated collection of houses, which may not even have been gathered together in a group.

Changes, 1086–1279

The Hundred Rolls of 1279–80 show that in the manors surveyed the proportion of demesne land is closely comparable to that implied by the numbers of demesne ploughs in Domesday Book, which might suggest a general continuity in manorial history. But a great many social and economic changes took place between 1086 and 1279. The Hundred Rolls use three main social categories: serfs, free tenants and cottars. Slaves had long disappeared. Some equivalence between the categories used in Domesday Book and those of the Hundred Rolls is suggested by places such as Walton, Cosby and Blaby (Leics) where sokemen predominated in 1086, and free tenants in 1279.[41] However legal and social developments in the twelfth and thirteenth centuries had made profound changes in peasant status.[42] The descendants of the former slaves had become servile peasants, both cottars and 'serfs', and a high proportion of the villeins were defined as servile. They were subject to the jurisdiction of their lords and owed a range of dues and services, including marriage fines and the annual payment of tallage. 'Villeinage' now became equated with servility. Some former sokemen were absorbed into the 'villein' category, so that at Willoughby Waterless (Leics), for example, despite a predominance of sokemen in 1086, there are very few free tenants and many more serfs in 1279.[43]

   While the category of unfree peasants expanded, and freedom was consequently defined more narrowly, at the same time the numbers of the free were growing from other directions. The process of colonisation of wood and waste in the twelfth and thirteenth centuries led to the creation of many new free tenures as lords were ready to attract settlers to their woods and wastes by conceding relatively privileged terms of tenure and modest rents and services.[44] We commonly find in our study area that assart land was held for money rent only. Peasants were sometimes clearing land on their own initiative, and developed a tradition of independence and freedom on which lords were unable to impose much discipline. As a consequence of these trends, the Hundred Rolls show a substantial proportion of land held in villeinage, 40 per cent, compared with about 28 per cent of the total in free tenure (the rest lay in demesne).[45]

But the small size of many freeholdings means that in any village the free tenants outnumbered the villeins.

Proportions of free and unfree peasants show much local variation in 1279. Serfdom predominates in Leicestershire, where the evidence relates to the south and west of the county, and likewise in the four northernmost hundreds of Buckinghamshire. The individual hundreds in the latter county differ significantly, with the hundred of Mursley showing a greater quantity of villein as compared with free land, but Bunsty and Stotfold both reveal slight majorities of free land. In far north-west Bedfordshire, there was more than twice as much free land as villein land. Individual villages such as Stevington, which had a clear majority of villein over free land, are in a minority.[46]

Surveys of individual manors of the late thirteenth and early fourteenth centuries can fill gaps in the Hundred Rolls. Those for Leicestershire show that the predominance of villein tenure was characteristic of other parts of the county besides the south and west.[47] In central and southern Bedfordshire the picture is more mixed, with some manors such as Chalgrave showing a predominance of free tenure, while others such as Kempston and Barton-in-the-Clay have a distinct preponderance of villeinage.[48] In Buckinghamshire the social structure of the southern part of the county, in particular the Chiltern Hills, was characterised by peasant free holders.[49] In Northamptonshire the surveys of church estates show a large numbers of servile holdings, but there were also some outposts where free tenure seems to have predominated, particularly in the east of the county, but also on occasion in the west, for example at Harlestone, a lay manor.[50]

Although areas with a predominance of villeinage might generally be expected to have experienced a more restrictive manorial regime than those with free tenants, the nature and scale of peasant obligations must also be taken into account. One of the most onerous burdens imposed on villeins was week-work, by which the tenant was expected to devote two, three or even more days each week to labour on the lord's demesne. This was required on a number of manors in Bedfordshire including those of Ramsey Abbey. However in Leicestershire this obligation seems to have been almost entirely absent.[51] As a result, despite the preponderance of villeinage in Leicestershire the services required of villeins seem to have been little heavier than those of some free tenants. Week-work also seems to have been absent from a number of manors in Bernwood Forest and the Chiltern Hills, in east and south Buckinghamshire, although it is found at some places in the Thames Valley in the extreme south of the county.[52]

Perhaps the absence of week-work on villein tenures in the late thirteenth or fourteenth centuries was the result of commutation of labour
services in exchange for money rents which is documented from the
twelfth century. However, the modest extent of manorial demesnes in
Leicestershire, both in the thirteenth century and in 1086, suggests that
such heavy labour service may always have been rare there.[53] In the
Hundred Rolls demesne land accounts for only 22 per cent of the total
in Leicestershire and in 1086 the county had the lowest proportion of
demesne ploughs of the four, at only 24 per cent. A tradition of demesne
agriculture on a limited scale may suggest a manorial economy that had
never needed, or perhaps had never been able, to command the more
extensive labour services of other areas, and one in which other types of
rent (above all money) had for a long time played a larger role. The
Chiltern Hills (another area where week-work is absent in the thirteenth
century), is also notable for the small proportions of demesne ploughs
found in Domesday Book.[54]

The extent to which peasants were under the control of their lords is
pertinent to the development of settlements in the twelfth and thirteenth
centuries, because in some cases nucleation may well have been taking
place within the period, and certainly expansion of all types of settlement
was underway. New rows or ends were added to nucleated villages, and
gaps in polyfocal villages were infilled; the extension of dispersed settlements involved the lengthening of interrupted rows, and the proliferation
of isolated farmsteads. We can envisage lords setting up servile tenants
in new holdings, and the peasants, both free and unfree, claiming land
for new houses, or subdividing existing tofts. The coincidence of free
tenure and dispersed settlements in the Chilterns provides the most
obvious correlation between social structure and settlements, but the
opposite situation, the coincidence between nucleated villages and serfdom, raises many problems to be discussed later.

Changes in yardland holdings

The yardland varied in size and even the acre itself might be based on
a local customary measure. The bulk of yardlands contained between 20
and 30 acres (8–12ha) of arable land but some extreme variations are
recorded, from 12 to 80 acres (5–32ha). As the yardland had been based
on the amount of land that could support a family, the size could have
depended on ecological factors such as quality of soil. This explanation
is supported by the tendency for yardlands in valleys to be smaller than
those on heavy clays or poor sandy soils; accordingly large yardlands are
known at Cranfield (Beds) and Harlestone (Northants).[55] Surveys listed

either 'standard' whole or half yardlands, or irregular tenements described in numbers of acres. Sibson (Leics), according to the survey of 1279–80, consisted simply of 28 yardland holdings. But at Sharnbrook (Beds), only a third of the holdings comprised whole, half or quarter yardlands while all the rest were described in terms of varying numbers of acres.[56]

The contrasts between standard and non-standard holdings to some extent coincides with the relative incidence of villein and free tenure. Standard holdings were above all held by serfs, while variable sized holdings are more common in free tenures; Sibson, for example, was dominated by villein tenure while Sharnbrook had more free holdings. It often appears that standard peasant holdings had once been predominant and that over time non-standard holdings became more numerous. A number of changes lay behind this process. Larger holdings were divided into half or quarter yardlands as the result of population growth and the consequent need to accommodate more people on the land. The peasant land market had developed in the thirteenth century, by which existing holdings also came to be fragmented by sale; lords were anxious to preserve if possible the integrity of the customary holding, as villeins' rents and services were levied on the basis of the standard units. There were no such inhibitions on free tenants, who could divide and sell their land as they wished, leading to tenements of many different sizes, often reduced to a minute holding of an acre or even less. The process of land clearance produced additional holdings of non-standard size such as at Caddington (Beds), thus accentuating the shift towards greater variability among free holdings, as asserts were usually held on free tenure.[57]

Whole yardlands were still numerous amongst thirteenth-century peasant holdings in Leicestershire, but in Bedfordshire and Buckinghamshire they are a rarity and far outnumbered by half or quarter yardlands. This more vigorous process of subdivision in the south may reflect both rapid population growth, and greater flexibility among lords who were prepared to accept subdivisions.

The local community

Not only were local populations organised in manors, they also belonged to communities bound to their neighbours by horizontal rather than vertical ties. Local communities or vills are often found acting in administrative roles, for example in assessing taxes (especially after 1334, when the village paid a lump sum) and in giving evidence or paying fines to the royal courts. They are also seen governing themselves by issuing by-laws, regulating agriculture and maintaining amenities such as roads.[58]

These activities show that local communities were fundamentally defined by their shared rights in the territory that they occupied.

The east midlands has some of the earliest recorded examples of by-laws, such as those for Newton Longville (Bucks), which were first committed to writing in 1290.[59] This class of evidence is rather more common in the east midlands than in much of the rest of the country, and it has been suggested that this may indicate a greater emphasis on the vill as a focus of organisation at an early date.[60] Although we know most about the by-laws which were issued in the lord's court, and therefore recorded in the court rolls, the status of the community as an entity separate from the manor, and capable of action independent of it, is clearly indicated by cases like Wymeswold (Leics) and Harlestone (Northants). In these villages, which were divided among a number of lords, by-laws and agreements about changes in the common fields were made by communities across manorial divisions.[61] The community clearly cut across distinctions of personal status and tenure.

In some cases the activities of communities went much further than the regulation of fields. From the early thirteenth century the community of Kingsthorpe (near Northampton) was itself the lessee of the royal manor and thus exercised all the rights and jurisdictions of the lord on its own behalf. This example may be an exception, but it illustrates a capacity for corporate action on a high level that was the potential of all communities.

The community's self-government was also reinforced by the involvement of villagers in running the parish. In many cases the vill coincided with the parish, and those that did not were usually combined with another township or townships to make up a parish. Rarely was a vill split between two or more parishes, in contrast with the frequent division of vills between manors. Like the vill, the parish bound communities together, ignoring manorial divisions, through the common obligations placed on them for the upkeep of the church building itself, the churchyard, and the goods of the church, such as furnishings, books and vestments. The church provided communities with an obvious physical focus, through which their identity could be expressed. That it was indeed such a focus of community interest may be indicated by the fact that in the late medieval period fines for the infraction of by-laws were often paid in part or, in the case of Wymeswold (Leics) wholly, to the church.[62] Villages had customs and cultures of their own, so that the inhabitants developed a self-conscious loyalty to the place in which they lived and worked.

Lords and estates

The character of manorial organisation and the nature of peasant communities were influenced by the type of lords and their varying demands. Although many minor lords held only one manor, for others the individual manor represented merely one element in a wider estate that could be scattered over the region or even over the whole country. The impact of a particular lord on a community was affected by the extent to which he was sole lord or whether lordship was divided.

The king

A striking example of the influence of a particular lord on local communities comes from the special case of royal manors which, even when they passed to other lords, were known as 'ancient demesne', so that the tenants enjoyed special advantages from their former association with the king. The king was a relatively undemanding lord, and his former tenants were protected from increased exactions.[63] Some manors of the royal demesne had peculiar inheritance customs; whereas the normal system was based on succession by the the eldest son, at the royal manors of Brigstock (Northants) and Rothley (Leics), either inheritance by the youngest son (ultimogeniture) or partible inheritance were practised.[64]

The king held land in all four counties in 1086, but they were widely scattered and accounted for only a minority of manors. However, they were very large and covered entire communities. Those in Leicestershire, furthermore, had land attached in the form of sokelands, which extended the king's influence as a landlord. Royal manors in 1086 clustered in Bedfordshire at Luton, Houghton Regis and Leighton Buzzard, and in Northamptonshire there was a contiguous belt of manors stretching across the area that later became Rockingham Forest, and into Rutland. Rutland as a whole may have had a special status as a block of royal lands, possibly part of the dower lands of the queen of England before the Conquest (Fig. 5.6).

Most of the royal manors of Domesday Book appear to have been possessions of the king since before 1066, but afterwards many were permanently granted away. By the end of the thirteenth century the king held only a few manors directly, such as those which could serve as bases for hunting expeditions, at Geddington in the forest of Rockingham, Silverstone in Whittlewood and Brill in the forest of Bernwood. In such places there were extensive parks, woods and wastes under forest law, as well as peasant tenants.

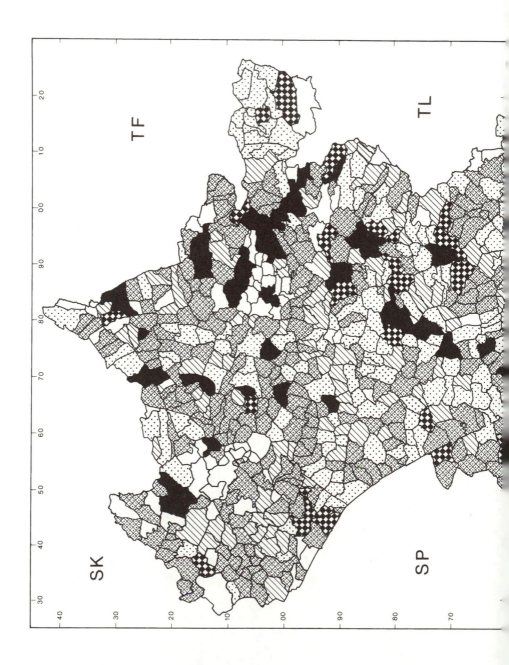

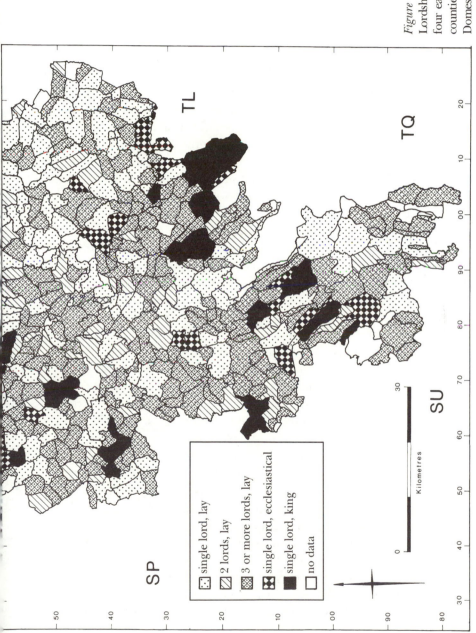

Figure 5.6
Lordship in the
four east midland
counties in
Domesday Book.

The Church

Ecclesiastical estates within the study area occupied a limited area in 1086. A number of major churches outside the four counties had one or two manors in the area, and these were clearly peripheral to their main interests, as in the case of Ramsey Abbey (Cranfield, Barton-in-the-Clay and Shillington in Bedfordshire) and the bishopric of Winchester (West Wycombe and Ivinghoe in Buckinghamshire). The only major monastic church actually sited within the four counties in 1086, Peterborough, held manors concentrated almost exclusively in the lower Nene valley and the Soke of Peterborough. These estates were well established, dating back at least to the tenth-century monastic reform movement. By 1086 almost half of Peterborough's lands were held by knights who fulfilled the abbey's military obligations to the king, but the rest of the estate remained under the direct exploitation of the abbey. The demesne manors of the older churches like Peterborough, that have been characterised as 'classical', tended to be large, often encompassing a whole village or a number of villages, with demesnes of hundreds of acres and a high proportion of servile peasantry owing heavy labour services.

In the century or so after 1086 ecclesiastical foundations increased as Norman lords patronised new religious orders, and this led to an increase in the amount of land in the hands of the church. These new monastic houses tended to be relatively small and their estates modest in extent. The largest, Leicester Abbey, had interests in more than a hundred places, mostly in Leicestershire. The holdings given to these new monastic houses consisted of small manors and parcels no larger than some peasant holdings, or just the right to collect a few shillings in rent. They were often given tithe income rather than landed property. Many of these new houses were also endowed with tracts of woodland and waste; in particular the Cistercians actively sought out 'wild' isolated places, which they then cleared. Some new monasteries were closely connected with the assarting that increased in pace during the twelfth and thirteenth centuries, such as Pipewell in the forest of Rockingham (Northants) and Old Warden (also known as St Mary of the Assarts) on the Greensand ridge in central Bedfordshire. Some Augustinian houses like Luffield in the forest of Whittlewood and Great Missenden (a foundation of the Arrouasian sub-order of Augustinians) in the Chilterns were also sited in woodlands and came to hold much cleared land. Older abbeys like Peterborough also took an active role in clearance, but assarts clearly made up a much higher proportion of the lands of these new monasteries.

The differing spatial, chronological and ideological circumstances of foundation gave the estates and manors of newer monasteries economic and social structures which were quite distinct from those of the older Benedictine houses. Their tenants were almost invariably only lightly burdened with labour services and paid largely money rents, so demesnes were cultivated with wage labour.

The laity

Most of the land within the four counties, throughout the eleventh to the fifteenth centuries, was held by laymen. Lay estates lacked the stability of those of many institutions, as a group of manors held by a family was not guaranteed to continue from generation to generation. Although some estates did develop an institutional status as honours or baronies and have a traceable continuity in the long term, even these were in many cases subject to amalgamation or division. Lay estates were subject to the uncertainties of inheritance, the sale and mortgaging of land, the transfer of land at marriage, or the creation of new fiefs. These all make the influence of particular lords on their estates difficult to detect.

The largest lay estates were those of the earls and barons, which comprised the lands of great lordships whose caputs lay within the east midlands such as those of Leicester, Bedford and Long Crendon (Bucks). These estates usually originated from the largest fiefs recorded in Domesday Book. Many individual manors within the study area were held by barons whose centres of power lay outside it, and few such lords held extensive lands in our area. The demesne manors of the great east midlands lordships bore some similarities to those of the older churches: they were often large, covering whole communities or large parts of them. They were the most likely among the lay manors to conform to the 'classic' manorial regime, with a large demesne and numerous servile peasants owing heavy labour rents, such as is found at Hanslope (Bucks), a manor of the Earls of Warwick.[65]

The lesser laymen – knights and 'gentry' – held more manors than any other type of landlord. Details of their estates are sometimes recorded in such family cartularies as those of Henry de Bray (whose lands lay principally at Harlestone, Northants) and the Hotots (with their main interests in Clopton, Northants, and Turvey, Beds), but we usually know less of them than of the magnates.[66] The differences between the estates of greater and lesser lay lords to some extent mirror those between the older and newer churches. The estates of the lesser lords tended to be made up of small manors and holdings which often constituted only a fraction of a vill. One type of manor had a high proportion of demesne land, but with a relatively small number of tenants burdened with only light services, so that demesne cultivation depended on hired labour and a permanent staff of servants. Another type had little or no demesne, but consisted mainly of tenants paying cash rents.[67]

Landlords could exercise an influence over settlement in a number of ways. Some were hostile towards peasant neighbours if they lived too close, in particular the Cistercian monks who removed the inhabitants from the 'deserts', where they preferred to found their houses, as is recorded after the foundation of Pipewell in Rockingham Forest.[68] The new monasteries, especially the Cistercians, rationalised their holdings into granges often as compact blocks of land, which required the purchase and exchange of land and sometimes resulted in the removal of existing peasants, as happened at Dishley, a Leicestershire grange of Garendon Abbey in the twelfth century.[69] The royal policy in the forests, of fining those who made assarts or purprestures (enclosures), might be seen as another example of superior authority working against settlement, but it seems that the crown did not oppose clearance of woodland over much of the forest, but was happy to allow it, in return for the income generated from the fines. The colonisers probably regarded payments to the forest courts as an acceptable cost, which was far outweighed by the advantage of acquiring new land. For most lords, tenants meant profit from rents and services, and they encouraged them, by renting out land for assarting in the woodlands or by allowing the subdivision of holdings in the nucleated villages. The extent of their contribution to the actual form of rural settlements is a matter for debate; the most appropriate candidates to be regarded as planners of villages must be those with large manors that encompassed tracts of land and settlements, such as the king, and the lay and ecclesiastical magnates. On the other hand it was the new monasteries and the knightly lords who, though they may have controlled only a section of a village, were closest to the ground, and most likely to be involved directly in the reallocation of land. The new monasteries also seem to have been capable of radical changes on their estates, including the creation of granges.

Towns, markets, trade and industry

We are not concerned here with the forms of urban settlement directly but with their impact on the countryside. In 1086 the only places of certain urban status in our four counties were the four boroughs at the head of each shire. There was also a small borough at Newport Pagnell in Buckinghamshire, and eight markets some of which were valued as high as £10 (Aylesbury) or £5 and £7 respectively at Luton and Leighton Buzzard. Most of these places with markets recorded in Domesday later became boroughs. A borough is recorded at Oundle (Northants) only forty years after Domesday Book, and at Peterborough within fifty years, and these may already have been unrecorded urban communities in 1086.[70]

In the course of the next three centuries the number of places granted the privileges of boroughs (burgage tenure, free disposal of property, fixed cash rents) grew to a total of thirty-nine. Some appear to have been founded anew, mostly in the twelfth and thirteenth centuries, including Dunstable (Beds), Fenny Stratford (Bucks) and Mountsorrel (Leics). Although all the boroughs had markets, not all achieved full urban status in terms of large permanent populations pursuing a variety of non-agricultural occupations. Brill (Bucks), for example, seems to have remained a village.[71]

While not all boroughs became towns, there were a number of other settlements which developed into towns apparently without the aid of borough status. Some of these were founded as new towns such as Market Harborough.[72] Others seem to have evolved via a process of gradual adoption of urban functions as the settlement filled a gap in the commercial network. Markets were also established in some 116 villages in the thirteenth and fourteenth century. As with the boroughs, some markets were successful, while others lapsed. That at Rothley (Leics) was transferred to Gaddesby in 1306 after its initial failure to attract commerce.[73]

The expansion in boroughs, towns and rural markets attests to strong commercial growth in the twelfth and thirteenth centuries. The market economy permeated the countryside, so that by 1300 everyone lived within a day's journey (11 km or 7 miles) of a market, and many would have a choice of two or three commercial centres. The distribution of markets was by no means even. There was, for example, no simple correlation between those areas with high densities of markets and those with greater population and wealth. In fact some of the wealthiest areas, such as the Ouse valley in Bedfordshire, had a relatively small number of markets, while the less well-populated Northampton Heights and the dip slope of the Chilterns were well furnished. One explanation for a local scarcity of markets was that a larger dominant town like Bedford, almost the only market in the Ouse valley, might monopolise the bulk of trade in its locality (Fig. 5.7).

Markets were often complementary, with small centres serving as collecting points for the larger towns. The hierarchy of town size helped to determine the extent of their rural hinterland, with the largest urban centres, like Leicester, trading over a radius of more than 20km (12 miles), but a very small town might expect to have regular contacts only within

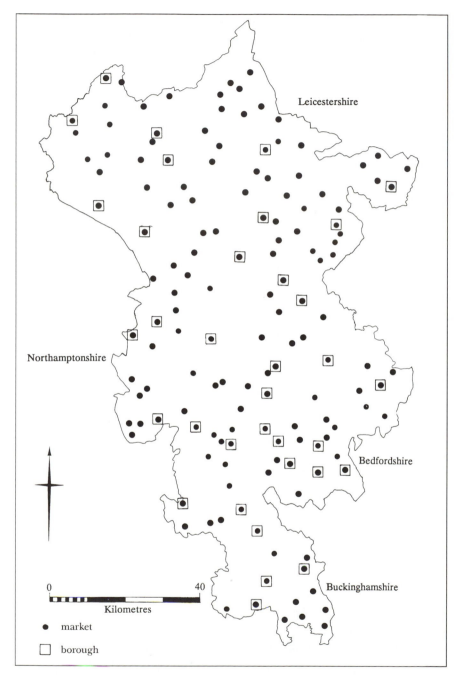

Figure 5.7 Medieval boroughs and markets in the four east midland counties. This records all known documentary references to boroughs and chartered markets before 1500.

8km (5 miles).[74] The lay subsidy of 1334 provides a comprehensive indication of the relative wealth and size of different towns, though there are
inevitable complications, like the inclusion of rural communities with
some towns for tax purposes. The largest towns of the study area, assessed
at more than £200 of taxable wealth were the county towns of Leicester
and Northampton, together with Peterborough, and Dunstable, a relative
new development. Luton, Leighton Buzzard and Melton Mowbray also
paid on more than £200, but their assessments included tax-payers in
the nearby countryside. Of the other county towns Bedford was assessed
at just under £200, while Buckingham rated less than half that. This
second rank of towns also included Brackley (Northants), Newport Pagnell
and High Wycombe (Bucks), with assessments ranging from £90 to £180.
The other thirty market towns paid tax on valuations as low as £25.[75]

The success of Dunstable, together with a number of other market
towns in south Bedfordshire and south Buckinghamshire, suggests the
commercial vitality of the Chilterns and their northern fringes, relatively
close to London. This region supplied, for example, fuel and timber to
metropolitan consumers.[76] A small market tended to serve its immediate
locality, but manors might buy and sell in remote markets, reflecting
commercial specialisation. Thus while the reeve of the Prior of Luffield's
manor at Lillingstone in north Buckinghamshire is recorded in the late
thirteenth century as selling grain to the local markets of Stony Stratford,
Buckingham and Brackley, that of nearby Thornborough was prepared
to carry grain a greater distance to Aylesbury, while also buying parts for
a plough there.[77] In the fourteenth century in south Bedfordshire manorial produce was sent direct to London, while on all the Bedfordshire
manors of Ramsey Abbey in the thirteenth century the obligations of the
villeins included services of carrying grain to a variety of places, including
London.[78]

Trade was linked with the development of industrial production in the
countryside. Cloth making is known from both urban and rural contexts,
but does not seem to have been a really major industry in the east
midlands. Attempts appear to have been made in the fourteenth century
to foster the cloth industry in the town of High Wycombe in the Chilterns,
while fulling mills are also recorded nearby at Chenies, and at Wendover
(in the thirteenth century).[79]

Perhaps the best evidence of all for rural crafts in the study area comes
from the pottery industry. Producers at Brill in Bernwood Forest and
Olney Hyde in Salcey, both in Buckinghamshire, Potterspury in Whittlewood Forest and Lyveden and Stanion in Rockingham Forest (all
Northants), served not just their local consumers but traded over distances

in excess of 100km (60 miles).[80] Plentiful clay and of course, fuel, were available in these woodlands, and the social structure of such regions with their smallholders and common rights, encouraged industrial development. The presence and availability of raw materials also fostered a number of other industries in royal forests, such as iron production in Rockingham and Whittlewood.[81] In western Leicestershire advantage was taken of the coal seams and slate quarrying.[82] At Barnack (Northants) the quarrying of the famous building stone was already a sizeable operation before the Conquest.[83]

The new towns of the twelfth and thirteenth centuries provide the best evidence for the active planning and encouragement of new settlements by landlords. Most of the boroughs show signs of regular street plans and measured burgage plots which resemble the layout of many villages with row or grid plans. Also some villages can be shown to have had market places added and other modifications made to their plans, probably at the time of the issuing of a market charter. However there are important differences between the villages and the new towns. The foundation of these towns involved major changes to the existing landscape and society, such as the diversion of roads, the allocation of a separate administrative zone within a rural manor, and the settling of a largely immigrant population. Villages seem to have been accommodated easily into well defined and agriculturally coherent territories, and their inhabitants were presumably people already in occupation. Towns, markets and trade had a more general influence on rural settlement, making the economy of the dispersed settlement of woodlands viable, for example, by providing outlets for the products of crafts and pastoral agriculture.

Depopulation

This chapter has been mainly concerned with the evidence for population growth, lordship, social structure and the development of the market during the formative period, when settlements were expanding. Much of the evidence for the physical form of medieval villages comes from shrunken and deserted sites, and we have seen that the distribution of abandoned settlements sheds light on the nature of the places and their inhabitants in their heyday as well as during their depopulation. Historical research helps us to understand the decline and fall of so many settlements.

The agrarian problems of the later middle ages had begun by 1341, especially in Buckinghamshire and Bedfordshire, where a total of 151 parishes were reporting a contraction of the cultivated arable.[84] This was not empty tax-dodging – any group of tax-payers could have used these excuses, but these complaints were concentrated in particular landscapes, notably the Chilterns, the greensands and the northern claylands of the two counties, and in some cases the decline in grain growing is confirmed in other documents of the time.[85] The Black Death of 1348–9 and subsequent epidemics affected our counties in much the same way as other regions, leading to a loss in the long term of about half of the rural population. This did not prompt the immediate collapse of many villages, but rather initiated a series of trends that gradually undermined many communities: lands fell vacant, thereafter to lie derelict, or to be converted into pasture, or amalgamated into peasant holdings which became much larger than those of the late thirteenth century.

Tenants who held more than one tenement often allowed buildings to fall into decay, and we find many references to the need for repairs: in the 1430s, at Watford (Northants), the lord paid for peasant buildings so as to maintain the housing stock of the village and the rental value of the manor.[86] The discipline exercised by lords slipped as the scarcity of tenants strengthened the hands of those who remained. Peasants were able to secure reductions in rents, and many migrated, including serfs, who were in theory bound to their lords' manors.[87] The tenants who remained found that there was little profit in large-scale cultivation of their holdings and used much of the land for pasture: peasants at Clipston (Northants) for example were keeping, in defiance of the customary limitation on numbers of animals, individual flocks of 100, 200, 300 and even 400 sheep.[88] Such actions threatened the long-term health of village economies that were based on a degree of co-operation between neighbours, and restraints on individuals.

Under such strains a few places lost their inhabitants quite early, such as Kingsthorpe in Polebrook parish (near Oundle, Northants), which appears to have been near to desertion by 1386.[89] More often villages are found to have had quite large populations at the time of the poll taxes of 1377 and 1380, but soon afterwards went into serious decline. Elkington in Northamptonshire, for example, which had 39 tax-payers in 1377, was reduced to a few farm servants by 1412, and Little Newton in the same county declined from 18 families in 1377 to 4 in 1449.[90] Many villages shrank physically in the fifteenth century as tenants migrated or families died out, and their holdings were taken over by neighbours who added them to their existing lands. Towards the end of the fifteenth century landlords were removing tenants and converting whole village territories to make way for new sheep pastures. For example, at Doddershall (Bucks) on 11 August 1495 a lawyer called Thomas Pigott, who had acquired the manor, enclosed it 'with fences and ditches', so that 24 houses were left to fall into ruin and 120 people departed 'tearfully'.[91] Rural depopulation was more often a long and slow process continuing well into modern times, like the protracted demise of Hardmead (Bucks), which did not finally lose its last villager until the nineteenth century, though it had suffered shrinkage in the later middle ages and enclosure in the seventeenth century.[92]

The decay of settlement was by no means confined to the village areas, and the records of manors with dispersed settlement tell the same story of decayed buildings and arable turned to pasture. Hamlets can sometimes be shown to have disappeared at this time, like Fastnidge in Wendover in the Chilterns.[93] But as the archaeological evidence shows, rarely among the dispersed settlement was the landscape transformed so dramatically as when a nucleated village and its whole field system was converted into a single pasture.

Notes

1   These generalisations are based on the Domesday text: A. Farley (ed.), *Domesday Book seu Liber Censualis Wilhelmi Primi Regis Angliae* (London, Record Commission, 1783), 1; and its geographical interpretation in H. C. Darby and I. B. Terrett, *The Domesday Geography of Midland England*, 2nd edn (Cambridge, Cambridge University Press, 1971), pp. 309–416; H. C. Darby and E. M. J. Campbell, *The Domesday Geography of South-East England* (Cambridge, Cambridge University Press, 1971), pp. 1–47 and 138–85.

2   *Rotuli Hundredorum*, 2 (London, Record Commission, 1818), pp. 321–3 and 334–55 for Beds and Bucks; J. Nichols, *History and Antiquities of Leicestershire* (London, 1795–8), 1, pp. cx–cxxi for Leics. The Bedfordshire return has also been translated: J. S. Thompson (ed.), 'The Hundred Rolls of 1274 and 1279', in J. S. Thompson (ed.), *Hundreds, Manors, Parishes and the Church* (Bedfordshire Historical Record Society, 69, 1990), pp. 3–63. Surviving early Lay Subsidy lists: A. Gaydon (ed.), *The Taxation of 1297* (Bedfordshire Historical Record Society, 39, 1959); S. Hervey (ed.), *Two Bedfordshire Subsidy Lists* (Bury St Edmunds, Suffolk Green Books, 1925); A. Chibnall (ed.), *Early Taxation Returns* (Records of Buckinghamshire, 15, 1968); W. Fletcher (ed.), 'The earliest Leicestershire lay subsidy roll, 1327', *Associated Architectural Societies Reports and Papers*, 19 (1887–8), 209–312 and 447–8; 20 (1889–90), 130–70; for Northamptonshire, *c.* 1301 (incomplete county roll covering eastern and western hundreds), PRO, E/179/155/31.

3   In the Hundred Rolls for Buckinghamshire, holdings are stated as held by people 'with their lesser tenants'; A. Jones, 'Caddington, Kensworth and Dunstable in 1297', *Economic History Review*, 2nd Series, 32 (1979), 316–27. On the other hand, tenants sometimes held land in more than one manor, and so might be counted twice: M. A. Barg, 'The social structure of manorial

freeholders: an analysis of the Hundred Rolls of 1279', *Agricultural History Review*, 39 (1991), 108–15.

4   J. Bennett, *Women in the Medieval English Countryside* (Oxford, Oxford University Press, 1985), p. 13; *DB*, 1, f. 219. 'Adult' males were those aged 12 and over. The Domesday calculation is based on the recorded population of both Brigstock and Stanion, which were included in the later manor.

5   *Ibid.*, p. 224; *DB*, 1, f. 149.

6   See these figures published in R. B. Dobson, *The Peasants' Revolt of 1381*, 2nd edn (London and Basingstoke, Macmillan, 1983), pp. 54–7.

7   County totals preserved in Remembrancer's account. Besides this there is also a body of surviving records for individual places in the study area as follows: Returns for Bucks, only the three Chiltern Hundreds in PRO, E/179/77/22; Returns printed for historic Leics in *VCH, Leicestershire*, 2, pp. 163–5; Returns for Rutland in PRO, E/179/165/21, 22 and 23; Returns for Northants in PRO, E/179/155/28. We are grateful to Dr R. M. Smith for allowing access to his computerised versions of the poll tax.

8   Printed in R. E. Glasscock, *The Lay Subsidy of 1334* (London, British Academy, 1974).

9   These generalisations are based on Darby and Terrett, *Midland England*; Darby and Campbell, *South-East England*.

10 J. A. Raftis, *Assart Data and Land Values* (Toronto, Pontifical Institute for Mediaeval Studies, 1974), pp. 98–155.

11 H. E. Hallam (ed.), *The Agrarian History of England and Wales, vol 2, 1042–1350* (Cambridge, Cambridge University Press, 1988), p. 199.

12 Raftis, *Assart Data*, p. 102.

13 Hallam (ed.), *Agrarian History, vol 2*, p. 198.

14 *Ibid.*, p. 195.

15 W. G. Hale (ed.), *The Domesday of St Paul's* (Camden Society, 1st Series, 69, 1858), pp. 9–13.

16 G. F. Farnham, 'Charnwood forest and the Charnwood manors', *Transactions of the Leicestershire Archaeological Society*, 15 (1927–8), 207.

17 H. E. Hallam, *Rural England 1066–1348* (Glasgow, Fontana, 1981), pp. 93–104.

18 B. M. S. Campbell, 'Agricultural progress in medieval England: some evidence from Norfolk', *Economic History Review*, 2nd Series, 36 (1983), 26–46.

19 D. Roden, 'Demesne farming in the Chiltern Hills', *Agricultural History Review*, 17 (1969), 9–23.

20 Raftis, *Assart Data*, pp. 29–34.

21 Hallam, *Rural England*, p. 118; Raftis, *Assart Data*, pp. 27–9; A. R. H. Baker, 'Contracting arable lands in 1341', *Publications of the Bedfordshire Historical Record Society*, 49 (1970), 7–17.

22 H. L. Gray, *English Field Systems* (Cambridge, Mass., Harvard University Press, 1915), pp. 17–82.

23 J. G. Jenkins (ed.), *The Cartulary of Snelshall Priory* (Buckinghamshire Record Society, 9, 1945), no. 129.

24 D. Roden, 'Field systems of the Chiltern Hills and their environs', in A. R. H. Baker and R. A. Butlin (eds), *Studies of Field Systems in the British Isles* (Cambridge, Cambridge University Press, 1973), pp. 325–76; instances in the study area found at Ilmer (Bucks), and Kempston and Thurleigh (Beds). See J. Wood, *Kempston* (Bedfordshire Parish Surveys, 2, 1984), p. 51.

25 For example, Roden, 'Field systems of the Chiltern Hills', pp. 352–3, which suggests irregular systems at Colmworth and Wilden.

26 H. S. A. Fox, 'The alleged transformation from two field to three field systems in medieval England', *Economic History Review*, 2nd Series, 39 (1986), 536–48.

27 It has been estimated from a survey of 1273 that the parish of Barrow (Leics) on the fringes of Charnwood contained *c.* 1,560 acres (630ha) of woodland and park and up to 8,000 acres (3,100ha) of waste at that time, Farnham, 'Charnwood forest', 148–9. While not quite so impressive, see the reference to 861 acres (332ha) of pasture in the vicinity of Boarstall that made up part of the endowment of the forestership of Bernwood, Stowood and Shotover forests in 1451: H. E. Salter (ed.), *The Boarstall Cartulary* (Oxford Historical Society, 88, 1930), no. 595.

28 P. Vinogradoff, *Villainage in England* (Oxford, Oxford University Press, 1892), pp. 458–9.

29 D. Hall, 'Late Saxon topography and early medieval estates', in D. Hooke (ed.), *Medieval Villages* (Oxford, Oxford University Committee for Archaeology, monograph no. 5, 1985), p. 64.

30 J. Thirsk, 'The common fields', *Past and Present*, 29 (1964), 3–25.

31 See the arguments in H. S. A. Fox, 'Approaches to the adoption of the midland system', in T. Rowley (ed.), *The Origins of Open Field Agriculture* (London, Croom Helm, 1981), pp. 64–111.

32 D. Hall, 'Field systems and township structure', in M. Aston, D. Austin and C. Dyer (eds), *Rural Settlement of Medieval England* (Oxford, Blackwell, 1989), pp. 194–6.

33 C. N. L. Brooke and M. M. Postan (eds), *Carte Nativorum. A Peterborough Abbey Cartulary of the Fourteenth Century* (Northamptonshire Record Society, 20, 1960), pp. 128–9.

34 See the case of Acklington (Northumberland), B. K. Roberts, *The Making of the English Village* (London, Longman, 1987), pp. 52–5.

35 The issues are discussed in D. Pelteret, *Slavery in Early Mediaeval England* (Woodbridge, Boydell, 1995), pp. 125–5, 176–7 and 241–2.

36 Hallam (ed), *Agrarian History, vol 2*, p. 65.

37 For an exposition of the character of the soke see F. M. Stenton, *Types of Manorial Structure in the Northern Danelaw* (Oxford Studies in Legal and Social History, 2, 1912), pp. 3–96.

38 *DB*, 1, f. 211.

39 A. K. G. Kristensen, 'Danelaw institutions and Danish society in the Viking age: sochemenni, liberi homines and Konigsfreie', *Medieval Scandinavia*, 8 (1975), 27–85.

40 C. Howell, *Land, Family and Inheritance in Transition. Kibworth Harcourt 1280–1700* (Cambridge, Cambridge University Press, 1983), pp. 114–46.

41 *DB*, 1, ff. 231, 234, 236 and 237; Nichols, *History of the County of Leicester*, 1, pp. cxvii–cxviii.

42 See R. H. Hilton, 'Freedom and villeinage in England', *Past and Present*, 31 (1964), 1–19.

43 *DB*, 1, ff. 232 and 236; Nichols, *History of the County of Leicester*, 1, cxi.

44 R. H. Hilton, *The Decline of Serfdom in Medieval England*, 2nd edn (London and Basingstoke, Macmillan, 1983), p. 19.

45 E. A. Kosminsky, *Studies in the Agrarian History of England in the Thirteenth Century* (Oxford, Blackwell, 1956), pp. 90–1.

46 Thompson (ed.), 'Hundred Rolls', pp. 56–7.

47 *VCH, Leicestershire*, 2, p. 173.

48 M. K. Dale (ed.), *The Court Roll of Chalgrave Manor* (Bedfordshire Historical Record Society, 28, 1950), p. xxii; F. B. Stitt, 'A Kempston estate in 1341', *Bedfordshire Historical Record Society*, 32 (1952), pp. 71–91; W. H. Hart and P. A. Lyons (eds), *Cartularium Monasterii de Rameseia* (London, Rolls Series, 1884), 1, pp. 474–86.

49 D. Roden, 'Field systems at Ibstone, a township of the south-west Chilterns during the later middle ages', *Records of Buckinghamshire*, 18 (1966–70), 43; *VCH, Buckinghamshire*, 2, p. 43.

50 For Badby and Newnham, A. E. Brown, *Early Daventry* (Leicester, University of Leicester, Department of Adult Education, 1993), pp. 73–4; for Wellingborough, F. M. Page (ed.), *Wellingborough Manorial Accounts 1258–1323* (Northamptonshire Record Society, 8, 1936), p. xxiv; for Kettering and Warmington, R. Lennard, *Rural England 1086–1135* (Oxford, Oxford University Press, 1959), p. 379; and for other manors Kosminsky, *Studies in Agrarian History*, p. 188. D. Willis (ed.), *The Estate Book of Henry de Bray* (Camden Society, 3rd Series, 27, 1916), pp. 12–14.

51 *VCH, Leicestershire*, 2, p. 173.

52 For Wichendon, R. Wigram (ed.), *The Cartulary of the Monastery of St. Frideswide* (Oxford Historical Society, 31, 1896), 2, pp. 195–7; for Brill, Salter (ed.), *Boarstall Cartulary*, pp. 199–205; and for Ibstone, Roden, 'Field systems at Ibstone', p. 43.

53 *VCH, Buckinghamshire*, 2, pp. 48–9.

54 *VCH, Leicestershire*, 2, p. 173.

55 The Cranfield yardland was 48 acres (19.5ha), while that at Harlestone could range from about 30 acres to as much as 80 (12–32ha), but seems most often to have been between 60 and 70 acres (24–28ha), Hart and Lyons (eds), *Cartularium Monasterii Ramesia*, p. 438; Willis (ed.), *Henry de Bray*, pp. 7–9, 31–4, 44 and 83–6.

56 Nichols, *History of the County of Leicester*, 1, cxiii; Thompson (ed.), 'Hundred Rolls', pp. 33–6.

57 Hale (ed.), *Domesday of St. Pauls*, pp. 6–7.

58 W. O. Ault, 'Village by-laws by common consent', *Speculum*, 29 (1954), 278–92.

59 W. O. Ault, *Open Field Farming in Medieval England* (London, Unwin, 1972), p. 19.

60 Hallam (ed.), *Agrarian History, vol 2*, pp. 640–1.

61 Ault, *Open Field Farming*, pp. 75–6.

62 *Ibid.*, p. 76.

63 M. McIntosh, 'The privileged villeins of the English ancient demesne', *Viator*, 7 (1976), 295–328.

64 R. Faith, 'Peasant families and inheritance customs in medieval England', *Agricultural History Review*, 14 (1966), 77–95; Bennett, *Women in the Countryside*, p. 14; G. T. Clark (ed.), 'Customary of the manor and soke of Rothley, in the county of Leicester', *Archaeologia*, 47 (1883), 125.

65 *Rotuli Hundredorum*, 2, pp. 343–6.

66 Willis (ed.), *Henry de Bray*; E. King (ed.), 'Estate records of the Hotot family', in E. King (ed.), *A Northamptonshire Miscellany* (Northamptonshire Record Society, 32, 1983), pp. 3–58.

67 Kosminsky, *Studies in Agrarian History*, pp. 256–82; R. H. Britnell, 'Minor landlords in England and medieval agrarian capitalism', *Past and Present*, 89 (1980), 3–22.

68 R. A. Donkin, *The Cistercians: Studies in the Geography of Medieval England and Wales* (Toronto, Pontifical Institute of Medieval Studies, 1978), p. 42.

69 *Ibid.*, p. 50.

70 *Domesday Book*, 1, ff. 148, 143 and 209; Darby and Terrett, *Midland England*, pp. 35 and 45; Darby and Campbell, *South-East England*, pp. 42–3 and 178–9; M. W. Beresford and H. P. R. Finberg, *English Medieval Boroughs: a handlist* (Newton Abbot, David and Charles, 1973), pp. 141 and 142.

71 *VCH, Buckinghamshire*, 4, p. 15.

72 W. G. Hoskins, 'The origins and rise of Market Harborough', *Transactions of the Leicestershire Archaeological Society*, 25 (1949), 56–68.

73 G. F. Farnham, 'Rothley', *Transactions of the Leicestershire Archaeological Society*, 12 (1921–2), 1.

74 One indication of a town's zone of influence comes from the range of places from which migrants came. See P. McClure, 'Patterns of migration in the late middle ages: the evidence of English place-name surnames', *Economic History Review*, 2nd Series, 32 (1979), 176–9.

75 Glasscock (ed.), *Lay Subsidy of 1334*.

76 J. A. Galloway and M. Murphy, 'Feeding the city: medieval London and its agrarian hinterland', *London Journal*, 16 (1991), 3–14.

77 G. R. Elvey (ed.), *Luffield Priory Charters*, 2 (Northamptonshire Record Society, 26, 1975), pp. 48–9 and 358–60.

78 P. L. Bell (ed.), 'Account roll for Higham Gobion and Streatley, 1379–82', in Thompson (ed.), *Hundreds, Manors, Parishes*, pp. 71, 76, 89, 103, 114 and 122; Hart and Lyons, *Cartularium Monasterii de Ramesia*, 1, p. 443; 3, pp. 302 and 308.

79 *VCH, Buckinghamshire*, 2, p. 128; 3, p. 117; 2, p. 60; A. Travers (ed.), *A Calendar of Feet of Fines for Buckinghamshire 1259–1307* (Records of Buckinghamshire, 25, 1989), p. 47.

80 M. R. McCarthy and C. M. Brooks, *Medieval Pottery in Britain* (Leicester, Leicester University Press, 1988), pp. 285–94.

81 Darby and Terrett, *Domesday Geography of Midland England*, p. 415.

82 F. Hartley, 'Coleorton', *Current Archaeology*, 134 (1993), 76–7; J. Hatcher, *The History of the British Coal Industry, 1: Before 1700: Towards the Age of Coal* (Oxford, Clarendon, 1993), pp. 159–62.

83 D. Parsons (ed.), *Stone: Quarrying and Building in England AD 43–1525* (Chichester, Phillimore, Royal Archaeological Institute, 1990), pp. 16–32, 187–206.

84 A. R. H. Baker, 'Evidence in the *Nonarum Inquisitiones* of contracting arable lands in England during the early fourteenth century', *Economic History Review*, 2nd Series, 19 (1966), 518–32.

85 E. Miller (ed.), *Agrarian History of England and Wales, vol 3, 1348–1500* (Cambridge, Cambridge University Press, 1991), pp. 107–8.

86 Northamptonshire County Record Office, Spencer MSS, roll 109.

87   Miller (ed.), *Agrarian History, vol 3*, pp. 631–2.
88   *Ibid.*, p. 69.
89   *Ibid.*, p. 74.
90   *Ibid.*, pp. 73–4.
91   I. S. Leadam (ed.), *The Domesday of Inclosures 1517–1518* (London, Long-
     mans, Royal Historical Society, 1897), 1, pp. 162–3.
92   P. S. H. Smith, 'Hardmead and its deserted village', *Records of Buckingham-
     shire*, 27 (1985), 38–52.
93   Miller (ed.), *Agrarian History, vol 3*, p. 112.

6

Explaining settlement form

In the previous chapters we have seen the varied forms taken by medieval settlements, and the diverse physical and historical influences that may help to explain their origin. In this chapter we will examine critically some of the general explanations that can be offered for the different types of settlement, in the light of the research on our four east midland counties. There is no direct documentary evidence for the changes in settlements in the crucial period between the ninth and twelfth centuries, so that any attempt at historical explanation must be based on comparison between the categories of information, to search for correlations that ought to help us to understand why, in particular, nucleated villages developed in some places but not in others.

Settlement patterns and field systems

In the four counties the medieval evidence for regular field systems of the midland type comes from the districts dominated by large and compact settlements, such as north Buckinghamshire and much of Northamptonshire. Where dispersed settlements prevailed, the fields tended to be irregular, consisting often of a combination of small enclosed crofts and numerous common fields, and at least part of the land was not governed by the routines of cropping practised in the midland system. In this coincidence between settlement form and agrarian regime, east midland villages are in accord with the rest of England, and this suggests that nucleated villages were a product of a development in agrarian methods.

Apparent exceptions deserve to be noticed. For example, at Harlestone in Northamptonshire, the various parts of this polyfocal village are spread out so widely as to invite the description of being dispersed. Yet if the settlement is viewed in the context of the whole parish, though not nucleated, it nevertheless lies in a restricted area around a rather large green, and is surrounded by the furlongs and strips of the regular field system. So while the village was more loosely organised than most, it cannot be regarded as an exception which disproves the general rule. Occasionally we find small hamlets that possessed regular two-field systems, such as Charlock (in Abthorpe) in Northamptonshire, and Evershaw (in Biddlesden) in Buckinghamshire, so the 'midland system' was not confined to large settlements. These two places lay in districts dominated by nucleated villages.[1]

The link between nucleated villages and regular field systems is strengthened by the likelihood that they came into existence at about the same time. Most researchers would agree that the critical period lies somewhere between 850 and 1200 for both nucleation and the formation of the midland system, with a strong likelihood in our area that the change occurred in the first two centuries of the time span.[2] This is not, of course, a mere coincidence, but arises from the functional connection between them. If land in a defined territory was to be laid out in great expanses of arable, then any small settlements scattered about the landscape could have formed an obstruction and their inhabitants would have been encouraged or forced to move to a central place.

The field system consisted of many scattered strips, whether by original design or as a result of the gradual fragmentation of parcels of land by the forces of inheritance, subdivision of holdings, and the land market, so that every tenant had a fair share of good and bad land.[3] Such a distribution helped to ensure that all members of the community had an equal commitment to the fields. In the same way, a residential arrangement whereby all of the tenants lived in close proximity gave all of them equally short and long journeys to arable, meadow and pasture both near and far. Regular rotations left a field lying fallow for common grazing, and this gave the nucleated village another function in relation to the fields, as part of the daily routine would have been the gathering of the animals together under the care of the common herdsman, who would then drive them out to pasture and return them at night to their individual owners – a much easier procedure if the peasants lived close together. The herdsmen's activities formed such a regular feature of village life that they rarely receive mention in documents, except when, as happened at Newton Longville in Buckinghamshire in 1422, a by-law was needed to remind members of the community that they had an obligation to supply food to the herdsman, who was evidently paid largely in kind.[4]

The midland system depended on discipline, and the submission of individuals to the interests of the whole community. The village's physical form, in which space was allocated to individual households, but where greens and streets were provided for collective use, as well as common facilities such as water supplies, the church and graveyard, reflected the delicate balance between private and public use of resources in the open fields. Individuals were responsible for the cultivation of the strips, but the fields and furlongs were subject to regulation by the community in such matters as the seasons for cropping and common grazing, the number of animals that could be kept in the pasture, and the maintenance of boundary markers. The documents show a tension between individual and collective interests – the lengthy series of by-laws issued at Newton Longville, already quoted, begin in 1290 and continue for more than two centuries. They provide excellent evidence for the community's interest in such matters as control over gleaning in the stubble, and keeping grazing animals away from the corn fields, but their constant repetition, and the need to punish those who broke the rules, points to the problem of keeping the individual inhabitants in line with the perceived interests of the whole group.

Opinion remains divided on the speed and the degree of organisation involved in the creation of villages and fields. The planned linear settlement, with rectangular tofts of equal size arranged in neat rows, so characteristic of the north-eastern English counties, corresponds to the most regular of field arrangements, in which the strips lay in orderly sequence in each furlong, so individuals had the same neighbours for every strip. When we encounter such places, we can envisage a single act of foundation, in which in a very short period a blueprint (so to speak) of a model village was imposed on a territory. When the regularity is not so marked, as at Badby (Northants), it might be argued that this represents a decline from an originally more systematically organised settlement.[5] But the regular settlements and fields could equally reflect a process of restructuring in the centuries after nucleation, and the existence in so many places of amorphous clusters of tenements rather than neatly planned rows suggests that we are dealing with many cases where the village accumulated at its site in a gradual and uncoordinated fashion, as a result of a series of decisions rather than a single act. Indeed, often the field system was more orderly than the village, and it seems likely that the nucleated village was really a by-product of the agricultural changes that encouraged the formation of the fields.

Having established the close link between nucleated villages and their fields, we still need to understand more about the reasons for the varied methods of agricultural organisation which influenced the different forms of settlement

Settlements and lordship

The role of lords is most clearly visible in the case of dispersed settlements because moated sites, at least a few of them manor houses, formed part of the scatter of dwellings, or were sited next to peasant farms (which might also be moated) along the roadside or in green-edge rows. Here lords (often minor lords) were participating in assarting with the peasants, but also no doubt helping to organise and encourage the clearance of wood and waste and the establishment of new settlements. It is often also in areas of dispersal that lords are found reordering the landscape, in the case of the new religious houses, by replacing peasant holdings with granges, and by parcelling out land to peasants in the process of colonisation. Lords seem also to be associated in some cases with the development of polyfocal settlements, because before they became nucleated settlements the different early foci, as at Wollaston (Northants), are found to be associated with the sites of the later manor houses of different lords. In such cases rival property interests may sometimes have helped to slow down the process of nucleation, and thus to preserve in the topography of the later medieval and modern village traces of its once separate predecessors.

In the case of the nucleated settlements there are a number of ways in which the lords could have either commanded or influenced the formation of new, compact settlements. In the period around the time of Domesday Book we presume the slaves were being settled on holdings of land, and this provided the lords with the occasion to measure out plots for peasant houses on part of the demesne, ideally near to the manor house. Only a few manors at the time of Domesday had slave populations numerous enough to account for *large* villages having been established in this way, and indeed many manors where slaves are recorded had four or less. But of course the numbers of slaves may have been much larger a century or two earlier. In fact, the ex-slaves often appear in later detailed surveys as smallholders, and the key to understanding village formation lies in explaining how the more substantial tenants, the yardlanders and half-yardlanders, who had the most important stake in the field system, came to be living in close association in orderly nucleated villages. One view maintains that the *ceorl* and the *gebur* of the tenth and eleventh centuries had themselves been settled on demesne land just like the slaves, and therefore we can easily discern the role of the lords as settlement planners because the whole village, not just that part of the settlement inhabited by the smallholding former slaves, would have been established in a similar way. One can see evidence of that process in place-names such as Charlton which refers to a settlement consisting entirely or mainly of a *ceorl* community.[6]

The problem with accepting the view that nucleated villages were laid out by lords, using the well-documented analogy of the new towns of the twelfth and thirteenth centuries, is that in eastern Leicestershire or the

Northampton Heights, village after village in close succession has a similar
form, and there can be no question of these being new settlements to
which immigrants would have been attracted and granted holdings, as
happened in the case of the new towns. The archaeological evidence tells
us that there were people living here before the villages emerged, and
we must presume that lords were reorganising an existing population, not
starting from scratch, and this makes some degree of gradual development
more likely. The analogy with the foundation of new villages by lords in
parts of Europe, on the largest scale in eastern Germany, but nearer to
hand in the Norman colonisation of Pembrokeshire, cannot be regarded
as an exact one because in those places the lords were conquerors establishing settlers of one ethnic group to supplant the native population, or
to serve as the basis of colonisation.[7] The notion that our villages were
founded by Danes as part of their programme of land acquisition cannot
work, because the distribution of nucleated villages does not coincide with
other signs of a Danish presence, such as place-names.

It has been argued with some persuasiveness that the upheaval involved
in forming a new settlement for an existing population needed the
dictatorial powers of a lord, who could compel peasants to uproot
themselves and move to a central settlement, and that a coherent plan
is more likely to be formulated successfully by a single authority than by
a committee.[8] In support of this view we can again invoke the new towns,
which were clearly set out according to a scheme preconceived by lords'
officials, as an example of successful co-ordination and implementation
of an idea. However, we should not forget that the mechanism by which
the inhabitants of the new towns were recruited involved an offer of
privileges and easy terms of tenancy.[9] Our villages contained many
tenants who were so heavily burdened with rents and services that it is
hard to believe that they had been induced to accept their holding by
advantageous conditions.

The problem here is that we are insufficiently informed about the
nature and powers of lordship in the crucial period. Those lords who
enjoyed continuous possession of their estates in the whole period from
the tenth to the thirteenth century can be shown from their later records
to have a secure grip over their tenants. Lords such as the monks of
Peterborough and Ramsey had evidently established a very strong control
of their subordinates by the thirteenth century, and it seems likely that
the origins of their power lie in the pre-Conquest period. Historians
of the secular aristocracy also tell us of the independent power wielded
by the new Norman magnates in the late eleventh and early twelfth
centuries, like the earls of Leicester, and the ordering of peasants into

line seems entirely in keeping with the behaviour of these buccaneering local dictators.[10]

As well as the lords themselves, there are references outside the region in the twelfth century to farmers and subtenants who bullied tenants and took initiatives in rearranging land and settlements which are only known to us when their behaviour attracted the notice of those in higher authority.[11] But these stories tell us of tenants being expelled, and of new holdings being created, but not of the planning of nucleated settlements. Similarly the archaeological evidence from Eaton Socon in Bedfordshire for the removal of the peasant tenants to make way for the castle does not record where the displaced people went, and whether they were provided with a neat row of new tenements.[12]

Perhaps the type of lord most likely to have pursued order and efficiency might have been the numerous lesser aristocrats, thegns in the pre-Conquest period, knights and minor gentry in the succeeding centuries, whose small manors gave them the incentive to make the most profitable use of limited resources, and whose continued residence on the spot made them especially knowledgeable of the local terrain. They had both an interest and the ability to re-organise in detail the land and peasant holdings. Smaller units of landholding, often in the hands of thegns, were appearing in large numbers in the tenth century, and small manors continued to multiply in the eleventh and twelfth centuries, spanning precisely the period of village development. The archive of the Northamptonshire Hotot family compiled in the thirteenth century reveals such gentry who were concerned with the purchase of a few selions or roods of land to expand or consolidate their demesne, and then made carefully written records of these acquisitions.[13] We could imagine a very similar process of purchase and exchange (and sometimes expropriation) necessary for the reorganisation of a settlement.

It is not too difficult then, to envisage the occasions, the powers and the motives that could have made the lords of our area into village planners. But there are many obstacles to accepting such a simple version of events. If lords were the decisive factor, then we should be able to observe certain geographical patterns. The estates of individual lords or types of lord should reflect estate policy by presenting some similarities in their settlements. To some extent this is found in the case of the manors of Peterborough Abbey, on which nucleated villages predominate, including those in the forests of Northamptonshire where, contrary to general experience, the settlement pattern (whatever the lord) consisted mainly of villages. In the case of Ramsey Abbey, the bulk of its Huntingdonshire manors coincided with nucleated villages, but its outlying properties in Bedfordshire were generally irregular in their settlements, and Cranfield in particular included a great deal of dispersed settlement. The ancient estate of the bishops of Winchester included the Buckinghamshire manor of West Wycombe, which in keeping with its Chiltern location, had scattered settlements, while the same estate's Hampshire and Wiltshire manors were often associated with nucleated villages.

It appears that the settlement forms were in keeping with those prevailing in the locality rather than being dictated by the policy of individual landlords. To sustain the argument that lords were prime movers in settlement foundation, it would be necessary to argue that they were very sensitive to local conditions, and only imposed nucleated villages in regions that were appropriate in ecology and agrarian economy. The older-established church estates provide the best means of testing the hypothesis because their continuous lordship goes back into the likely earliest period of village formation.[14] Likewise royal estates have considerable antiquity and contain a variety of settlement forms. We can be less confident of the long-term history of lay estates, though places that were held by aristocrats at the time of Domesday were likely to have been in the hands of similar lords in the previous century or two.

Another approach to the problem is to examine the overall geographical spread of the lords of different types in the eleventh and subsequent centuries, to see if the distribution of nucleated villages coincides with, say, knightly and other lesser lay lords, or old church estates. The conclusion is of course negative, because in village regions like eastern Leicestershire the nucleated settlements belonged to a great variety of lords and types of lord, but are found to be of similar form. Again the geographical circumstances seem to have had more influence on settlement than lordship did.

A further obstacle to the assumption that lords were the principal agents in village planning lies in the frequency with which manors and townships failed to coincide. Divided lordship was common at the time of Domesday. Indeed there is an extreme example like the now nucleated village of Lavendon in Buckinghamshire where there were nine lords in 1086.[15] This need not have been a very recent degeneration from an earlier simple world where village and manor occupied the same territory. For our area, places such as Hatley (Beds), in the tenth century, and Sharnford (Leics), appear in pre-Conquest wills as divided between lords.[16] The argument that nucleation required a single directing agency loses some of its force when we find that lords would have needed to come to an agreement on the planning of the village. If a committee of lords has to be envisaged, why not bring the tenants into the decision making as well?

Alternatively, perhaps lords influenced the process of settlement nucleation in more subtle ways than the advocates of seigniorial planning sometimes allege. Although the countryside consisted of a patchwork of lordship, with types of lord jumbled together regardless of the form of settlement, there may be some patterns in the overall social structure. One ingredient in the character of a region might be the prevalence of freedom and this is indeed a feature of the Chilterns with its dispersed settlements. Similarly, in much of southern Leicestershire in the thirteenth century, peasant society was dominated by villeinage, and here nucleated settlements are especially numerous, and the same correlation can be noted in northern Buckinghamshire. So lords of all kinds enjoyed in these regions greater power to manipulate tenants, while in mainly free districts the tenants were in a better position to resist such pressures. Part of that seigniorial power may have been the imposition of a type of settlement conducive to more effective social control and economic efficiency – the nucleated village. And yet the geographical evidence is by no means consistent or conclusive, because in north-west Bedfordshire we find a high proportion of free tenants living in nucleated villages, and there is a smattering of the same phenomenon in otherwise mainly servile areas such as south Leicestershire.[17]

There is a chronological problem here, because our evidence for peasant status comes mainly from the thirteenth century, and as we have seen, the definition of villeinage changed around 1200. So at the time when the villages formed, perhaps as early as the tenth and eleventh centuries, could the status of the peasants have been completely different? This is not a likely explanation, because ancestors and predecessors of the thirteenth-century villeins can be shown to have been tenants already expected to do labour service and in other ways to be under considerable lordly control before serfdom was given a new and strict definition. And in the case of a number of Leicestershire villages, such as Walton, Beeby and Blaby, their tradition of freedom goes back before Domesday, when in these places a significant number of sokemen is recorded.[18]

Perhaps we are expecting too much of our medieval lords – we attribute to them the powers and ambitions of planners, whereas in reality their role in nucleation may have been more indirect. They built their manor houses and founded churches, so providing the villagers with a nucleus around which to establish their dwellings. They settled their slaves and servants in cottages near the manor house, contributing an important stage in the process of nucleation. They no doubt wished to manage their demesnes in the most profitable way and, as the largest and most powerful landowner in the village, had a major say in the organisation of the fields.

Lords pressurised the peasants into giving more money and labour as rent, and forced them into systematic farming methods which would provide a living for themselves and a surplus for their superiors. All of these would therefore have propelled the inhabitants of a territory towards nucleation.

But obviously not all lords had this effect because many places failed to nucleate, and some free peasant communities were able to form a nucleated village without coming under the lord's direct influence. The advice was given to an ecclesiastical lord by the author of the *Rectitudines*, on how to run an estate in the early eleventh century or even a little before: 'The customs of estates are various . . . Nor do we apply these regulations to all districts . . . If we learn better, we will eagerly delight in what we learn and maintain it according to the custom of the district in which we then live. Wherefore one must delight among the people to learn laws if one does not oneself wish to lose honour on the estate'. In other words, lords had to live by and respect local custom. Although this was a counsel of perfection, offered in moral terms, it does not suggest that lords imposed alien rules on tenants easily or lightly.[19]

Local communities

If the role of the lords cannot be seen in any clear-cut way as the sole or even principal agents of village planning, we need to turn to look at the people who lived in the settlements. The peasants, and particularly their collective organisation of the village community, inevitably had a part to play in the adoption of new agricultural methods and settlement planning. This is demonstrated for a few villages which appear not to have had lords, or at least not in the conventional sense. We have seen already that the inhabitants of Tilbrook (Beds) consisted of twenty sokemen who had enjoyed some autonomy before 1066, and the only agency that could have remodelled the fields and the village would have been these twenty people acting collectively. Likewise in the case of the sokes of Leicestershire, we find groups of peasants living in places remote from their parent manor, with no demesne to give their lord a strong presence or direct interest in the agriculture of the village, and again ordinary inhabitants were the most likely creators of the nucleated villages.[20]

The peasants had a strong interest in their own place of residence and work, and also the means to carry out a complex reordering of their lives. They were directly concerned with the cultivation of the fields, and had an intimate knowledge of the local terrain and soils. They were entirely dependent on the resources of one place for their survival, unlike lords, many of whom held properties in a number of localities. And there is abundant evidence of the ability of villages to elect officials, collect money, gather information and take decisions. They could provide answers for the inquests sent from higher authority, or carry out the difficult task of assessing and gathering taxes or collective dues owed to lords. From the eleventh century onwards we know that on occasions they took on responsibility for the management of their own manors when they became collective lessees, as at Kingsthorpe (Northampton), dispensing with officials appointed by the lord, and providing an agreed annual sum of money from rents and the profits of the demesne.[21]

In the great majority of villages the lord maintained a direct presence, and the community worked in conjunction with the lord. By-laws often originated from the knowledge and concerns of the villagers, who were most likely to be aware of imperfections in the management of the fields and the behaviour of their neighbours, but were crucially combined with the authority of the lord, who could lend his weight to the legislation by having the regulations announced and enforced in his court. The lord's officials would presumably make sure that the by-laws did not infringe his interests, and would be more than happy to collect the money that erring villagers had to pay for infringing the rules.

It might be said that the issuing and enforcement of by-laws shows a routine administration at work, very different from the radical changes that took place in many of our villages when peasants were uprooted and fields laid out. It could also be argued that those documented examples of major changes, such as the revision of the allocation of land between fields at Harlestone (Northants) in 1410, which involved agreement by the lords and a committee of villagers, comes too late to be helpful to our specific enquiry – such co-operation between lords and 'the whole of the villagers' could belong to an age of more sophisticated government, and after the loss of population in the plague epidemics had enhanced the bargaining power of the peasants.[22] However, a record of an apparently similar agreement at Segenhoe (Beds) in the twelfth century provides unusual evidence of a reallocation of land in the period of village formation.

In a narrative account of the history of Dunstable Priory's property in Segenhoe, a canon or official of the Priory in the thirteenth century reported that in this village of divided lordship, as a result of the upheavals of a time of war (likely to be a reference to the anarchy of the reign of Stephen, in 1135–54), lands were found to be occupied unjustly.[23] The solution involved the combined authority of the two lay lords, who took action in the manor court, and that of the villagers, represented by six old men. All the tenants (knights, freemen, and 'all others') gave their common assent, and surrendered their lands to the lords, and they were then measured (by the perch, 'as if newly conquered') and assigned 'reasonably' to each tenant. Here we have an explicit account of a transformation similar to that involved in nucleation and planning. We are told without ambiguity that both lords and villagers were involved; that fairness of distribution was one of the principles behind the process; and that a measured survey took place. This is a very precious record. Its only drawback as evidence is that it was written some time after the events; however, the Priory would have had no obvious motive to distort the means by which its lands were assigned, and even if we adopted the view that the whole narrative was invented, it shows how a near contemporary would *expect* such a process to be carried out, which is almost as useful for our purposes as an exactly contemporary description of the episode.

If we allow that the peasant communities could have been the initiators of the reconstruction of their own villages and fields, or at the very least played a major part in the decision to change by granting their consent, and would then provide the means of reorganisation by electing old, wise and reliable peasants to implement the process, this would help to explain the tendency for a number of adjacent villages in districts such as north Buckinghamshire and east Leicestershire to have adopted broadly similar forms of settlements and fields. Individual communities were not islands unto themselves, but had many contacts with their neighbours. Indeed in some cases they were formally connected by rights of intercommoning, even to the point that they shared the grazing of each other's fallows. Thus we find at Newton Longville and Bletchley in 1310–11, and at Dunton and Mursley in 1345 (all in north Buckinghamshire) that changes to common fields were made jointly.[24]

In addition to these necessarily coincidental innovations, there must also have been a good deal of learning from example and imitation, as new ideas spread from one community to the next. It is sometimes said that if fifty or a hundred contiguous villages were all laid out in similar fashion, this must be the result of some simultaneous cataclysmic event such as a destructive war or the acquisition of the whole area by an invader. But in the eighteenth century, when there was no such wholesale devastation or conquest, schemes for the enclosure of fields were adopted in village after village over whole districts, with a similar layout, simply through the diffusion of similar perceptions of improvement.

If we accord the community a role in nucleation, we still do not resolve the problem of the reason for their actions. The Dunstable writer compared the radical restructuring of Segenhoe to the results of a conquest, but this was a metaphor, and we do not need to invoke great political crises to explain mundane local events. Instead it may have been the result of a change in ideas, even a fashion, just as eighteenth- and nineteenth-century estate owners, Chartist radicals and paternalistic town planners built 'model' villages along preconceived lines. But the suspicion remains that there were hard practical considerations behind nucleation: so much was at stake in the fields – not just the prosperity but the very survival of the cultivators – suggesting that they were under economic or demographic pressures to make radical changes in their way of life.

Settlement patterns and population

The pressure on resources which may have produced the need for regular field systems could have been the result of population increase.[25] Indeed a coincidence has often been noted in other parts of the country between areas of villages with regular field systems and areas with higher levels of medieval population, while areas of dispersed settlement and irregular agrarian organisation generally have lower population densities. However, in the glaring exception of East Anglia, which included some of the greatest concentrations of people found in the country, indeed in Europe, settlements often consisted of irregular rows stretched along green-edges, and field systems were (at all times that we can observe them) irregular in layout and organisation.[26]

Some settlement forms in the study area do accord with the distribution of population. Many districts with a predominance of villages have high recorded populations in Domesday Book, sometimes exceeding 50 per square mile (19 per sq km); these include the river valleys of the Ouse, Nene, Welland, Wreake and Soar. Areas of dispersed settlement, including the Chilterns and the north Bedfordshire clay vales, have correspondingly low densities of people. The rule does not always work, however, as some districts with numerous nucleated villages, including the forest of Rocking-ham and much of the Northampton Heights, have low recorded densities in 1086, in some cases at least as low as those of areas of dispersed settlement, and these two districts are themselves very different in land use, one containing much woodland and the other very little. It might be argued that the settlement pattern had experienced its formative stages perhaps a century or two before 1086, so that the densities recorded in Domesday are not relevant. However, the precise chronology of settlement change remains uncertain, and nucleation may still have been continuing at the time of Domesday or even later. And in any case such a basic characteristic as the relative density of people that the land supported is

unlikely to have gone through a complete transformation in a few generations, and indeed did not in the centuries after 1086.

While areas of dispersed settlement tended after 1086 to remain less
densely populated than the village-dominated districts, their levels of
population had by the fourteenth century risen as high as, if not higher
than, those of the village areas in 1086. However, despite the development
of a comparable population density by *c.* 1300, no process of nucleation
resulted. Therefore, even though they must have experienced competition
for grazing and other economic pressures,[27] these problems did not
prompt them to reorganise themselves into nucleated settlements. The
post-Conquest population growth in these areas seems instead to have
led to the multiplication of hamlets and farmsteads. Many of these are
not recorded before the twelfth or thirteenth centuries and in some cases
the documents tell us at this time of the foundation of new small settlements.[28]

By contrast most places with nucleated villages are mentioned in Domesday. This could mean that villages may have been the product of a
particular period. It would appear that there was a 'village moment' when
nucleated settlements formed in a particular set of conditions. Thus, after
the twelfth century, the moment had passed, and similar circumstances
(such as high densities of people) produced different results. We are
reminded of the appearance of assarts in the documents at about the same
time. When new land was cleared in the eleventh century, it seems to have
been incorporated into the open fields and was added to the yardland
holdings of the villagers. In the twelfth century new clearances were given
a special title, assigned their own form of tenure, measured in acres, and
often held in severalty or in furlongs outside the main field system.[29]

Was the landscape simply too full by the twelfth and thirteenth centuries
to accommodate new villages and their territories? With land already
extensively divided up amongst established communities, there was
limited space for laying out the extensive field systems that villages
required. It is significant that, when some new large settlements did
appear in the twelfth and thirteenth centuries, these were invariably urban
settlements or market centres. The towns such as Market Harborough
(Leics) had no need of extensive agrarian resources of their own, and
could therefore develop in much less space than that needed for villages.
It may also be that the establishment of stronger property rights for free
tenants, who were brought under the closer protection of the crown by
the legal reforms of the late twelfth century, and who were able to defend
their common right under the Statute of Merton in 1236, made radical
reorganisation of the countryside increasingly difficult. So while in theory

a large parish with dozens of hamlets and farmsteads could have been converted into a nucleated village, unscrambling the entrenched properties of hundreds of tenants would have required superhuman efforts of negotiation and persuasion. The landscape was too far advanced in its organisation and layout to allow for drastic change.

The area of dispersed settlements tended to have the more dynamic population growth in the twelfth and thirteenth centuries, and an area like eastern Leicestershire appears to have experienced a smaller degree of expansion in comparison. However, some settlements grew rapidly like Brigstock (Northants) through extensive assarting, but nevertheless retained a nucleated form. Perhaps there were greater restrictions on the location of settlement because it lay in the royal forest of Rockingham, but other royal forests in the study area such as Whittlewood, Salcey and Bernwood, are notable for a more mixed settlement pattern. Again it appears that a large village had formed within the period of the 'village moment', and it was likely to continue on that path. In the same way we ought to note that for all the fluidity of settlements, and the many changes that were implemented, there is very little evidence for the disintegration of a nucleated settlement before the crises of the later middle ages. Village formation seems to have endowed those settlements with a measure of stability.

Though expansion in the twelfth and thirteenth centuries is particularly associated with the creation of dispersed settlement, there are also some settlements that may have developed into villages only subsequent to 1086. These are places with insufficient population recorded in Domesday Book to be regarded as more than hamlets. Places like Redmile in the Vale of Belvoir (Leics); Fleckney in High Leicestershire; Everdon in the Northampton Heights; Charlton in the Charwell valley (Northants); and Foscott in Whittlewood (north Bucks) all have a recorded population of less than five households in Domesday Book (indicating less than thirty people).[30] This suggests that not all villages resulted from the reorganisation and nucleation of numerous pre-existing settlements and that some may have grown from small beginnings. But again it appears that in the districts in which these settlements lay there was a predisposition to follow a 'village track', while in other environments population growth encouraged the proliferation of small settlements.

We can conclude that the density of population had some relationship with settlement patterns. Those districts with greater peasant numbers in the eleventh century were most likely to have a high proportion of nucleated villages. But population density was not the only factor behind the development of villages because there were important exceptions to the rule such as the thinly populated, though village dominated, districts such as the Northampton Heights, and because the rule did not work at all in such places as East Anglia. Rising numbers of people in the thirteenth century did not precipitate a wave of nucleations because the 'village moment' had passed. In some ways village society helped to prevent very high population levels. While the more flexible landscape and social structure of the dispersed settlement districts allowed them to find room for newcomers, nucleated villages, the territories of which had a high proportion of arable by the twelfth century, could not absorb migrants in such large numbers. Indeed, both the custom of primogeniture, and the prejudice against excessive subdivisions of yardlands, often held on customary tenures under lords who feared fragmentation of the tenements on which rents were levied, meant that many nucleated villages did not expand much in the twelfth and thirteenth centuries. The inhabitants of villages must have been sending many of their younger sons and daughters into colonising districts or towns as their opportunities at home for acquiring land and a living were limited.

Settlements and the state

We are led to make some connections between settlements and political circumstances because the period of nucleation coincided with the assertion of royal power over the newly-formed kingdom of England in the late ninth and tenth centuries. The vill was indeed part of the hierarchy of government, and ultimately the success of the state in such matters as maintaining law and order depended on this, the smallest unit of administration. It has been argued that the coincidence between the peasant holdings and the fiscal assessment of the village suggests that the village was called into existence to serve the needs of royal administration. A symmetry is also found in the number and location of strips in the open fields which corresponded to the number of yardlands. As it is generally agreed that the hidage assessments were imposed by the state, originally long before 900, but were revised in a systematic way in the tenth and eleventh centuries, the villages and fields could have been founded at the same time, and the orderly schemes of this early administration continued to influence the form of the settlement until modern times.

Those who attribute the imposition of regular settlement and field patterns to a central authority sometimes hint that the Danish invaders were responsible, and this would accord with some greater degree of regularity visible in the villages of the north-east of our area, where Danish influences were stronger. Alternatively the landscape could, it is obliquely suggested, have been reorganised to a new blueprint when the kings of Wessex acquired the land from the Danes in the early tenth century, as the moment of English 'reconquest' (or rather conquest, because the previous rulers had been the kings of Mercia) gave an opportunity for radical change.

There are various difficulties in accepting this account of events. Much of the evidence for the numbers of yardlands comes from a much later period. Although contemporaries did have a notion of a new order following a conquest – it is mentioned in the Dunstable account of the Segenhoe replanning mentioned above – it is hard to imagine that the incoming Danes or English were faced by an uninhabited *tabula rasa* on which they could impose a brand new pattern. We no longer think of the Scandinavian invaders as ultra-violent savages, and even those who believe that they arrived in considerable numbers, not just as a handful of aristocrats, would not suppose that the whole of the Danelaw (and especially its south-western fringe) was settled anew by tens of thousands of Danish immigrants. Likewise the rulers of England would have retained as many of the Anglo-Danish population as possible, as they are unlikely to have had reserves of manpower to repopulate the area after any imagined mass expulsion.

So in other words, the conquerors, both Danish and English, would have had to deal with a countryside containing people, fields, lords, and all the complications of rights and customs that would in a practical spirit have to be respected and moulded, and not swept aside. The west Saxon rulers were anxious to proceed by some degree of conciliation, hence the continuation of Danish customs in the conquered Danelaw. The weight of probability again lies in favour of gradual and piecemeal development, in which models of villages and fields were diffused across a region, rather than a single cataclysmic transformation. The observed regularities could have resulted from reorganisation at a later date, perhaps in the twelfth century.

A further problem arises from the geographical limits of the regularly planned villages, as apparently only parts of the Danelaw or only small districts within the English king's extensive tenth-century conquest received the supposed new imprint of village organisation. After all, the dispersed settlements were subject to the same system of taxation, and could have been involved in the same planning process, yet were allowed to develop along a very different path. We might also expect to find the models for midland nucleated villages in Wessex, if the idea came with the new rulers, but such counties as Hampshire and Wiltshire exhibit a great variety and complexity of settlement form.

The state is more likely to have had an indirect influence on the development of villages. The demands made by the higher authorities encouraged and impelled the inhabitants to organise themselves in a disciplined fashion – which strengthened the internal governing machinery of the vill. The need to pay taxes and meet the other demands of the state may well have added to the pressures on communities to make their farming more efficient. The need to share the obligations owed both to the state and the lords fairly would have made the need for standard holdings, with approximately equal resources and duties, all the more desirable. The lives of the rural communities should not therefore be seen as a dialogue simply between lords and peasants, but to have involved a third party, the state; and the institutions of lordship, village community and government developed together on a similar time-scale.

Settlements and the market economy

The establishment from the ninth to the thirteenth century of a hierarchy of towns, and a network of markets both in towns and villages, could have influenced rural settlement in three ways: firstly by bringing into being new nucleated urban settlements; secondly by providing a model for settlement planning; and thirdly by changing the character of the rural economy through the growth in demand for agricultural produce, goods and services.

The foundation of boroughs by lords in the twelfth and thirteenth centuries undoubtedly added to the number of large nucleated settlements, but in a very specialised category. Most boroughs developed the urban economy that their lords expected, attracting settlers by favourable terms of tenure and the prospect of a busy market, and consequently their inhabitants gained their livelihood from a variety of non-agricultural occupations. Some however retained at least a partly rural character: Lutterworth in Leicestershire, for example, or Oundle in Northamptonshire, grew out of villages rather than being established on a separate, new site, and consequently townspeople and peasants lived in close proximity in the same place.[31] Some intended town foundations were unsuccessful, like Brill (Bucks), which was granted borough status in the thirteenth century, but failed to attract a sufficient number of traders and craftsmen to be regarded as a functioning town.[32] Nevertheless it stands out in its locality as a larger and more regularly planned settlement than its neighbours. In some cases, like Culworth (Northants), the grant of a market charter led to the addition of planned elements to an existing settlement, making the nucleated village larger, but also giving it an element of planning that it would have lacked as a primarily agricultural community.[33] In districts of mainly dispersed settlements, like the Chilterns, the only sizeable nucleated settlements were the boroughs and the market villages.

The second way in which urbanisation can be linked to the development of rural settlements lies in the possibility that the regular villages followed the example of town planning. The argument in support of this view depends on the assumption that planned towns were established earlier than the planned villages. Towns outside our study area, such as Winchester, were apparently given a regular grid of streets, with rows of plots along the main street as early as *c*. 900. The earliest settlement resembling a planned village in our four counties, Stratton in Bedfordshire, was laid out at some time in the tenth or eleventh century.[34] It is also often assumed that planning of many villages came at a second stage after nucleation, perhaps as late as the twelfth century, by which time a proliferation of small market towns could serve as local models. The similarity between towns and villages lies in the arrangement of houses and plots along streets and the use of standard units of measurement.

The objections to this view lie in the lack of early clearly planned towns in our study area, with Northampton for example offering no very orderly guide to village founders. The chronology of village planning is still very uncertain, depending as it does on insecure dating of pottery. Town and village plans are actually different, with the rather narrower urban plots presenting a much more concentrated built-up space than would be found in most villages. Now that we have realised that the dispersed settlements, which are totally unlike towns, exhibit some signs of deliberate organisation, the proposal can be made that planning is found both in towns and the countryside, but with each plan adjusted to the needs of the place, its economy and the landscape. Historians have become increasingly sceptical of the assumption that towns provided centres of innovation from which ideas diffused into the country.[35] The valid part of the theory surely lies, however, in the recognition that orderly settlement arrangements formed part of early medieval mentality. The ideas were applied everywhere, and spread from place to place, but not necessarily on a one-way track from town to country.

Finally, the growth of the market had an important influence on the workings of the rural economy and society, which could have fed back into field systems and settlement forms. The urbanisation of the tenth and eleventh centuries had given the four counties by 1086 two sizeable towns (at Leicester and Northampton) and at least half a dozen smaller trading centres; and the next two centuries saw the mushrooming of urban communities and markets until by the late fourteenth century between 15 and 20 per cent of the population were town dwellers.[36] The London market was also drawing on the resources of the southern part of our area in the thirteenth century, and this is unlikely to have been an entirely new phenomenon.

The inhabitants of the towns would have demanded supplies of food and raw materials from the countryside, and this would have drawn the peasants as well as the lords' demesnes into production for the market. In exchange the craftsmen, increasingly concentrated in towns, would have relied on rural customers for their living: cloth, leather goods and metal wares would have figured prominently among urban exports to the villages, and indeed we have concrete evidence for this in the finds of town-manufactured pottery, such as Stamford ware, on rural sites. The commercial orientation of the peasant economy is demonstrated in the ability of the lords to demand at least a small quantity of money rent by the eleventh century, such as the 30 shillings rendered annually by the thirty-seven peasants of Great Bowden (Leics).[37] Cash payments increased greatly in the twelfth and thirteenth centuries. Excavation of rural sites occupied in the thirteenth century provides ample evidence for a growing division of labour, and the rise of a modest peasant consumerism: houses were built on stone foundations, with professionally carpentered super-structures, and the inhabitants owned quantities of non-local pottery and pieces of functional and ornamental metal work.[38] Also in the thirteenth century, reversing an earlier trend, craft production was spreading in the countryside.[39]

The repercussions of all this for settlement and field layouts must firstly be related to the priorities of agricultural production. The midland field systems were adopted to achieve a balance between arable and pasture. The fallow field ensured that the animals would be provided with some grazing as the arable extended over the bulk of the available land. The balance was primarily designed to give peasant families a guarantee of subsistence, since a high proportion of the food produced, and especially the grain, was consumed within the village. It also preserved the sustainable agriculture of the village territory, as the manure from the stock, the resting of the land, and the use of leguminous crops kept the arable from total exhaustion.

But in addition to these priorities, the compromises that lay behind the field system involved some surplus of production, especially in the form of wool, milk products and meat, or of certain types of cereals for which the village had a limited demand (notably brewing grains).[40] So the beginnings of the market may have had some influence on agricultural management of the village territory in its formative stages, and continued to affect its subsequent development. These were matters for collective decisions, but we should also note the growing emphasis on individual property rights in the period: the closer definition of the strips of each holding, and the concern with precise demarcation of toft boundaries. As a further reflection of the market, villages and dispersed settlements alike contained an increasing number of cottage tenements, as wage-earning and craft work gave smallholders the chance to make a living by selling their labour.

None of these trends was confined to one type of settlement rather than another. While such trends may have fed into the combination of stresses and pressures that led to nucleation, the influence of the market was felt more in the areas of dispersed settlements. In these areas agriculture had a strong pastoral element with consequent market orientation, and landholding and the management of resources both tended to put greater emphasis on individual property rights. The dispersed areas had a stronger tendency to experience industrial development and to see the proliferation of smallholdings.

Settlements, topography, *pays* and landscapes

Terrain is an obvious influence on settlement form, in that the open fields of the nucleated villages often occupy the broad expanses of claylands found in eastern Leicestershire or the Northampton Heights, while the wooded valleys and ridges of parts of the Chilterns provide space only for patches of arable fields, and farmsteads with small territories. However, human ingenuity is not always constrained by physical conditions, and we must be sceptical of dogmatically deterministic explanations of the phenomena that we observe.

A plausible influence on settlements might be sought in the soils and their use in agriculture. Nucleated villages frequently occur in the river valleys and on the more hospitable limestone claylands. To be more precise, 45 per cent of all known settlements on alluvium and river gravels, and 64 per cent of all known settlements on cornbrash (in our area exposed along river valleys), are nucleated. On the Northampton sands (a river valley soil) 60 per cent, and on limestone 48 per cent, are nucleated. By contrast only 32 per cent of all settlements on chalk, and a mere 13 per cent of those on clay with flints, are nucleated. Dispersed settlements were prevalent on the chalk and greensands of the southern part of the study area, on much of the heavier clayland, and in the harsher environment provided by the rocks of Charnwood in the north. But these statistics themselves show that the divisions are not absolute, and that a significant percentage of nucleated settlements occupied soils that usually were associated with dispersed settlements. We can observe too many exceptions for any rules to be accepted without qualification – the clays of north central Bedfordshire, for example, have nucleated villages, interrupted rows and green-edge settlements.

It would be more satisfactory to identify soil and terrain as important contributions to the formation of distinctive *pays*. We can classify a considerable part of the area that we have studied as consisting of either champion or woodland *pays*, and these types of countryside are defined in terms, not of a single feature of their physical or social structure, but by a bundle of characteristics. Champion countries were traditionally thought to contain nucleated villages, midland field systems, extensive arable farming, and a tendency for a high proportion of the inhabitants in the thirteenth century to be classified as servile. This contrasts with the non-concentrated settlement, irregular fields, tendency to pastoralism and freedom of the woodland *pays*.

We have already seen that differences between the *pays* were more complicated than these two broad subdivisions will allow. For example, the wolds of the higher claylands of Leicestershire and Northamptonshire, which shared many characteristics with the champion, form a distinct *pays* because villages tended to be smaller and the people poorer, and they had developed a primarily grain-growing economy relatively late, after a phase of pastoralism (with a proportion of woodland) in the pre-Conquest period.[41] Similarly, woodland *pays* contain at least two types of landscape, the most extreme contrast being between the nucleated settlements of Rockingham (paralleled by other woodlands outside the region, such as Wychwood in Oxfordshire) and the dispersed settlements of much of the remaining woodlands. An ingredient in causing this distinction may have been the imposition of forest law, or at least inconsistencies in its implementation.

The use of the concept of *pays* raises the problem of identifying regional cultures. The different ways of life implied by the varied methods of organising the countryside cannot be explained by any single determining factor. A combination of circumstances moulded the character of each region, and we can think ourselves fortunate if we can identify even a handful of the strands that created the whole web of history that lay behind them. In some cases a self-consciousness among the inhabitants of a region can be identified. For example, the Arden district in neighbouring Warwickshire had its own customs. Perhaps the Chilterns had a stronger sense of identity than any other *pays* that we have observed in this study, beginning with its Roman opulence, and extending up to its distinctive later medieval agricultural practices such as the use of horses in ploughing, while most of the rest of England remained faithful to the ox.[42]

While we can write with some confidence about the *pays* and define their characteristics in the thirteenth century and later, doubts remain about their period of origin. Was there greater uniformity in the rural scene of, say, the ninth century, when dispersed settlements seem to have prevailed everywhere? The distribution of Romano-British sites points to an important concentration of activity in the river valleys, a relatively thin and intermittent use of the high clayland, but a strong preference among the rich for sites in the Chilterns – clearly there were *pays* in the Roman period but their character differed from those of later periods. A recent study of the wolds suggests that radical changes occurred between the eighth and the twelfth centuries. It appears then that the medieval *pays*, like many other aspects of the culture of the period, were formed in roughly the same period as the villages, the towns and the state.

Conclusion

To some extent this discussion of the causes of varied settlement forms has had a negative tone. Every single agency that could lie behind village nucleation – lords, communities, population growth, the state, urbanisation, soils – has been found inadequate *on their own* to account for the observed differences. One reason for the failure of monocausal explanations has been the assumption that there must be a practical, economic reason for change, while we have shown that both material and mental forces must be taken into account. Settlements were objects, but they were also ideas. In thinking about their origin, we must consider both the pressures and constraints deriving from demography, farming methods and lordship, which pushed people to make a choice, but also the mechanics by which decisions were made and implemented. We must see rural settlements as important cultural artefacts in themselves, but nonetheless part of a larger picture. At the beginning we recognised the utility of linking the settlement with its fields, and at the end they can be seen to form part of the whole package of characteristics making up the *pays*. In putting forward a more positive view of the origins of rural settlements in the next chapter, we must observe the agrarian and landscape context of the villages, hamlets and farmsteads.

Notes

1 G. R. Elvey (ed.), *Luffield Priory Charters* (Northamptonshire Record Society, 22, 1968), vol. 1 p. 221; (Northamptonshire Record Society, 26, 1975), vol. 2, pp. 119–20.

2 D. Hooke, 'Open field agriculture, the evidence from the pre-Conquest charters of the west midlands', and H. S. A. Fox, 'Approaches to the adoption of the Midland system', in T. Rowley (ed.), *The Origins of Open Field Agriculture* (London, Croom Helm, 1981), pp. 39–63 and 64–111; H. S. A. Fox, 'The agrarian context', in H. Fox (ed.), *Origins of the Midland Village* (Leicester, Papers for the Annual Conference of the Economic History Society, 1992), pp. 53–67.

3 For example, C. J. Dahlman, *The Open Field System and Beyond* (Cambridge, Cambridge University Press, 1980), pp. 141–5

4 W. O. Ault, *Open Field Farming in Medieval England* (London, George Allen and Unwin, 1972), p. 122.

5 A. E. Brown, 'Badby, Northamptonshire', *Medieval Settlement Research Group Annual Report*, 6 (1991), 19–21.

6 For a discussion of the significance of place-names in *ceorl*, see H. P. R. Finberg, 'Charltons and Carltons', in H. P. R. Finberg, *Lucerna: Some Problems in the Early History of England* (London, Macmillan, 1964), pp. 144–61.

7 A. Mayhew, *Rural Settlement and Farming in Germany* (London, Batsford, 1973), pp. 50–84; J. Kissock, 'The origins of the village in south Wales', *Medieval Settlement Research Group Annual Report*, 5 (1990), 6–7.

8 P. D. A. Harvey, 'Initiative and authority in settlement change', in M. Aston, D. Austin and C. Dyer (eds), *The Rural Settlements of Medieval England* (Oxford, Blackwell, 1989), pp. 31–44.

9 M. W. Beresford, *New Towns of the Middle Ages* (London, Lutterworth, 1967), pp. 191–225.

10 D. Crouch, *The Beaumont Twins: The Roots and Branches of Power in the Twelfth Century* (Cambridge, Cambridge University Press, 1986), pp. 38–57 and 155–70.

11 M. Chibnall (ed.), *Charters and Custumals of the Abbey of Holy Trinity, Caen*, Records of Social and Economic History, new series, 5 (London, British Academy and Oxford University Press, 1982), pp. 44–5, shows Simon de Felsted carrying out changes in Essex; R. H. Hilton (ed.), *The Stoneleigh Leger Book* (Dugdale Society, 24, 1960), pp. 32–3, depicts the high-handed behaviour of Ketelbern de Canley in Warwickshire.

12 P. V. Addyman, 'Late Saxon settlements in the St. Neots area: I. The Saxon settlement and Norman castle at Eaton Socon, Bedfordshire', *Proceedings of the Cambridgeshire Antiquarian Society*, 58 (1965), 38–52.

13 E. King (ed.), 'Estate records of the Hotot family', in *Northamptonshire Miscellany* (Northamptonshire Record Society, 32, 1983), pp. 1–58.

14 E. King, *Peterborough Abbey, 1086–1310* (Cambridge, Cambridge University Press, 1973); J. A. Raftis, *The Estates of Ramsey Abbey* (Toronto, Pontifical Institute of Medieval Studies, 1954).

15 Lavendon can be compared with Colmworth (Bedfordshire), where settlement is dispersed, which had only one lord. *DB*, 1, ff. 145, 146, 148, 152, 153 and 213.

16 Hatley was divided between two people in the will of Ethelstan Mannessune (986), M. Gelling, *The Early Charters of the Thames Valley* (Leicester, Leicester University Press, 1979), p. 19. A hide at Sharnford (Leics) appears in the will of Wulfric Spot (1002 × 1004), C. Hart, *The Early Charters of Northern England and the Northern Midlands* (Leicester, Leicester University Press, 1975), p. 71; its assessment in 1086 was 4½ carucates.

17 J. S. Thompson (ed.), 'The Hundred Rolls of 1274 and 1279 for Bedfordshire', *Publications of the Bedfordshire Historical Society*, 69 (1990), 27–63; J. Nichols, *The History and Antiquities of Leicestershire* (London, 1795–8), 1, pp. cx–cxxi.

18 *DB*, 1, ff. 231 and 237.

19 D. C. Douglas (ed.), *English Historical Documents, vol. 2, 1042–1189*, 2nd edn (London, Eyre Methuen, 1981), p. 878; for the date of this document, see P. D. A. Harvey, 'Rectitudines Singularum Personarum and Gerefa', *English Historical Review*, 108 (1993), 1–22.

20 *DB*, 1, f. 230.

21 C. C. Dyer, 'The English medieval village community and its decline', *Journal of British Studies*, 33 (1994), 407–29.

22 J. Wake, 'Communitas villae', *English Historical Review*, 37 (1922), 406–13.

23 P. Vinogradoff, *Villainage in England* (Oxford, Oxford University Press, 1892), pp. 457–8.

24 For Newton Longville and Bletchley see H. E. Salter (ed.), *Newington Longville Charters* (Oxfordshire Record Society, 3, 1921), pp. 18–20; and for other examples, note 54 in chapter 2 above.

25 J. Thirsk, 'The common fields', *Past and Present*, 29 (1964), 1–25.

26 T. Williamson, 'Explaining regional landscapes: woodland and champion in southern and eastern England', *Landscape History*, 10 (1988), 5–13; and also B. M. S. Campbell, 'Population change and the genesis of common fields on a Norfolk manor', *Economic History Review*, 2nd Series, 33 (1980), 188–91.

27 See D. Roden, 'Demesne farming in the Chiltern Hills', *Agricultural History Review*, 17 (1969), 9–23.

28 See for instance J. G. Jenkins (ed.), *The Cartulary of Missenden Abbey: Part 1* (Records Branch of the Buckinghamshire Archaeological Society, 2, 1938), p. 130.

29 P. D. A. Harvey, *The Peasant Land Market in Medieval England* (Oxford, Clarendon Press, 1984), pp. 13–15.

30 *DB*, 1, ff. 233, 220 and 144.

31 J. Goodacre, *The Transformation of a Peasant Economy* (Aldershot, Scolar Press, 1994), pp. 8–21; G. Foard, personal comment.

32 *VCH, Buckinghamshire*, 4, p. 15.

33 For a discussion including examples from the study area, see C. C. Taylor, 'Medieval market grants and village morphology', *Landscape History*, 4 (1982), 21–8.

34 M. Biddle and D. Hill, 'Late Saxon planned towns', *Antiquaries Journal*, 51 (1971), 70–85; *Medieval Settlement Research Group Annual Report*, 6 (1991), 35–6; 7 (1992), 33.

35 R. H. Hilton, *English and French Towns in Feudal Society* (Cambridge, Cambridge University Press, 1992), pp. 53–104.

36 These figures are based on calculations by C. Dyer from the poll tax.
37 *DB*, 1, f. 230.
38 D. G. and J. G. Hurst, 'Excavations on the medieval village of Wythemail, Northamptonshire', *Medieval Archaeology*, 13 (1969), 167–203; J. S. Wacher, 'Excavations at Martinsthorpe, Rutland, 1960', *Transactions of the Leicestershire Archaeological Society*, 39 (1963–4), 1–19.
39 R. H. Britnell, *The Commercialisation of English Society, 1000–1500* (Cambridge, Cambridge University Press, 1993), pp. 114–15.
40 Fox, 'Agrarian context', pp. 64–7.
41 H. S. A. Fox, 'The people of the wolds in English settlement history', in Aston *et al.* (eds), *Rural Settlements*, 77–101.
42 J. Langdon, *Horses, Oxen and Technological Innovation: The Use of Draught Animals in English Farming from 1066–1500* (Cambridge, Cambridge University Press, 1986).

7

The evolution of rural settlement

We have seen in the previous chapter that no single factor will adequately explain the variations in the medieval settlement pattern of the east midlands, or indeed of any other region. At the same time, however, the factors that have been addressed are clearly all associated, to a greater or lesser degree, with differences in the types of settlements. To expand our understanding of the changes at work we need to consider the information in different ways and attempt new approaches to the subject. In doing this we must incorporate all the factors that are involved in these changes, and acknowledge the complexity of the relationships between them.

The physical evidence

Firstly, archaeological evidence shows that the date at which nucleated villages were created can be narrowed down to the period 850–1200: only exceptionally are large settlements found earlier than the ninth century and few rural nucleations developed after the thirteenth. The creation of larger settlements was not a single process, and villages experienced periods of planning, replanning, growth and shrinkage.

While nucleation occurred in a specific period, albeit one of a few centuries, dispersed settlements such as hamlets and farmsteads appeared and disappeared over a millenium and more: they are known from archaeological evidence such as pottery scatters between 450 and 850, and appear extensively in documentary sources in the twelfth to fourteenth centuries, often as apparently new sites. We can therefore identify the period between the mid-ninth and early thirteenth century as including the 'village moment', when villages formed in those places prone to nucleation. Elsewhere, the 'village moment' passed by uneventfully, with a continued proliferation of farms and hamlets. Our fundamental problem is to identify what it was which made some places 'prone' to nucleation, or which enabled other places to resist nucleation.

Identifying the factors governing this tendency to nucleation leads us to a second fundamental point. There must be a strong relationship between the form of settlements and the type of land in which they are found. The nucleated villages are strongly associated with 'champion' country of extensive arable cultivation and tend to occur in the major river valleys and the undulating limestone country of the centre and north of the area studied. Elsewhere, the stony clay and chalk of the Chilterns, the sandstone heaths and the heaviest claylands generally have dispersed patterns of settlement. This is also true of other parts of England beyond the study area. Evidently, there are physical or geographical variations influencing settlements' susceptibility to nucleation. But there is no simple bipartite division: we have observed considerable variations within the two broad types of settlement; in some districts both types occur; and apparently similar formations of soil and geology do not consistently support the same settlement patterns.

Thirdly, the demographic expansion which is well documented between 1086 and c.1300, and which probably began a century or two before 1086, affected settlement development by providing the impetus and opportunity to expand the size of villages and hamlets or to create new farmsteads, but did not itself cause settlements to be reordered into nucleated villages. Our explanation must take into account the fact that levels of population as high in the dispersed regions in the thirteenth century as those of the champion regions in the eleventh century did not precipitate nucleation: why had the 'village moment' passed in some regions without actually activating the mechanisms which formed the village?

A further factor, which may be critical to our understanding of the processes influencing the appearance of variety in the rural settlement pattern, is the consistently strong association between nucleated villages and regular common-field systems. The inhabitants of nucleated villages depended heavily on arable cultivation, while those who lived in dispersed settlements seem to have combined more pastoral husbandry with their cereal cultivation, and are sometimes found involving themselves in rural industry. Regular common fields probably appeared during the 'village moment', and the creation of such a field system around a settlement marked the point at which it was necessary to gather the inhabitants into a nucleated village. Certainly, it spelt the end for most of the other dispersed hamlets and farmsteads within the village territory.

Finally, nucleated and dispersed settlement show different patterns of conservatism and adaptability to changing circumstances. Nucleated villages were created by radical movements in habitation and the organisation of fields, but once in existence they persisted. They might be subject to replanning, but they maintained their field systems through both the expansion of the twelfth and thirteenth centuries and the subsequent reduction in both population and demand for grain. While the majority retained some form of open-field husbandry until the modern enclosure movement, a few went into terminal decline and lost most or all of their inhabitants, from the fourteenth century onwards. Dispersed settlements show more flexibility, able to receive more immigrants in times of expansion and to slim down without experiencing total disaster from 1350 onwards. These then are the factors that need to be accounted for in any explanation of the origins of the nucleated village. But before attempting to weave together these threads into an explanatory hypothesis, we must explore the wider historical circumstances.

Historical contexts

There is general agreement on the formative character of the period between the ninth and thirteenth centuries. It saw the emergence of medieval civilisation and also of many features of the modern world, such as the European states, the network of towns and of course the rural settlement pattern. Some scholars, notably in France, have identified a revolution, dubbed the 'feudal transformation', taking place around the year 1000 which saw the final disappearance of features of the ancient world such as slavery, and the advent of a new aggressive aristocracy, wielding strong jurisdictional power based on castles, and forming feudal relationships which bound together lords, knights and peasants.[1] At the same time, the first united kingdoms of England and Germany, which represent the birth of the modern states, can be located in the tenth century. For Italian historians the communes and the city-states were born at the end of the eleventh century, at about the same time as the fortified nucleated villages, the result of the process of *incastellamento*. For students of religion the reformed papacy was a product of the upheavals of the late eleventh century, and ushered in a period of centralised government of christian life from Rome, with associated changes in local churches. Economic and social expansion accelerated, according to most schools of thought, either in the late Carolingian period (ninth century) or the tenth century, and was certainly in full swing from the eleventh century to the thirteenth, with urban growth, a greater volume of trade and the extension of cultivation at the expense of marsh and forest.[2]

We cannot simply and vaguely associate changes in rural settlement with growth in the economy and in social and political organisation, because of the varying effects of these common influences in different regions. We ought to take note of some themes in recent thinking about this period which may help us to view our villages in a broader comparative light. At the beginning we should remind ourselves of the planned character of many villages, and their specific form. The rectilinear shapes of tofts and rows are not the shapes that would occur by chance or whim. To make a single comparison, the east midland villages and indeed English villages in general are never round or radial, as found in the *wurten* or *rundling* settlements of Germany, the former type being characteristic of the North Sea coast (and also in the Netherlands), once thought to be the original homeland of the English village. Radial settlements have also recently been identified in parts of Wales.[3] The laying-out of the English village was a deliberate decision, or series of decisions, by people who had a particular idea of the shape that a village should take: ranged along a street or in a grid.

A recent synthesis of European history of the period 950–1350 by Bartlett concentrates on the periphery of the continent – western Britain, eastern Europe, the reconquered lands of Moslem Spain – and argues that important characteristics of the society and politics of the 'core' countries (originally the old heartland of the Carolingian Empire, now France, western Germany, the Low Countries and northern Italy, but later including most of England) were, often after a phase of conquest, imposed on the newly won territories.[4] These social and political features included: the bishoprics and their accompanying network of churches; aristocratic institutions and migratory noble families; a military technology based on the castle, cavalry and archers; and towns and villages as instruments of colonisation. Bartlett is referring to villages as institutions, especially the free and privileged communities set up in the Slav lands of Germany and Moslem territory in Spain, but he notes the systematic planning of villages in many parts of the continent.

Bartlett's emphasis on the free village, and the assumption that the distribution of villages is easily explained in environmental or ethnic terms, do not accord with our findings, but the identification of a general tendency towards models and blueprints in the period can help us a great deal. This was a great age of legal codification, with a growing homogeneity in the law, but above all it was an age when particular institutions spread by example and imitation. Motte and bailey castles, and their stone successors, are found in many parts of Europe and clearly belong to a generic type. When towns were founded their lords often gave to the new inhabitants privileges borrowed from a place with well-regulated customs. In Spain, the laws of Cuenca-Teruel were widely adopted, just as the privileges of Magdeburg spread all over eastern Europe. In England the laws of a small and obscure Norman town, Breteuil, were granted to dozens of new boroughs in the twelfth and thirteenth centuries. The numerous Cistercian monasteries were following the rule observed by the first house, Cîteaux in Burgundy, and the similar ground plans and architecture were used by the scattered houses of that order. The Cistercians and other ecclesiastical, royal and aristocratic patrons all played a role in the diffusion of the Gothic style which gave a homogeneous appearance to churches over much of Europe.

Clearly then we are dealing with a society which had notions of how institutions, settlements and buildings should be organised and constructed, and was anxious to find good working models on which new foundations could be based. It was an imitative age, which was ready to adopt and emulate. And of course these ideas were all interlinked in a complex network. New castles, monasteries and towns were often sited together: the income which provided for the castles and churches was generated from the stimulus to the market from the new towns. Cistercian monasteries were often founded in underdeveloped areas such as eastern Germany, where new secular settlements were also being laid out.

The village fits well into these interlocking elements of planning, both in terms of the role of the peasants as primary producers providing incomes for their social superiors through rents, tithes and taxes, and in the element of imitation involved in the diffusion of village planning. When a village and its fields were restructured in accordance with a model of rectangular tofts, rows of houses, and furlongs and strips, just like dozens of neighbouring places, the local planners were in tune with the general tendencies of their time. The dispersed settlements also contained orderly and planned elements. An interrupted row or a green-edge settlement does not lack logic or discipline. And the inhabitants of dispersed settlements were involved in the development of the *institution* of the village because they formed communities with control over part of their territories.

Another approach to the period is to see it as an age which saw the advance of reason. Law and government became more systematic, and the advances in the use of money meant that revenues could be calculated more readily. The spread of the abacus allowed governments and lords to strike the balance of accounts and plan their activities effectively.[5] Agriculture was increasingly geared to the market, and growth in more precise ideas of property, and equitable divisions of the burdens on tenants, encouraged the use of measurement in the layout of tofts and fields. The use of written records helped strengthen individuals' awareness that they possessed specific parcels of land, and gave them greater certainty in their obligations to their lords. Thirteenth-century villagers accumulated small archives of documentation of their holdings, deeds in the case of freeholders, and 'copies of court roll' for the customary tenants, from which they derived greater confidence and a stronger sense of individual property.[6]

In the specific sphere of social and economic development it is useful to see the high middle ages as an age that was moving towards relatively small units of government, landholding and lordship.[7] The Carolingian Empire which broke down in the ninth century had been constructed on an elephantine scale. In England (as on the continent) before 900 we find huge estates, in which economic activity needed constant movements of people and goods from the outer fringes of the land unit to its centre. Between the ninth and twelfth centuries economic life was based on the more intimate and manageable level of the township and manor. Again our villages, with their relatively small territories, are very much in accordance with the general tendency of their age. And this was not a scale of operations appropriate only to the vertically linked institutions of states, estates and lordship, but also to the lateral associations of townsmen and peasants which formed an important basis for social activity.[8]

A further historical generalisation about the period between the ninth and thirteenth centuries is that it saw the emergence of a Europe of regions. On the continent these had a political identity, even a political independence, as the counts and dukes inherited the powers of the former Carolingian Empire. In England there are numerous indications of variety among regions – the emerging language of middle English developed differently in the west midlands, east midlands and Kent.[9] In Kent and parts of East Anglia, custom favoured partible inheritance, while most of the country practised primogeniture.[10] Local styles of timber building were developing in the thirteenth century with frames based on crucks in the west and north, but box framing in the south-east, no doubt preceded by other variations in methods of construction.[11] A large area including the counties around London looked to the market of the capital, and many of the younger inhabitants went there to make a living. Other rural populations lay within the orbit of regional capitals such as York, Norwich, Bristol and the lesser towns, such as Leicester and Northampton.[12] Some areas were given a common identity by their experience of conflict with neighbours, as on the Welsh and Scottish borders. Others were brought together by their dependence on a great river as a major artery of communication, as in the case of the Trent, the Severn or the Great Ouse.[13] Many regions had distinctive local agricultural products, which gave them a common diet and method of production – an extreme example being the oat cultivation and upland pastoralism of the Pennines and the Peak District.[14]

However, if we map these different social, economic and topographical zones of influence, they do not neatly coincide and allow us to define clear self-contained regions. Rather they overlap in complicated ways. Differences in settlement types and field systems formed another, very important, ingredient in defining regional societies and cultures, reflecting partly the different environment, but also the traditions and loyalties of their localities. The study of settlement patterns gives us another insight into a complex and shifting society, very different from our own, and yet leaving to us an important legacy in the ordering of the rural landscape. The emphasis has been placed here on culture because, whatever the economic influences behind nucleation, the precise form that villages took had a basis in ideas and attitudes – contemporaries planned and constructed villages according to clear notions of what a village should be. They adopted rational measures and were anxious to fix boundaries in the light of notions of property rights, and they did so within territorial units.

It is worth exploring the cultural dimension of settlement design and not just the economics of farming systems, because we cannot be certain that there were gains in agricultural productivity as a result of the adoption of regular field systems and the grouping of those working them in a central location. When corn yields are recorded in detail in the thirteenth and fourteenth centuries, some of the poorer results come from the regions dominated by midland field systems, and the most likely places to rise above mediocrity were in the non-nucleated regions, such as parts of East Anglia, which reduced the area of fallow, and farmed flexibly and intensively.[15] Some agricultural historians are not fully convinced that the eventual enclosure of the open fields produced much immediate increase in productivity either.[16] If we are to invoke practical reasons for the adoption of the new methods in the ninth to twelfth centuries, it would be to introduce order and rationality into the confusion of private property and shared assets that had arisen from piecemeal development, with an emphasis on providing fair shares and equal access to resources as a means of restoring peace and ensuring future co-operation.

Hypothesis for settlement evolution in the east midlands

If historical evidence and thinking can illuminate the cultural environment within which settlements changed, archaeology can contribute to the subject its holistic view, in which settlement change can be viewed within a broader perspective of the whole society and its material culture. Systems theory can be applied to our subject: this assumes that any human society should be viewed as a whole system, similar to a biological organism, made up of a number of interacting components or subsystems. Changes to one part of the system caused sympathetic changes elsewhere, which aimed to maintain the *status quo*. If this could not be achieved, part or all of the system might be altered or, if the change was extreme or cumulative, cease to function.[17]

This approach, which is useful in establishing the interrelatedness of all parts of an organism, has its limitations when applied to human societies. Human societies make constant decisions and take appropriate actions in the face of changing circumstances. In addition, human societies are often more successful than physical organisms in adapting to change. It is perhaps most useful to regard a systems approach as providing us with a model of growth, stability and change, rather than a direct analogy.

Systems approaches can more usefully be combined with ideas about evolution to produce a model for the way in which human societies adapt and change. Here, human society can be regarded as analogous to a species which evolves by adopting new modes of behaviour or physical characteristics in response to the environment. Such adaptations occur either in response to a change in external circumstances which threatens the species' viability, or to enable it to exploit a newly available ecological niche or opportunity. Human society likewise evolves by changing the nature or function of its economic and social component parts, partly by conscious intelligent adaptation and innovation, and partly as a result of changes imposed from outside.

We can envisage societies as complex systems made up of political, social and economic institutions, which are subject to survival, growth or extinction over time. But because we are dealing with societies capable of rational decision-making, the mutations, or innovations, or the discarding of elements, will be the result of intellectual or social processes such as emulation or imposition.[18]

Theoretical frameworks are not so commonly applied to medieval archaeology, but more often to remote prehistoric periods when the evidence is entirely archaeological, and much of the information on social organisation or political change has necessarily been based on inference or analogy. Medievalists have the advantage of information derived from abundant documents as well as the physical remains of the past, but the evidence is still limited. To the eternal frustration of historians concerned with settlement, there is no surviving document containing an order that a village should be planned, or a record of villagers making a decision to nucleate.

To understand the underlying dynamics, we need a theoretical framework which will produce a logical explanation of the development of settlements which is flexible enough to accommodate the observed regional and local variations, and also the influences of the historical process, but with specific meaning.

Seventh to eleventh centuries

For the first five centuries after the collapse of the Roman province, until the ninth century or later, rural settlement generally consisted of small dispersed settlements, most densely scattered on lighter and more fertile soils. Many of them were abandoned some time after 850, and were replaced by villages.

The nucleated villages were associated with agrarian systems based on extensive arable fields. The widespread appearance and survival of such settlements and fields indicate that these changes must have conferred benefits, or at least were thought to have been beneficial, for the people who adopted them. The new system was chosen selectively, and many communities persisted with old forms of habitation and fields, presumably because they were also perceived as advantageous for them. The new agrarian landscape spread over the mixed limestone and clay soils, but there appears to be some correlation with soil type, as those areas which did not develop nucleated settlements include greensand and the very heavy boulder clays. The areas where the nucleated village was the dominant form of settlement in the middle ages, appear to have had consistently higher proportions of arable land in cultivation in 1086, which is likely to reflect a long standing bias towards cereal cultivation.

One possible reconstruction of events would be to assume that a high dependence on arable cultivation was associated with increased population, demand on land, and the beginning of market opportunities, all of which may have threatened to exhaust the soil. This need not have posed an immediate problem, as new land would have been available within the settlement territory to be converted to cultivation, but a point would have been reached when the supply of land for expansion ran out. Neighbouring groups of cultivators would become more possessive over the remaining land, leading to the need to delineate increasingly firmly the limits between territories, which is reflected in the charters of the tenth and eleventh centuries with their careful and exact descriptions of boundaries. The difficulty with this idea is that theories of over-population and ecological crisis have been applied to the thirteenth century, when densities of people were much higher. And even for that period the theories have not been proved.

Another hypothesis would be to emphasise the internal boundary problems of groups of cultivators within their territories. As the exploitation of land became more intensive, competition would be increased for access to meadows, pastures and woods which were still shared, while, as the rest of the land became a complex patchwork of individual fields, subdivided no doubt by inheritance and exchange, quarrels would arise over boundary marks and fence-lines. A major problem would have been the adjustment of the balance between arable and pasture, and the difficulties of reconciling the rival demands of both must have resulted in numerous incidents of straying and trespassing animals, or of parcels of grazing land being overburdened with beasts.

The system, that is of a society increasingly dependent on arable farming, would have been threatened both with difficulties in production and with growing friction between neighbours. Converting some of the remaining pasture to arable would have left the animals nowhere to feed, and their manure was the source of fertiliser which would have propped up yields. Mechanisms for maintaining law and order imposed rules for settling disputes and transferring land. A peaceful option for a long term resolution of their difficulties involved the inhabitants reorganising their numerous farms and hamlets into common fields where the problems of competition would be minimised. The animals of the whole community were pastured together on the land which lay fallow or awaited spring cultivation. The land was subjected to a cycle of fallowing which gave it a chance to recover some fertility.

The large fields subdivided into strips allowed the easy management of the collective flocks and herds of grazing animals, which offset the troubles associated with travel to the scattered parcels of each holding. The layout and management of fields did not represent a complete departure from previous practice, but grew out of it. There had been shared lands and scattered parcels before, and land had been fallowed, though perhaps more irregularly through variants of the infield–outfield arrangements which gave pieces of land many years to recover after a period of continuous cropping.

The task of reorganising arable cultivation would have needed a co-ordinated effort by all those participating in the exploitation of each territory, both lords and peasants, though we do not know who took the lead, or to what extent coercion was involved. The assumption must be made that the uprooting of those living in dispersed farms, and the laying out of the new large fields, took place when competition for land had reached a high level. Lords provided a focus for the new village by building a manor house, a church, and settling slaves and servants near that centre.

A further factor must have been restrictions on the supply of new land, or on changes in use, both from communities anxious to preserve their access to grazing and woods, and from kings and lords who were conserving hunting grounds.

Another influence from outside the communities of cultivators came from the market economy, which is apparent from the archaeological evidence for Saxo-Norman pottery having been made on a large scale and traded extensively, and from at least the early tenth century the growth of urban populations dependent on activities other than farming. Those settlements already tending to large scale grain production were thus further encouraged to produce a tradeable surplus. This development gave the lords a further incentive to maximise their social control – already they would have played a major part in regularising the landholding of the new villages, because they favoured standard tenements. Now they could hope to profit from the market both from demesne production and tenant rents.

The possibility cannot be ignored that the decision to change was preceded by some recession – perhaps cultivators had begun to abandon their holdings because of difficulties in production, or a temporary opportunity was created by a short-term fall in population, which gave a breathing space and left land vacant, so there was not a crisis of congestion and demand for resources. If later, better documented changes can serve as a parallel, notably the reordering of fields in the early enclosures of the fifteenth century, or the first wave of enclosures of the early eighteenth, a time of relatively low population pressure may have been conducive to radical departures from existing practice.

In other regions, however, this adaptive evolution of fields, boundaries and settlements was not followed. Where the arable contribution to the economy was less dominant, the pressure on the land never reached the point at which a transformation of the landscape seemed either necessary or desirable. Although the areas of continued dispersed settlement were subject to the same factors, such as increased population or the emergence of markets, nonetheless the availability of additional land for cultivation, their pastoral interests, or opportunities to make a living from the woods and wastes, insulated them from radical changes.

According to an evolutionary framework, a process analogous to natural selection meant that those communities, in the regions with a bias to arable cultivation, which reorganised themselves became better equipped to survive and thrive. This adaptation, once introduced and established, probably spread by emulation: the nucleated settlements and regular open fields in so many communities across the east midlands show so many similarities as to suggest that, as the success of the nucleated open-field village became evident, the idea spread following a standard model. The large number of nucleated open-field villages suggests that they were indeed a successful adaptation to circumstances, and one which subsequently showed a remarkable resilience. While small settlements were being abandoned or shifting site almost continually between the fifth and the ninth centuries, most village settlements occupied in the tenth and eleventh centuries survived for hundreds of years, and many are still inhabited. The new nucleated villages were evidently preserved, perhaps by virtue of being set within their encircling fields, and a system was established which, unlike its predecessors, was able to maintain some measure of equilibrium.

The use of an evolutionary model might suggest that the process of nucleation occurred gradually over a long period of time – perhaps a century or two. This could have occurred in a piecemeal fashion, as individual families moved one by one from their isolated farms to holdings near their fellow villagers, or through a series of replannings. But we should not ignore the possibility that, while the nucleation came about as a response to widespread evolutionary pressures, the actual restructuring of the village happened quite suddenly. So radical was the transformation in the layout of houses and fields, and so difficult was it for the unitary plan of the nucleated village to coexist with the old arrangement (how could an open field function if there were significant numbers of houses and enclosed fields still scattered over the village territory?) that we can envisage the whole resettlement occurring in one year, after the harvest, involving everyone in a massive relaying of boundaries and construction of new houses. Evolutionary development may therefore have culminated in a revolutionary upheaval.

Eleventh to thirteenth centuries

By the late eleventh century some nucleated villages had already formed, and Domesday Book records in many districts the extensive arable cultivation characteristic of such village economies. In the succeeding two centuries we assume that nucleation was continuing, where it was not already complete, both because the pressure that lay behind the earliest nucleation continued, and because we can expect emulation of the model provided by neighbours. Village formation spread into the limestone claylands, where nucleated settlements are found seemingly without archaeological evidence for occupation earlier than the eleventh or twelfth centuries. It is likely that this period saw the growing together of adjacent small nuclei to form the polyfocal villages. It may also have seen the subdivision of larger places, to form double settlements such as those called 'upper' and 'lower', or 'great' and 'little'. Villages that had already coalesced into a single settlement went through a variety of changes, such as general expansion, the addition of new sections, and the restructuring of the whole settlement with a regular plan – it could be that many of the regular rows and gridded settlements were laid out at this time.

All of these changes must be related to adaptations of agrarian systems – cereal-growing predominated among the villages, within well-defined territorial boundaries. The population increased, but space in many villages was too limited to accommodate very many more households than existed at the time of Domesday. Holdings were divided to make half- and quarter-yardlands, and cottage holdings were created. Archaeological evidence shows that new tenements were laid out over former arable fields. Production was increased both to feed these extra people, and to supply the growing market for foodstuffs from the towns and those sections of the population who lacked direct access to land. Some technical innovations show an adaptation to new circumstances such as intensification of crop rotations, occasionally by changing from a two-field to a three-field system, but most commonly by planting part of the fallow field. The commercialisation of rural society was also encouraged by lords who increased their demands of their tenants, especially for payments of rents and dues in cash, or by the state stepping up its requirement for taxes. In general the nuclear villages maintained a degree of equilibrium; the system worked, and adapted to the changes in external circumstances.

In the areas of dispersed settlement, the documentary rather than the archaeological evidence likewise shows the twelfth and thirteenth centuries to have been a period of great growth in the number of farmsteads and hamlets. More houses were added, like beads on a string, along the interrupted rows and green-edge settlements, and the density of isolated farmsteads increased. Gaps in rows tended to fill, though rarely to the point that rows became continuous. Existing agricultural holdings were subdivided, and woodland clearings were expanded by assarting. These tendencies are reflected in the archaeological record by the proliferation of moats, which were especially numerous among dispersed settlements, and in addition the new monasteries of the twelfth century and their granges show the development of other types of high-status isolated settlement. There was, however, some movement towards nucleation here too. Some large agglomerations grew up through the merging of former separated hamlets, and the new market towns and market villages were associated with large, planned settlements.

The dispersed settlements were subject to the same changes in population, commercialisation and pressure from lords as nucleated, champion regions. They accommodated larger increases in numbers of inhabitants than did the villages, often experiencing more than a tripling in their population. Their inhabitants were able to add to the arable area by assarting, but retained their varied resource base. They were more pastoral in their farming, and exploited the woodlands for charcoal and for the manufacture of iron and pottery. They felt the impact of market growth, and many markets and small towns were sited in, or on the edge of, zones of dispersed settlements. They were probably more innovative in agricultural technique, as in the Chilterns, and were given an advantage by the flexibility with which their fields were managed. The greater legal and tenurial freedom enjoyed by the inhabitants aided their capacity to adapt to new trends.

However, this growth did not lead to the adoption of nucleated settlements in these regions. The tendency for agglomerations of market villages and polyfocal settlements did not transform the overall character of the settlement pattern. The dispersed regions as they expanded did not adopt nucleation, even when they exceeded the high population densities which in the eleventh century were associated with the appearance of nucleated open-field villages. By the thirteenth century the 'village moment' had passed, because the adoption of open-field, nucleated villages was no longer a useful adaptation. Nucleated settlements were closely packed in the village districts, so there was no room for new nucleations. In the dispersed areas the extension of new settlements and fields with established property rights made the formation of villages more difficult. Evolutionary forces in the dispersed regions never impelled them to adopt nucleation: the inhabitants were able to continue successfully to exploit their economic niche, and the adoption of nucleated settlement systems conferred no advantage.

Fourteenth to fifteenth centuries

In this period many nucleated settlements contracted, in some a few tofts were abandoned; in others, sections of villages shrank away, and for a minority whole villages were deserted. Equally dramatic shifts in the associated fields led to conversion of strips or furlongs into temporary or permanent grazing, and sometimes to the enclosure of all of their fields for pastures. In areas of dispersed settlement there was some thinning out of farms and hamlets, but not on such a scale as to empty a territory, as happened to some villages. Indeed there is some evidence for the foundation of new settlements, as some cottages were built on wastes, and the leasing of demesnes and granges led to the building of new farms. As among the nucleated villages, the fields were often converted from arable to pasture, but not with the same catastrophic loss of livelihood to the inhabitants.

The loss of so many settlements was associated with demographic decline, beginning in some places with the famine of 1315–18 and continuing as a result of the Black Death of 1348–9 and subsequent epidemics. Cereal prices declined as demand fell, while the opportunities for pastoral agriculture improved. Tenants became more independent of their landlords, and a stratum of prosperous tenants and demesne farmers was beginning to engross holdings and increase production for the market, regardless of the interests of their neighbours. They were inhibited in their production by the lack of labour that could be hired.

All of these developments put stress on the tightly-knit village communities and strictly-regulated fields. It may have been as difficult to scale down cultivation of such fields as it had been earlier to raise productivity. As weeds grew and unfenced pasture disrupted the old routines, peasants were tempted to migrate. They were no longer restrained from leaving by their lords, and may have been disgruntled by the aggressive behaviour of their neighbours. Potential immigrants who might have replaced them were repelled by the decayed state of the communities. The nucleated settlements had the same conservative tendency in death as they showed in their origins – once they had been deserted, they were rarely repopulated, as their lords and the graziers who occupied the new enclosed pastures developed a strong interest in the profits that could be made from extensive animal husbandry.

But even more remarkable was the capacity of the majority of villages to survive. They had developed as a system appropriate to an age of growth but, when tested in a crisis, only a relatively small number succumbed, and the majority were able once more to evolve new methods of production and social structures to suit changed circumstances. We can see in this period more than in any other the 'survival of the fittest' at work, in which smaller and in other ways ill-favoured settlements went to the wall, while the rest adapted and kept a reduced population.

The dispersed areas were better equipped to withstand the changes that proved so disastrous for some villages. Their more varied economies, and ability to change the balance of their farming from arable to pasture, together with their greater interest in non-agricultural activities, made them much more resilient and more easily responsive to market forces. They lost people to epidemics and from migration just as the villages did, but as they were less restricted by lords, they did not experience the same urge to migrate as the manor relaxed its authority. They were not bound so tightly into communities and subject to rules governing their husbandry, so they did not experience the same conflicts and certainly not the collapse in common-field agriculture which overtook some villages. Abandoned farms and hamlets might be repopulated after an interval, or replaced as the settlements shifted within territories.

Conclusion

A combination of historical and archaeological approaches to the problem of rural settlement hints at the many structures and changes which gave rise to varied forms and patterns. Beginning in a countryside with characteristics affecting the suitability of the land for settlement and exploitation, and which had already undergone important developments in land use in the pre-medieval millennia, a series of cultural, economic and social changes led to the evolution of different types of rural settlement and landscape. We have used the idea of evolution to explain successive phases of settlement. But this should not be taken to mean that one form of settlement represents a higher stage of development. The old view that the village was superior to the hamlet and isolated farm, and that extensive cultivation marks a civilised advance beyond a more primitive pastoralism, cannot be sustained.

Of course we must be impressed by the orderly plan of many villages, and the ingenious logic of the interlocking features of the open-field system. But in terms of yields and technical progress, the non-village economy may have had the edge. As we have seen, the village developed, adapted and survived the successive episodes of growth and recession in the middle ages, but the countryside dominated by hamlets and farmsteads went through more rapid expansion, and then proved more resilient in managing the subsequent shrinkage. All forms of settlement have evolved and adapted, and each type had its strengths and weaknesses. Village and non-village patterns do not represent progressive and backward ways of living in the countryside, but simply reflect different traditions and different paths of development. We have had to stop the story around 1500, but the persistence of the forms of medieval settlement, which were still dominating the rural scene when the first comprehensive maps were drawn in the early nineteenth century, and which still survive in large measure at the present day, provide remarkable testimony to the debt of the modern world to the creative energies of our medieval predecessors.

Notes

1 G. Bois, *The Transformation of the Year One Thousand: The Village of Lournand from Antiquity to Feudalism* (Manchester, Manchester University Press, 1992); P. Bonnassie, *From Slavery to Feudalism in South-Western Europe* (Cambridge, Cambridge University Press, 1991); A. Verhulst, 'The decline of slavery and the economic expansion of the early middle ages', *Past and Present*, 133 (1991), 195–203; T. N. Bisson, 'The "feudal revolution"', *Past and Present*, 142 (1994), 6–42.

2 These issues are discussed in *La Croissance Agricole du Haut Moyen Age: Chronologie, Modalités, Géographie* (Centre Culturel de l'Abbaye de Flaran, Xe Journées Internationales d'Histoire, Auch, 1990).

3 Mayhew, *Rural Settlement and Farming in Germany* (London, Batsford, 1973) pp. 30–3 and 61–4; J. Kissock and M. A. Aris at the 'Medieval Settlement in Wales' conference, held in December 1994 at Bangor, Gwynedd.

4 R. Bartlett, *The Making of Europe: Conquest, Colonization and Cultural Change 950–1350* (Harmondsworth, Allen Lane, 1993). For useful comments on this, C. Wickham, 'Making Europe', *New Left Review*, 208 (1994), 133–43.

5 A. Murray, *Reason and Society in the Middle Ages* (Oxford, Oxford University Press, 1978), pp. 141–87.

6 M. T. Clanchy, *Memory to Written Record, 1066–1307*, 2nd edn (Oxford, Blackwell, 1993), pp. 46–51.

7 R. Fossier, *L'Enfance de l'Europe, Xe–XIIe siècles: Aspects économiques et sociaux* (Paris, Presses Universitaires de France, 1982), emphasises this process, called by him *encellulement*.

8 S. Reynolds, *Kingdoms and Communities in Western Europe, 900–1300* (Oxford, Oxford University Press, 1984).

9 A. McIntosh, M. L. Samuels, M. Benskin, *A Guide to a Linguistic Atlas of Late Medieval English* (Aberdeen, Aberdeen University Press, 1987), p. 9.

10 R. Faith, 'Peasant families and inheritance customs in medieval England', *Agricultural History Review*, 14 (1966), 77–95.

11 N. W. Alcock (ed.), *Cruck Construction. An Introduction and Catalogue* (London, Council for British Archaeology, Research Report, 42, 1981), pp. 5–24.

12 E. Ekwall, *Studies on the Population of Medieval London* (Stockholm, 1956); P. McClure, 'Patterns of migration in the late middle ages: the evidence of English place-name surnames', *Economic History Review*, 2nd Series, 32 (1974), 167–82; S. A. C. Penn, 'The origins of Bristol migrants in the early fourteenth century: the surname evidence', *Transactions of the Bristol and Gloucestershire Archaeological Society*, 101 (1983), 123–30.

13 C. Phythian-Adams, 'Introduction: an agenda for English local history', in C. Phythian-Adams (ed.), *Societies, Cultures and Kinship; 1580–1850: Cultural Provinces in English Local History* (Leicester, Leicester University Press, 1993), pp. 1–23.

14 H. E. Hallam (ed.), *Agrarian History of England and Wales, vol 2, 1042–1350* (Cambridge, Cambridge University Press, 1988), p. 381.

15 B. M. S. Campbell, 'Land, labour, livestock, and productivity trends in English seigniorial agriculture, 1208–1450', in B. M. S. Campbell and M. Overton (eds), *Land, Labour and Livestock: Historical Studies in European Agricultural Productivity* (Manchester, Manchester University Press, 1991), pp. 144–82.

16 R. C. Allen, 'The two English agricultural revolutions, 1450–1860', in Camp-
    bell and Overton (eds), *Land, Labour and Livestock*, pp. 236–54.
17 Among the numerous writings on systems theory in archaeology, see
    D. L. Clarke, *Analytical Archaeology*, 2nd edn (Bristol, Arrowsmith, 1978);
    I. Hodder, *Reading the Past* (Cambridge, Cambridge University Press, 1986),
    pp. 18–33 assesses its achievements and limitations.
18 For a review of these approaches see S. Mithen, 'Evolutionary theory and
    post-processual archaeology', *Antiquity*, 63 (1989), 483–94.

Index

Numbers in italics refer to pages showing figures.